Fighting for Home

Fighting for Home

The Story of
Alfred K. Oates
and the
Fifth Regiment, Excelsior Brigade

Christopher Ryan Oates

Warren Publishing • Charlotte, North Carolina

WARREN PUBLISHING, INC.

Cornelius, NC 28031
© 2006 by Christopher Ryan Oates
Book design by TheBooksetter.com

This is a work of dramatic non-fiction. The events and persons in this book were heavily researched with documents, newspapers, letters, and secondary sources. The author has chosen to tell the story in a narrative style to heighten the emotions Oates and others felt in this most perilous of times in American History.

This book was set in Adobe Caslon Pro and BlackChancery, with Palatino on the title pages and dust jacket. Chapter numbers and drop capitals are in Adobe Rosewood Standard, a type face featured on the Civil War poster found on page 82.

Printed in the United States of America

May, 2006

LB 2006924495
ISBN 1-886057-12-5

To My Own Family

This work could not have started without the help of my father, Robert Oates, who found Alfred Oates' letters in the attic of his childhood home and has acted as my proofreader and agent, and my grandfather, Walter Ryan, who transcribed Alfred's cursive handwriting into the infinitely more readable Times New Roman. I must thank all those at Roxbury Latin who gave me the education to attempt such an endeavor while I was still in high school, especially Chairman of the History Department Stewart Thomsen, Assistant Headmaster Michael Pojman, and Headmaster F. Washington Jarvis. While a freshman at Brown University I worked on this project with the late Professor Jack Thomas, who suggested the current narrative style and the inclusion of large sections of Alfred Oates' letters. It was during my time under Professor Thomas' guidance that this manuscript developed from a rudimentary collection of names and battles into a fast-moving story around a central figure. Associate Professor Michael Vorenberg provided further advice on the work, especially with finding a publisher. I must also thank Dean Armando Bengochea, who took the time to look at the work of a freshman and recommend me to a Professor Emeritus who only worked with seniors. Cathy Brophy at Warren Publishing, Inc. has been of immense help getting this book from a computer file to a physical book. Without any assistance of these people or the support of my Mom, sister, grandfather, grandmother, aunts, uncles, cousins and friends, what you are holding in your hand would not exist. I thank all of them.

Table of Contents

List of Illustrations

Prologue

Chickahominy Swamp, Virginia

May 25, 1862

The boots tramped over Bottom's Bridge as Private Alfred Kingston Oates and the rest of the Excelsior Brigade crossed the last river that stood between the Union Army of the Potomac and the Confederate capital of Richmond. The air was quiet and the reports of cannon seldom heard. Private Oates marched with the trappings of war all around him, past long, dirty columns of men, horses, wagons and cannon. Fields were stripped bare, villages reduced to burnt timbers. Rebellion had worn hard on this corner of Virginia.

The brigade halted and Oates threw his knapsack onto the clover field he would call his home that night. Soldiers milled about erecting tents and lighting cooking fires while falling to discuss the war. None could guess when or if the Rebels would stand to fight, but they all knew that the Union would soon prevail. Three weeks earlier, in the nightmarish battle at Williamsburg, the brigade had lost a quarter of their number yet had still whipped the Rebels. They were pursuing the fleeing Confederates right up to the doorstep of Richmond and the end of the war seemed near. Before long, Oates reflected as he chewed his dinner, the Excelsior Brigade, proven in battle and with their old general Daniel Sickles back, would help crush the rebellion and he could gloriously return home.

Daniel E. Sickles, Congressman turned acquitted murderer turned recruiter and commander of the Excelsior Brigade. Pictured here after he had attained the rank of major-general of Volunteers. Courtesy Library of Congress.

Chapter One

The Politician General
New York City
June, 1861

The locomotive screeched into the station and Dan Sickles debarked to find his hometown of New York City in a tumult of patriotic activity. The fever had built during the contentious election of 1860. Tensions increased after South Carolina's secession from the Union that December and exploded on April 12, 1861, when rebel forces shelled their countrymen at Fort Sumter in Charleston Harbor, plunging the nation into the biggest crisis of its short history. By June, militia units from New York were shipping to Washington to defend the capital, and the city Dan Sickles stepped into was one in the flurries of war.

He descended upon City Hall Park to find his soldiers, the best the State of New York had to offer, he claimed, hungry and dirty with some drunk and unruly. Sickles had staked his reputation on this new unit, but to anyone who passed their encampment, the brigade looked like the refuse of society. He would not tolerate lack of discipline or such a mark against his name. Immediately, he ordered his men to Crosby Street where he had them all given a haircut and a shave for 10 cents apiece. With the barber earning a fortune, Sickles dashed off to line up ferries. The men, newly shorn and faces raw, were immediately transported to an unused racetrack on Long Island. There Sickles began to demonstrate theirs and his potential. He charged his sub commanders, politically connected citizens aspiring for military glory, to take out their army manuals and, in what was being repeated across the country at the time, try to mold civilians into soldiers.

What a difference it was for Sickles from less than a year earlier. In November of 1860 he was a politician without public support, the least desirable position anyone could have. Descended from a long line of Knickerbockers, he had worked his way up the ranks of the Tammany Hall political machine to become an admired Congressman who served his party, rewarded his friends and was constantly climbing upwards. Sooner than he could imagine, he fell to such depths of unpopularity that he didn't even bother to run for reelection. The story of his downfall was swift, and unfortunately for Sickles, known by his constituents.

In 1857, when Dan Sickles arrived in Washington for his first term as United States Representative from the Third New York District, he came with his young wife Teresa on his arm. The two had married in 1852, already the subject of gossip. When they exchanged vows, he was 34 and she, the daughter of one of his friends, was 16 and pregnant (it was also rumored that he had had an affair with her mother years before but this was never proved nor forgotten). Notwithstanding her controversial start with Sickles, Teresa grew to be considered a fine wife and once in Washington the two moved in the highest social circles. One of those they encountered and befriended was Philip Barton Key, U.S. Attorney for the District of Columbia and son of Francis Scott Key, author of "The Star-Spangled Banner." Before very long the latest talk of the capital was an ongoing affair between Teresa and Key.

It seemed that everyone in Washington knew of the affair, except for Sickles himself. That ended on February 24, 1859, shortly before Sickles was to begin his second term, when he received an anonymous note telling him of the liaison. Sickles, a well-known adulterer himself, who had once brought a prostitute with him onto the floor of the New York Senate, was distraught. Weeping, he showed the note to a friend, Congressional Clerk George B. Wooldridge, in the lobby of the House of Representatives. On the night of Feb. 26, he confronted Teresa with the note and forced her to write a detailed confession, which she signed with her maiden name.

The next day, still agitated, Sickles saw out of his window Philip Key standing on the sidewalk signaling to Teresa. This is when, as Sickles reported later, he lost control. In a rage he grabbed two derringers and one revolver and thundered out of the house. Key bolted but was chased down by Sickles in Lafayette Park, across the street from the White House.

"Key you scoundrel, you have dishonored my home! You must die!" Sickles shouted.

Raging forward, Sickles fired his first gun. The bullet grazed Key. Key turned and ran for his life. He threw his opera glasses at Sickles, trying anything that might stop the armed madman pursuing him. Sickles fired again. This time he aimed well. The bullet hit Key in the groin. Key stumbled towards a tree, begging Sickles for mercy. He called for help, but the passersby were too shocked and afraid of the wild-eyed Representative to move.

Sickles cocked the gun, and pulled the trigger. Misfire. He cocked again. He pulled the trigger and the gun cracked and the smell of gunpowder filled the park air. The bullet hit Key in the chest, fatally wounding him. Key slumped over, bleeding his life away, as Sickles put away his gun and walked home. A United States Congressman had committed murder, in daylight, with dozens of citizens watching the grisly end to an affair.[1]

For most politicians, murder would have ended their careers. Sickles, however, was no ordinary politician. He turned himself in to the Attorney General soon after the murder and his cell was the jailer's comfortable office. Sickles' friend Edwin Stanton, future Secretary of War under Lincoln, agreed to defend him in court. They pled temporary insanity — a first in American law — yet it was not temporary insanity but rather public opinion that was Sickles' true defense. His case centered on the wicked Key, lustfully seducing the young Teresa and vilely betraying his friend. Sickles was merely a wronged husband, out of his mind with grief. The trial was widely reported in the papers, mostly in favor of Sickles. Stanton directed the charade so well that when the verdict was read (not guilty, of course) the jury stood and cheered. The handsome Sickles walked free, a noble Victorian gentleman who had successfully defended his honor and home. He stood at the height of popularity and a national hero.

Soon thereafter, Teresa asked her husband for forgiveness, pleading that she knew she had sinned and wished only to reconcile. Sickles kindly took her back, and at this point the press turned on him. The newspapers reviled him for forgiving one who had so cruelly betrayed him and forced him into his recent trials. It became apparent that the combination of those who were still shocked Sickles had killed Key, those who supported rival Tammany candidates, and the large numbers who now had lost respect for the forgiving Sickles constituted the majority of his district. Fallen from favor, he did not seek reelection in 1860. When Lincoln entered Washington in early 1861, Sickles exited. To all who cared to watch anymore, his career appeared to be over.[9] But he would not be finished yet. After a few months in the shadows he encountered a stroke of fortune and found the opportunity to propel himself to an even higher level of fame than he had ever enjoyed. The United States was going to war with itself.

Immediately after the bombardment and surrender of Fort Sumter, President Lincoln issued a proclamation calling for 75,000 troops to suppress the insurrection in South Carolina (open rebellion had not yet spread beyond the Palmetto State). Dan Sickles saw a chance to serve his country and reclaim his former popularity. He petitioned Governor Edwin Morgan of New York for permission to raise a regiment of infantry. Governors during the Civil War were largely responsible for the recruiting of the army, each state having been given a quota from the Federal government to fill. With populous New York City largely Democratic, Gov. Morgan, a Republican, needed all the political support he could find. He approved Sickles' petition.

With the help of Captain William Wiley, an old Tammany Hall colleague, Sickles went into action. The Tammany strings began to be pulled, handbills were soon printed, and within two weeks he had eight companies of 100 men each. A regiment consisted of 10 companies, and with that goal easily within reach, Gov. Morgan encouraged Sickles to continue recruiting and authorized him to raise an entire brigade of five regiments. Sickles was a politician by nature and he used his innate talents to launch a massive campaign to raise the required number of men.

When Sickles began recruiting his brigade, he immediately visited his old friend Charles K. Graham. Graham was a military veteran, having served in the United States Navy from 1841 to 1848, during which time he took part in the Mexican War. He resigned after Winfield Scott captured Mexico City, and returned to his hometown of New York to study engineering. Graham was also a veteran of Tammany politics. In 1857 he was appointed construction engineer of the Brooklyn Navy Yard - a position of power and patronage.

Graham was patriotic and wished to serve his country again. He joined Sickles in his quest to save the Union. Persuading a man of influence, one of military experience moreover, to help recruit and eventually fight was a victory for Sickles. But the real victory was what Graham brought to the fledgling brigade besides himself. He convinced, through words or through example, more than 400 workers of the Navy Yard to lay down their hammers and winches and pick up the rifle and the bayonet.

Graham's response served to propel Sickles even farther onward in his campaign to create the greatest brigade in the Union. New York City alone was not large enough to recruit a whole 5,000 man strong brigade, especially when other regiments, companies, and independent units competed for the fighting men of the North's largest city. Sickles therefore looked beyond the limits of Manhattan, and soon attracted companies from as far away as Paw Paw, Michigan, and as near as Staten Island. Sickles' secretary, Theodore Launer, claimed that "no fewer than seventeen regiments, and one hundred and twenty additional companies, making in all twenty-nine thousand men [had] applied within six weeks" to join Sickles' brigade.[3] No doubt Launer was exaggerating to increase Sickles' reputation, but the truth under the posturing was that the recruitment drive was phenomenal.

However, Sickles soon ran into problems. He had named his brigade the "Excelsior" Brigade, taking the name from New York's state motto, which means "Onward and upward." By taking the state's motto as his brigade's name, not only did he assert his men's aspirations to a higher purpose, but he also dedicated it to represent the State of New York. The problem was that, demographically, it did not represent the whole state. Those who came from outside New York City never made up more than a few of each regiment's ten companies. They predominantly came, like Graham's Navy Yard workers, from the city itself or very close by. Farmers and townspeople from Republican upstate regions began complaining to Gov. Morgan about their absence in the "state" brigade. Morgan, who had been elected by these farmers, could not afford to alienate his base of support. Further, he had grown uneasy with the idea of a brigade dominated by political rivals (Sickles' original regiment had been billed as "Democratic in politics, but Union to the very marrow of the back bone").[3a] Morgan had only allowed the Tammany-run brigade to exist because New York needed soldiers. But now the presence of the brigade threatened recruitment of other men. Upstaters did not want their state's brigade full of city men and might not enlist if they were not satisfied. Morgan had an opportunity to discredit a Democrat and boost overall recruitment at the same time.

Citing the lopsided locales of enlistment, Morgan ordered Sickles to disband 32 of the 40 companies he had already raised.

Dan Sickles was outraged. He was raising men for the Union, and he had performed better than anyone could have expected. He was doing it all for his country (he said), but now he was being ordered to send away 3,200 willing volunteers. Sickles did not even consider his brigade under the authority of Gov. Morgan. He had recruited the men himself with no help from the state government and so he viewed it as an independent brigade, dedicated to serving the Union and not responsible to anyone below the national level. The men currently assembling in City Hall Park answered to Sickles, and he answered to the President. It was as simple as that — Gov. Morgan had no business interfering in Sickles' affairs.

Sickles set out to correct what he saw as a misguided and perilous order. He left on the first train for Washington and won a meeting with the President. He urged Lincoln to federalize the troops; put them under the authority of the national government, out of the hands of the petty Morgan. Lincoln had no immediate answer, and could only promise it would be solved in due time. Sickles returned to New York, his future in the hands of the Federal Government.

Sickles was encouraged by the state of events. He had managed to borrow a circus tent from P.T. Barnum, and now had a home for the brigade headquarters on Staten Island where the brigade had its newest camp. Sickles had been lucky to find a campsite so close to New York City. It was near Forts Washington and Wadsworth, near the Verrazano Narrows, and in an isolated setting where he could better enforce military discipline. The land was muddy, soft, and surrounded by thick woods. He named it Camp Scott, after Winfield

Charles K. Graham, Brooklyn Navy Yard engineer turned colonel of the Fifth Regiment. This picture was taken after he left the regiment and had been promoted to brigadier general. Courtesy Library of Congress.

Scott, General-in-Chief of the Union armies, the man who had the authority to use or pigeonhole the Excelsior Brigade. Dan Sickles was ever the politician.

What was more, Sickles had heard rumors of some excellent news. The Secretary of War had finally decided on the situation of Sickles' men. Federal agents had arrived in New York to swear in the brigade as United States Volunteers, not state units like every other volunteer unit in the Civil War. Secretary Cameron had sent word that Sickles' Brigade was to be accepted into the service of the Federal government and therefore free from the control of New York and Gov. Morgan.

Under the hot sun of early summer, Sickles' men filed down the beach to officially take up service in the Union army. It was over two months since the seceding forces had bombarded Fort Sumter on April 12. At that time Sickles was a nobody, an outcast who had fallen from the heights of popularity and become a social and political leper in his home city. In the time since, he had risen out of the ashes of his old career and turned to a military life. Now, on June 20th and the following few days, he watched the individual men who had trusted him with their lives, who had been moved by his speeches and handbills and whose patriotism he had stirred. As they took the oath of allegiance to the United States of America, Sickles could smile. There were still problems to be dealt with — he was half a million dollars in debt from personally covering the brigade's costs, the men were still raw, the camp not yet built — but those were for later.

Sickles had climbed out of ignominy and failure to reach a position of impor-

Cartoon in Baltimore newspaper from early 1861. It shows Sickles recruiting his brigade from the dregs of society in the Five Points, one of the least respectable sections of Manhattan. Likely drawn by a political enemy of Sickles. Courtesy Brown University Library.

tance with his men. Raising the brigade was difficult and had almost slipped away when the men waiting in bureaucratic limbo had begun to desert to other units in large numbers. But Sickles had persevered and held onto thousands who wanted to fight under him. Looking down the beach he saw almost four thousand men who looked to him as their leader. He watched as they were sworn into the service of the government. The uncertainty was over. The Excelsior Brigade was born.

Camp Scott. July 25th

Dear Mother

I write these lines to
you in good health
hoping to find you enjoying
the same. We have had very
stiring times seince I wrote
to you last. On Monday the first
regiment got orders to march & at
5 oclock in the afternoon they
marched out escorted by 2nd & 3rd.
We did not like to see them go before us
because the friends rifles was with
and it appeared like if part of our
company was going. Then on Wesin
day morning the 2nd Marched out
& in the afternoon the third went,
We are the only ones occupying
the camp ground as the 4 regiment is
encamped 1 mile away. All week
the has been one continuell string
of wagons passing in & out hauling
tents, baggage. ammunition &c.

Chapter Two

The Soldier

Camp Scott, Staten Island

July 5, 1861

The cannonball skipped across the waters of New York Harbor before plunging into distant Long Island and embedding itself in the land. Oates and five others grabbed hold of the rifled cannon and pushed. The wheels of the gun had sunken six inches into the sand, and the squad launched themselves at it to lift it out and continue the testing. They fired off a few more rounds, observing how the rifled barrel of the cannon gave the projectiles spin and accuracy. Oates gazed at the projectiles shooting across the waves until his stomach began to cry out for food, and the soldiers headed back to camp for the night.

It had been another long day in his new life as a soldier. The Assembly for Buglers call had rung out across the camp at five a.m., alerting Oates that he had only fifteen minutes until the buglers sounded Assembly and the day started. When they did, from canvas tents dotting the landscape, men appeared rubbing their eyes and in various states of dress all headed to the parade ground. Orderly sergeants dressed the sleepy lines, Reveille sounded, and the men were off to their daily routine. First came breakfast, not much more than coffee and salted beef. Soon morning duties were sounded and some went off to picket — guard duty around the perimeter of the camp — others to fatigue duty where they fetched water, dug latrines, and cleaned the streets of camp.

At ten was drill call, and the Excelsior Brigade labored in the slow process of learning how to fight. Marching was the most important of the drills. Battle tactics of the day descended from the Napoleonic times when fights were won by elaborate maneuvers and fast advances. If the men could not follow the orders of their officers in a hail of bullets and fog of smoke, the unit would disintegrate and fall easy prey for the massed volleys of the enemy. And so the new soldiers drilled, marching left, right, left, right. For some units few of the men knew their left from right, and had bundles of straw and hay tied to their feet and drilled to the commands of "straw-foot" and "hay-foot." This was not necessary in Oates' company. They had recruited early and almost every man among them was at least somewhat schooled and spoke English.

The recruits then moved onto musket drills. Until supper they sweated in their new government issued uniforms under the hot July sun, learning with outdated muskets from 1830 that weighed fourteen pounds. The procedure to fire was complex but needed to be ingrained into every soldier's hands so the unit could fire rapidly in battle when an extra volley could separate victory and survival from defeat and death. Early in the war the presses and public on both sides of the Potomac were pushing their governments to action, but neither yet had the disciplined, lockstep army that battle required. War would have to wait until these inexperienced volunteers learned the trade.

The afternoon had slowly given way to evening and Oates and his regiment ended their drills. The men walked back to their tents to drop off their muskets when a great booming sound reverberated across the summer air. They followed the noise, which repeated itself again and again, and found on the beach a squad of artillerists trying out a new rifled cannon. Oates watched as the cannon roared and belched smoke, and a little black speck shot across the sky and buried itself in the ground on the other side of the harbor. It was a great show for the men, but by the supper hour they men were tired and more than ready for their few hours of free time they enjoyed each day.

Private Alfred Oates approached his tent and dropped his musket near his sleeping area. It had been over two months since he had left his home in Pittsburgh to join the army and serve his country in its time of need. Like most of the volunteers in the North and South, he had never been in an army before. In fact,

Regiment at drill on Staten Island. The round teepe-like tent at the right was the Sibley tent, designed in the 1850s by Henry Hopkins Sibley who would become the Confederate commander of the South's failed New Mexico campaign. Courtesy New York State Military Museum.

when the United States was last at war, with Mexico, Oates was a twelve year-old boy clutching at the side of a ship that would take him from his old life in England to his new life in America. But when the Confederates in South Carolina fired on Fort Sumter, Oates had no hesitation to sign up to defend the country in which he had grown to manhood and the home and friends he had made since age twelve. Oates joined with a company that was forming in Pittsburgh under a man named John Glass and they crossed the Appalachians to join a new brigade being created by the famous Dan Sickles.

Oates and his messmates walked around camp with the sun still hanging in the sky, lingering on in the lengthy summer twilight. After supper the friends from Pittsburgh walked the streets of camp seeing who were these brothers-in-arms with whom they would be serving alongside for three years or until the war ended. Oates' Pittsburgh company had arrived in New York to find that they had been placed in the Fifth Regiment of the brigade, led by the former engineer Charles K. Graham and that they were Company A of that regiment.

Oates and his group of friends walked through the clean streets of camp towards the areas of the other companies. They stayed clear of Companies G, H, I, and K, which were made up of the dockworkers Graham had brought with him to the brigade and were reported to be rough types. They worked their way around the other parts of the camp and met other young men like them, eager to fight the great battle that would save the Union and win immortal glory for themselves.

Fifth Regiment at drill on Staten Island. Note the regimental band with fife and drum leading the drills. Courtesy New York State Military Museum.

There were some from Boston, they must be in Company D. Lots of New Yorkers, Company C was from Long Island and E from Manhattan, and even fellow Keystoners, farmers from Tidioute in the northwestern part of the state. All of these men seemed to be going somewhere, and Oates and his friends followed along to see another wonder of this military life.

The men were all ambling towards Company B, the most famous of all the companies. These men Oates knew, or at least had heard about them. They were a company from the U.S. Zouave Cadets - part of a fad of military entertainment that had swept the country in the years preceding the war. The Victorian Era was the age of the romanticized soldier, and there were few that attracted more to the American mind than the Zouaves of the French Imperial Army. Based on the flamboyant dress of Berber soldiers from the mountains of France's Algerian colony, the Zouaves became the pride of the French army and the epitome of

the beau-ideal soldier. Wearing tasseled hats, short blue jackets with gold trim, and bright red pantaloons, the Zouaves charged into the enemy ranks with a coolness and bravery that captured the imaginations of the American public when it heard of these European lions.

If there is one thing that Americans are particularly adept at, it is imitation. Almost immediately after word of the Zouaves made it to the New World, American Zouave companies sprang up across the country. They were militia companies, citizens who trained for war in the case of emergency, a tradition carried over from colonial days. There was no need for actual military training for these Zouaves and they mostly existed as entertainment for the Americans who would go out to the local common and watch these bright young warriors perform elaborate maneuvers and display their marksmanship. Zouave associations toured the country, and when the war rolled around presented themselves as the crack warriors Lincoln (or Davis, for the few southern Zouaves) desired.

Pvt. Lorenzo Clark, a Zouave in Company B. Courtesy Michael McAfee.

The company that became Company B of the Fifth Regiment, Excelsior Brigade had all the normal experience of American Zouaves, the drill, close-order maneuvers, etc., but they had something else that few other Zouaves had and that mattered much more than the red pants. They had veterans.

Civil War Zouaves were almost all Americans aping Frenchmen, but Company B somehow had actual French Zouaves. There were only ten or so of them, but they were enough to enthrall the young Americans who were both eager and frightened at the idea of battle, and looked to the old soldiers for some indication of what war was like. These Frenchmen had fought in the Crimean War — Britain, France and the Ottoman Empire against Russia in 1855. They had been in the central battle of the war, the siege of Sebastapol, and had charged over the ramparts at Malakoff - part of the defenses of Sebastapol. Like most veterans, the French liked to talk about their victory, and found a willing audience in the young recruits. The Zouaves had even made a model of Malakoff outside their tents for the Americans to view. Pvt. Oates described it as, *"made of wood and mud and they have all the entrenchments dug in front of it just the same as the allies made. The top is all surrounded with 100's of small sand bags, you can see the marks of the cannon balls on the tower. Their cannons are made of small bottles. They had it illuminated last night."*[4] Oates and others, young men who had left their homes to enter into the company of strangers and into a new world of war, must have looked with awe at the model wondering how long until they would have to storm such a fortification themselves."

Oates turned his back to the miniature Malakoff and headed down the streets of the camp back to his tent. It was growing darker and darker and Oates found men of his company trying to enjoy the last minutes of the day. Some were playing cards or checkers, other sitting playing music, others listening to the music, and many were simply talking of what they had done that day and speculating how long before they were sent south. Oates entered his tent, crawled over to his spot of ground and, as he would do so often for the rest of the war, took out a pen and paper.

Camp Scott July 5, 1861

Dear Mother,

I write to you in good health hoping to find you the same. I do not think you get all the letters that I sent you for I have wrote about 10 to you. I suppose you would like to know how we spent the 4 of July. We have 3 rifle cannon here and at sundown on the 4 they fired a salute of 100 Guns. We had a dress parade from 10 till 12 o'clock and a grand review by General Sickles. He made us a very good speech. And was heard by thousands. We had a splendid fireworks in the evening and a ball at night wich ended at 12 o'clock. For Camp life we had a nice 4th. There was a great many people here and our company all turned out in full uniform ours and a boston company was the only company on the grounds that had wite shirts on the only fault I could find with the days fun that they did not give us some more food. I went out after dinner & bought some ginger bread and was eating it & a lady & gentleman came up to me & asked me what time we dined. I sayd we had just had our dinner. They wanted to know if we got enough to eat. & I sayd we could eat more if we could only get it. He took me into the Suttlers & I got a good dinner and a plate of ice cream & they gave me their directions and sayd for me to call and get my meals when I went to N. York, but you do not find many people like them here. I am sorry to say that some of our company got drunk & kicked up a fight in the company and the rest was mad at the officers for not putting them in the guard house . . .

Oates stopped for a moment to think of what else there was to say. Like most soldiers in the Civil War he wrote home often. He had never before taken part in anything so grand as suppressing the rebellion and was eager to tell his family and friends back home every new and amazing thing he saw. Letters were also the only way to receive news from home, and the Pittsburgh company, alone in Camp Scott hundreds of miles away from where most of them had spent all their lives, were not eager to lose connection with what they were fighting for. For Oates these were reasons for his many letters over the course of the war, ninety-nine surviving with likely an equal number lost over the years, but there was another reason closer to his heart. These letters he had, the small pieces of paper tucked away in the letter case given to him by his sweetheart Nancy Robinson, were all that now connected him to his family, the one thing in his life he had always known.

Oates was born February 19, 1836, a Monday, in Manchester, England. The Oates family had its roots in neighboring Yorkshire and Alfred's branch had moved to Manchester recently, likely in the early days of the Industrial Revolution when Manchester was the center of English industry and full of jobs. Yet America promised a still better life and Alfred's parents decided to leave the troubled Old World and chart a new life in the New. At the age of 12, Alfred Oates left the only world he had known to travel down the road to Liverpool and onto a docked steamship, the *Home*. After a five-week passage across the Atlantic, the weary family consisting of 12-year-old Alfred, his mother Sarah, and 16-year-old sister Elinor, landed at Staten Island, having arrived in America.

Alfred's father John and older sister Eliza had preceded the rest of the family. John Oates had a job in Pittsburgh as a bookkeeper and the rest of the family joined him there. The family lived near the East Commons in Allegheny City, what is now Pittsburgh's North Side. There the family lived and grew. Alfred went to school and then worked a coal refiner, all the while becoming a patriotic American proud of his new country and ready to defend his new home.

When Oates left Allegheny with his company he did not want to lose his home forever, even though he knew it was a possibility he would never return, and so he wrote whenever he could. It was most often with pen and ink, but sometimes with pencil. He wrote on patriotic stationary adorned with eagles and Columbias and Washingtons when available, which was not often. In fact, often there was no paper at all to be found. The common practice became for any letter from home to include the materials for a reply: paper, ink, envelope, and stamps.

Oates wrote mostly when he was in camp, but always immediately after a battle to reassure his family he was still in the land of the living. All letters were written, *"in a crowd of 8 or 10 Soldiers, some singing, talking and kicking up noise enough to make one crazy."*[5] Yet still he wrote, and he made sure that he stayed close to what he was fighting for.

> . . . *Six of us went to Fort Washington this morning. It is the gratest peace of stone work I ever saw. When I entered the gate it put me in mind of some of the old Buildings of rome. It is 4 stories high & from the inside it is all arched and their is not a stick of wood in it. I have got some peices of stone for sister, it is very pretty. I wrote a letter to Willy & one to Guy Freeborn & two to Bob Whitehall I will stop writing until the mail comes and see if I get any letters so that I will have some room. they have stopped Franking our letters. The mail just come in and I did not get any. You ought to see us crowding around when the mail comes. I think we will be kept here a month or so and then we will be sent to washington. We will get our arms & equipment next week, I suppose we will soon got mattresses to sleep on. I got them letters that was in Franked envelopes & it puzzled me at first to know how you got them. We expect two more companys from Pittsburgh. How do you think we wash a white shirt? We get a tin cup & put a hot stone in it and it heats it first. I saw the trial of Cunningham but did not hear of his sentance. I think taking it all that we treated better here than they are in some camps. Except camp Wilkins and they are as well off as at home. But we have the cleanest camp for you could not find a chip or a peice of paper in any of the streets in the camp. I must conclude for tattoo is beatting & we will have to put out the lights in awhile.*
>
> *Your Affectionate Son,*
> *Alfred K. Oates*

The bugle call rang across the fields and beaches to let the Bay Staters, Pennsylvanians, and New Yorkers of the Excelsior Brigade call the men to one final assembly of the day. The bugle call was not as elaborate as others the men heard during the course of the day, not like Dress Parade which was arranged for three buglers to play in counter-point, but nonetheless, it gave the bugler, "quite full scope as a soloist."[6]

The men gathered on the parade ground for the last roll call of the day. With the strains of Tattoo lingering in the air, and the low crash of the tide beating on the shores of Staten Island, Company A of the Fifth Regiment sounded their names. The light was nearly all gone as the men shouted in order. At a time of day when in years past they might have walked home from work, or opened the door on the way to visit friends, the thousands of the Excelsior Brigade asserted their existence. They were a single body training in the practices of war, having left their homes to defend them. For Oates, home and family were dear to him and he would not let go of them easily. Still, he stood there with the salt wind whipping around him and his comrades ready to go to war, charge into the cannon, and fight the enemies of this country where he had spent his life since childhood and where his family had set its roots.

Chapter Three

Patriotism

Lower Maryland

October, 1861

O
ctober 3, 1861 found Oates and his comrades in the Excelsior Brigade testing their new marching skills. Under autumnal foliage, the entire Excelsior
Brigade was heading back to Washington. For hours that day, Oates had
been on the road, trudging through Maryland and the clouds of dust raised by
thousands of feet in front of him. Finally, though, the Fifth regiment crested a
hill and the men spied the Anacosta River as it flowed slowly into the Potomac.
They saw the open field near the village of Good Hope in the southeastern part
of the District of Columbia, their home for some weeks before all this marching
had started. The First and Third Regiments of the Brigade had arrived a few days
before and set up camp. Oates and his regiment made the last few hundred yards
to their campsite and gratefully threw off their gear. They had been marching for
almost two weeks in what was considered enemy territory, and they would be back
at work constructing forts the next day, but the rest of the night they had off to
enjoy themselves and their brigade's first demonstration of military bearing.

The North had been whipped into a fervor when Fort Sumter was shelled, but
any emotion the people had felt was incomparable to the shock and anger they felt
when news came on July 21, 1861, of the Union defeat at Bull Run. On the fields
of northern Virginia, near a rail center where commerce used to travel to and from
all corners of the nation, Americans had fought Americans and thousands had
died. The battle had been a horrid display of the armies' inexperience. There were
few tactics involved and the battle did not end when one side was outmaneuvered
or outfought, but when the green Union forces panicked and "skedaddled" all the
way back to Washington. To the citizens of the North it showed that the rebellion
would not be easily suppressed and to the soldiers it showed that they had much
training to do before they were proper soldiers.

That day, twenty men of Company A crowded in Oates' tent (it was a big tent)
anxiously awaiting the tapping of the telegraph. The initial news was promising.

The Union forces were gaining ground and had routed at least one Confederate brigade. The men clapped each other on the back, claiming victory for the Union and assuring themselves that Sickles would keep them in New York until hostilities ceased in a few weeks or so. There was no sense in fighting when their country had already won the war.

Then more reports came in, and the messenger who brought them looked dazed. The battle had been lost. The Confederate forces had put to flight the entire Union army. All that now stood between the enemy and the White House was a disorganized rabble of recruits fighting not Confederates but wagons and carriages on the road to Washington.

Not long after the men had finished digesting the news, activity increased at Camp Scott. With the path to Washington open, every man loyal to the Stars and Stripes who knew how to step left, step right, was summoned to protect the Capital. The Excelsior Brigade was leaving New York and heading to the seat of war.

The First Regiment had the honor of departing camp first. However, they were still in the middle of recruiting and did not yet have enough men for a full regiment. To fill their ranks they drafted on the Fifth Regiment for one hundred men. One day after Bull Run, with the First Regiment stealing men from his own regiment, Oates got his first experience in the sufferings of war.

> "The boys was very much afraid that they would take some out of our Company, but the major sayd He would see them in Hell first. The men they picked on was most Irish and a good many of them up in years. They refused to go. And they called out our company with guns, & drew us up in a line behind them & read the Articles of War to them. & then he asked them if their was any not willing to go. an old man steped out of the ranks & wanted to speak. But Major Farnam of the 1st Rignt drew his revolver & made him step in ranks. This Farnam was captain of the Slave Watch Wanderer & he is one of the hatefullest men I ever saw. We had to drive them down to the Boat at the point of the bayanot. We did not like the job but we had to do it & the dust was ancle deep & we had to run over 2 Miles & O Lord such a set of looking devils you never saw, our uniforms looked liked gray it was so dusty . .. What hurt me the worst was an old Irish Woman that had come to see her husband and when he was ordered to fall in she did not get another chance to speak to him. She run the 2 miles & kept up with us. I asked the man to come off & talk with her till the boat started. But the officers pushed him on and would not let him speak."[7]

Charles K. Graham, their colonel, promised the men that he would get every one of them back into the Fifth Regiment, but he knew that action on that matter would have to wait. Camp Scott was fast being broken down and a few days later the Fifth Regiment received their orders. Soon they too were carried across the waters of New York Harbor towards the Potomac and war.

When Oates and the Excelsior Brigade hopped off the train in Washington in late July, they found themselves in a busy city. The flower of the North had been called to arms, and most of those arms were now in the city of Washington. The debacle at Bull Run - the Union army routed within a day's march of the Capitol - had demonstrated the vulnerability of Washington. Now all available units were called to its defense, and most of those were at work constructing a ring of forts around the city that would, by 1865, make Washington the most heavily defended city in the Western Hemisphere. Into this whirlwind stepped Oates, and he could only stick with his company mates as the brigade was whisked off to open ground and told to start building.

For over a month Oates did what he had done in Camp Scott. The brigade, largely untrained, drilled most of the day. They cleaned camp, stood picket, and constructed forts, but mostly they were dedicated to developing their own military talent. In August it was still the campaigning season, which in the temperate climate of the eastern United States lasted from the end of the muddy season in the spring until the onset of the cold and snow in winter. There was still a chance the Union commander, a talented "Young Napoleon," Major General George B. McClellan, would head out to meet the Rebels in battle before the snows set in. It was especially likely given the disposition of troops. The Union army had abandoned all ground south of the Potomac, and the Confederate army under Joseph Johnston was encamped on the south bank directly opposite McClellan's army on the north bank. Should battle occur, the Excelsior Brigade, one of the few truly cohesive large units in the army, would be at the front of the advance. Therefore, the Excelsior Brigade and Oates trained, marched and learned how to shoot.

The Fifth Regiment had recently been given Enfield rifles, the pinnacle of small arms technology at the time. The Enfield was actually a rifled musket, which meant that instead of firing a round ball through a smooth barrel, the Enfield fired a conical bullet through a barrel with spiraled grooves cut into it. The spirals spun the bullet, much like a spiraled football pass, giving it stability in flight. This method had been known for some time, but because the bullet needed to fit the spirals almost perfectly, it needed to be almost the same diameter of the gun barrel and so was difficult to ram down the barrel in battle. Rifled guns weren't practical for general troops until a French army captain, Claude Minié, developed a conical bullet with a hollowed base. When the gun was fired the hot gases in the chamber (and inside the hollowed bullet) expanded, increasing the caliber of the bullet momentarily and fitting it into the grooves. The common soldier could now insert the bullet easily and still have it fit perfectly upon exit. The other key aspect of the Enfield was that it fired a .58 caliber bullet (width of .58 inches). This meant

ELLSWORTH'S AVENGERS,

RESPECTFULLY DEDICATED

TO THE

EXCELSIOR BRIGADE, U. S. V.

Commanded by Gen. Sickel, of N. Y.

AIR —Annie Lisle.—By A. L. HUDSON.

Down where the patriot army,
　Near Potomac's side,
Guards the glorious cause of freedom,
　Gallant Ellsworth died.
Brave was the noble chieftain,
　At his country's call,
Hastened to the field of battle,
　And was first to fall.

> CHORUS.
>
> Strike, freemen, for the Union,
> 　Sheath your swords no more;
> While remains in arms a traitor,
> 　On Columbia's shore.

Entering the traitor city,
　With his soldiers true,
Leading up the Zouave columns,
　Fixed became his view.
See that rebel flag is floating,
　O'er yon building tall!
Spoke he, while his dark eyes glistened,
　Boys, that flag must fall!

> CHORUS.
>
> Strike, freemen, for the Union,
> 　Sheath your swords no more;
> While remains in arms a traitor,
> 　On Columbia's shore.

Quickly from its proud position,
　That base flag was torn,
Trampled 'neath the feet of freemen.
　Circling Ellsworth's form;
See him bear it down the landing;
　Past the traitor's door,
Hear him groan, Oh! God, they've shot him,
　Ellsworth is no more.
　　CHORUS.—Strike, freemen, &c.

First to fall, thou youthful martyr,
　Hapless was thy fate;
Hastened we as thy avengers,
　From thy native state.
Speed we on, from town and city,
　Not for wealth or fame,
But because we love the Union,
　And our Ellsworth's name.
　　CHORUS.—Strike, freemen, &c.

Traitor hands shall never sunder,
　That for which you died;
Hear the oath our lips now utter,
　Thou, our nation's pride.
By our hopes of yon bright heaven,
　By the land we love,
By the God who reigns above us,
　We'll avenge thy blood.
　　CHORUS.—Strike, freemen, &c.

NEW SONGS.

Yankee Boys so Handy, O!
Jeff Davis' Dream.
Yankee Generals.
Down the River.
Good Ship Cumberland.
Whack Row De Dow.
We'll Follow the Flag.
Stars and Stripes, Nos. 1 & 2.
Our Country's Flag.
Good Bye, or Soldier's Farewell
Col. Owen's Irish Volunteers.
Father Abraham,
Vive l'America,

Sons of Columbia.
Save the Union.
Death of Lyons.
Ellsworth's Avengers.
Death of John Brown.
Old Mountain Tree.
Battle of Fair Oaks, Va.
We are for the Union.
We will have the Union Still.
I Want to be a Soldier.
Captain with the Whiskers.
To a Soldiers Sister
Irish Volunteers,

Secession Wagon.
Goose Hangs High.
God Save the Union.
Hail to the Union.
Torn Flag.
Abraham's Daughter.
Liberty Tree.
Effie Lane, [600,000 more,
　Coming Father Abraham,
That's What's the Matter.
Jockey Hat and Feather.
Kingdom Coming,
Rock Me to Sleep, Mother.

Johnson, Song Publisher, No. 7 N. 10th St. Phila.

Patriotic song that accompanied the Excelsior Brigade to Washington. Col. Elmer E. Ellsworth was the commander of the 11th New York Infantry Regiment, a Zouave unit and was killed while taking down a Confederate flag during the Union occupation of Alexandria, Virginia, the first significant Northern casualty of the war. Library of Congress.

that the British-made Enfield could use the same ammunition as the .577 caliber American made Springfield rifled musket, eliminating possible problems with
supply. The Fifth Regiment was finally outfitted with all the proper equipment for
war. Graham had promised them a new uniform, a pair of shoes, a cap, knapsack,
haversack, and canteen even if he had to pay for them out of his own pocket. It is
not known whether he had top resort to such a method, but by the time the air
turned chill and the leaves showed their colors, the soldiers of the regiment had
their equipment.

Trudging through Maryland, Oates saw the Excelsior Brigade's newspaper
correspondent riding along the lines taking notes as he gazed at the surroundings. On September 15, the legionnaires of Sickles had assembled on their parade
ground and marched out. For the next two weeks the brigade marched up and
down the countryside of Lower Maryland. The government feared that Rebel
infiltrators might use the Southern-sympathizing region as a base of operations
within the Union, and Lincoln wanted the Confederates off of his side of the
Potomac. The brigade's official orders were to stop any flow of war material or
information to the Rebels, and they busied themselves looking for Rebel agents.

The newspaperman Oates had spied was the correspondent of the New York
Times, a rising paper in the city but with nowhere near the circulation numbers
of the powerful Herald or Tribune. Newspapers were widely read by all American
citizens and the reports appearing in broadside were the vehicle by which all public information was disseminated. The more well-known military units had correspondents attached to them who sent back regular dispatches. For the Excelsiors,
this newspaperman was "Nemo." He kept pace with Oates and the brigade, jotting
down the names of the villages the Excelsiors visited and inspected. As was usual
for the papers, he wrote in a rhetorical and inflammatory manner to stir the blood
of New Yorkers against the evil secessionists. For example, Nemo described the
village of Port Tobacco as "the grand centre of treason in Southern Maryland." "It
is a small village, lying at the head of a short, broad, shallow branch of the Potomac
River . . . The creek was once navigable to the river, but it has gradually filled up,
and with the characteristic inertia of these people, nothing has been done to remedy it. Until now it is useless almost for navigation, having only about two feet of
water within a mile of the village.

"The inhabitants are intensely treasonable in their sentiments, and the soldiers of the Union were very much of an eye-sore to them. The men were silent,
but the women gave free vent to their feelings of hatred. But this mattered little.
The Negroes were true to the Union and to us, and the most valuable information
was gained."[8]

For two weeks the brigade stormed through the woods and swamps of southern Maryland where the whites were less dignified than the blacks. The commanders reported having caught a great number of Rebel agents (whether this is
true or not is indeterminable), and that their job was done. The brigade marched

back into Good Hope and Oates picked up his shovel as Nemo rushed off to submit his story.

Although army life was difficult, the men did not want to leave it. All had volunteered and dedicated themselves to the cause of restoring the Union. One of Oates' comrades was a 15 year-old boy from Hanover, Massachusetts who had run away from home to fight for his country. This boy, Winfield Scott Guerney, joined what would become Company D of the Fifth Regiment. While his mother, "in her anxiety for his welfare," made all efforts to get him discharged from the Excelsior Brigade and sent back home, Guerney wanted to fight and had written home to tell his mother so.

Camp Good Hope,
Washington, D. C., Sept. 7, 1861

Dear Mother:

It is with regret and sorrow I learn that you are trying to clear me from the army. If you succeed in doing it, I shall never come home. I was about to send you some money, but I will never sent home one cent to aid you in getting me out of the army; so, mother, if you want to see your boy again, don't attempt it.

You wanted to know how I feel about going to fight. Mother, I and all of us listen for the long-roll of the drum to call us to arms. Every eye is placed on the messengers, as they ride through our camp to the Colonel's tent, expecting that every new one brings an order to march. Mother, I am ready for the battlefield. I came here to fight the secessionists, and I will fight them, although I fall at the first discharge of arms. I cannot die a more glorious death.

Mother, this is no hasty thought of mine. If it be my lot thus to fall, than I am ready; if to go safe through the war, then I shall be safe. Don't look at the worst side of things, but keep up a stout heart.[9]

The story of Winfield Guerney, who remained in the army, was appreciated and understood by the men of Excelsior Brigade. These men were volunteers. They had willingly left their homes, when it was quite easy to sit out the war, to fight for the Union. They had signed up because they believed that the current crisis threatened their country and way of life enough that defending Lincoln's government was defending their own homes.

Further, they had volunteered for the Excelsior Brigade, a brigade whose general spoke as ardently as possible of taking the war into the homes and hearths of the South and forcing the Rebels back into the Union. They had signed up to fight and intended to do so. It was true that Oates' companions sometimes would have preferred not to fight at all. When news of victory at Bull Run came into the tents, the men were happy to say that Sickles would keep them out of battle until the war was over. In general, however, the men viewed battle not as a place of danger but a place of glory. And they wanted to win glory and win the war. Later, when Sickles was having problems with his divisional commander, General Joseph Hooker, it was rumored that the Excelsiors would be transferred to another division which was guarding roads around Baltimore. This proposition was met with disgust from the brigade. Oates wrote home that, *"We would not like it at all, too much like Home Guards."* There was an honor in being in a combat brigade, and actually being in combat. The rebellion provided that opportunity, and the Excelsiors did not want it to slip away. In the first year of war, before they had been tempered by flying lead and exploding steel, they were eager soldiers. They had signed up for battle, and they wanted it. Even if it ended in "glorious death."

    Oates was standing picket outside camp one night when he heard movement in the woods a ways over. He silently motioned the other men on the picket line to him and they gathered to confer. Others had heard it too; he was not imagining things, a constant worry when on picket, watching for approaching enemy. Oates' small group argued about what the noise could mean, but there was little doubt as to what they needed to do. They went to investigate a possible intrusion.

    The Excelsior Brigade was once again posted in southern Maryland, with the Fifth Regiment encamped near that "intensely treasonable" village of Port Tobacco.[8] In that area it was the habit of the Rebels on the Virginia shore to paddle across the Potomac at night to pick up news of all the Union preparations. Oates and company crept through the woods, keeping an eye out for any Confederates with loaded muskets. One of them spied something in the woods that had not been there earlier, and the men slowly moved in. Soon they could make out a shape in the moonlight. It was a boat. Not a large boat, but big enough to carry a squad of men. There must have been Rebels crossing the river that night, and this must be their boat. The rebs had carried it far out of the water and hid it in brush, but it had been found all the same. Now those Rebels were about to be stranded on the wrong side of the Potomac. Oates and company quickly swept the branches off of this "splendid boat."[10] It was full of bullet holes, not enough to make it un-riverworthy, but enough to show it had been used for target practice by training Confederates or discovered by Union pickets before. Either way it was enemy property, and Oates and the rest of the picket line, after making a brief sweep for the Rebels it had contained, hauled it back to camp. The next night it was used against its former owners. Twenty men of the Fifth Regiment paddled across in it to the Virginia shore for their own reconnaissance.

    The Excelsior Brigade's stay in Good Hope after their first reconnaissance to southern Maryland was short-lived. The Fifth Regiment (except Company D, which had been detached for an extended march to Leonardstown, Maryland) entered the borders of the District of Columbia on October 3. While in Good Hope the men were largely confined to camp with only five passes to Washington issued to each regiment per day. The Excelsiors, besides drilling constantly, finished construction on three forts, which Gen. McClellan designated Forts Stanton, Carroll, and Greble, that commanded the approach to Washington from the south. How-

ever, they were soon redeployed to southern Maryland. Rebel activity along the
lower stretches of the Potomac called the Excelsior Brigade out of the camp only
a few weeks after they returned to it.

By October, 1861, a small crisis was brewing on the Potomac. Midway between

JACK TARS, AHOY!!
Let us Open the Potomac!

WANTED IMMEDIATELY
FOR CO. I, 5th REGIMENT,
EXCELSIOR BRIGADE,
50 ABLE-BODIED SEAMEN
TO COMPLETE THE COMPANY.

The Regiment is now at the Seat of War, and is commanded by Col. CHAS. K. GRAHAM, once a
"Reefer;" and Capt. ARTHUR WILKINSON, of Co. I, was once a "Skipper" in the Merchant service.
The Company is intended to operate in the Inlets of the Chesapeake, and on the Potomac, and will
see a full share of active service and glorious adventure.
☞ All Sailors who prefer Active Service and Fresh Beef, to midnight watches and salt junk,
are invited to join.

APPLY AT 17 BROADWAY, IN BASEMENT,
Or at Office of Excelsior Brigade, Staten Island Ferry, New York.

Baker & Godwin, Printers, Printing-House Square, Opposite City Hall, New York.

*Recruitment poster for Company I of the Fifth Regiment from the autumn of 1861. The action
in the inlets of the Chesapeake mentioned refers to the regiment's posting near Port Tobacco and
Matthias Point. Library of Congress.*

Washington and the Atlantic the river took a sharp bend and the Virginia side jutted out in the river. On this piece of land, Matthias Point, the Confederates had constructed batteries, each consisting of 4 to 6 cannon. The Rebels were now able to fire on ships approaching the Point, rounding it, and steaming away. In the time it took a ship to proceed the five or six miles past the batteries, the Confederates could have taken dozens of shots at it. Currently the Rebels were wretched marksmen and had only a few cannon, but if strongly fortified, Matthias Point would be able to shut down the Potomac to all Union shipping. The river was one of Washington's lifelines and one route by which supplies entered the capital for the army. Lincoln could not afford to lose his water highway; something needed to be done.

As Matthias Point was directly opposite Port Tobacco, Maryland, the Union officials called upon the only men with experience in that area, the Excelsior Brigade, to build a fort on the Maryland side to counter the Rebel batteries. Once again the Excelsior Brigade struck camp and began marching southward.

Oates knew why he was in Port Tobacco. The men in the regiments read the newspaper and knew of the situation at Matthias Point. Indeed, the whole North knew of the grief the batteries were giving Washington. The presence of an entire brigade opposite Matthias Point, the construction of a fort, and the Union gun boats patrolling the river all indicated that the government was serious about eliminating these Confederate cannon.

The first couple of weeks in Port Tobacco were entertaining for Oates. He still had to construct forts, as he had in Good Hope, and he still had to drill, but in his free time he was able to watch the war. He wrote home that, *"we go down to the river whenever we get a chance and watch Uncle Sam's gun boats shelling the batteries."*[10]

As much as it was enjoyable to watch, there was a lingering feeling that he and his brigade would quickly need to rise from the sidelines and enter the fights. Talking matters over while sitting around the campfire eating oysters they had stolen from the officers, the men knew they were too close to the action to be far removed from the danger. Once when Oates was by the river enjoying himself shooting ducks, *"a gun boat just out from in under their batteries and made directly for us. We did not know whether it was a Rebel or a union gun boat. There was only 6 of us and we thought we had better leave on short notice."*[10]

Oates wrote that with the situation as it was, it was inevitable that they would be sent across soon. He did not know that Col. Graham was already making all the necessary preparations for that trip. The Fifth was uniquely suited for the job of destroying the batteries. Company I of the Regiment was full of former sailors who, as one recruitment poster put it, "prefer Active Watches and Fresh Beef, to midnight watches and salt junk."[10a] The company was commanded by Captain Arthur Wilkenson, a skipper in the merchant service before the war. Graham, who likely knew Wilkenson before the war at the Brooklyn Navy Yard, put him to work immediately upon reaching Port Tobacco.

Capt. Wilkenson was ordered to seize a number of small boats and man them with crews of sailors from his company. These boats, with Wilkenson at their head, sailed across the Potomac to reconnoiter the shoreline and note the creeks and inlets around Matthias Point. Before Graham could draw up a plan of attack on Matthias Point he needed reliable information on the lay of the land and the number of Confederates stationed there. For two weeks Company I, covered by the 12-pound cannon of the Union gunboats *Freeborn* and *Island Belle*, paddled nightly across the river in their confiscated boats, one of which was the Rebel one Oates had found in the brush. Soon Col. Graham decided from the information at hand that there was not a Confederate presence on Matthias Point "sufficient to oppose the landing of troops."[11] Acting Master William T. Street of the U.S. cutter *Dana* volunteered his vessel for the expedition and the naval component of the operation was led by Acting Master Arnold Harris, captain of the *Island Belle*. During the evening of November 9, the *Island Belle* with the *Dana* in tow, ran up the Port Tobacco creek and 400 picked men of the Excelsior Brigade embarked to put an end to the pesky Confederate batteries. One of these was Oates, and he described the expedition in a letter home.

Camp Finton, Port Tobaco, Nov 12th, 1861

Dear Mother, Father & Sister's,

I received a letter from Willy, Sally, & Mother & was very glad to here from the Children. I answered their letters and directed them to Sewickley. I am in good health indeed never was better in health. Last Sunday was a beutifull day & it is the Soldiers day of rest. at 5 o'clock we have a dress parade, and after that was over on Sunday last we was congratulating ourselves on a good night sleep when orders came for not one of us was to leave our avenue till after 10 o'clock at night. About 7 o'clock they took 60 out of our company & gave us 40 rounds of fresh Cartridges & orders our company to fall out in line with nothing but our Overcoats on.[1] All the boys were guessing wat it was for but we did not know. they formed us in line with some others of the Rigiment (400 in all). And informed us not to speak or wisper nor to shoot a gun under pain of death no matter what we saw or hurd. They took all the Revolvers and knives from them that had them & then marched us down to a point in the bay whare their was the gun boat Island Belle & a Cutter awaited for us. We embarked on board & at a few minutes to 3 o'clock they Steamed across the River. Then we was informed that we was going to Matthias Point. We landed after a good deal of trouble for they could not get the boats close to

---

1   The men were most likely ordered to only wear overcoats so that, should there arise the need for swimming. The heavy uniforms normally worn would have dragged many soldiers down to their deaths.

shore on account of having to heavy loads on. The word was jump out Boys
wich we did. But not with pleasure for the water was very cold & was up to
our Back sides. & we formed in line of battle & stood their for an hour shiv-
ering like dog's not with fright but with cold. But the word came for us to
march forward and it was dark yet & we did not know but what they might
be 10,000 Rebels about us. We marched forward about 3 or 4 Miles & then
day broke and then we could see the Sacred soil of Virginia. It is a butifull
country about their. We could not see the Rebel troops but saw several squads
of their Mounted Pickets. Two of their Pickets mistooks us for their own men
& road close to us & they was dressed just like our french Zouaves. We shot
one of them the other made his escape. We advance to a spendid farm & their
destroyed a the Barn full of Wheat and 18 Stacks of wheat. While we was
destroying the barn I saw 3 Mounted Rebels way down the road watching us
but they kept out of the way of our rifles. After we destroyed all we could we
began to return towards the shore & destroyed all the houses we come across.
We saw a beutifull house that had been shelled by the gun boat it looked
awfull. You have no idea what civil war is till you see it. Their was some
of the crew of the gun boat went on shore with us. They are the fearless set
of Devils I ever saw. The Rebel pickets had taken possesion of the house that
had been shelled, so we burnt it down to also the barn and 2 out houses. We
returned to the shore about 9 o'clock & had got ready to embark for the Gun
boat when the Officers on the Gun Boat saw the Rebels coming. Their was 2
companys of Artillery and 4 Rigiments of Infantry. They was a general rush
the river bank to get in line of Battle. & their we stood 400 of us one the same
spot of Ground that Leutenant Ward with his 60 men was killed. Their we
stood & looked at one another & thought, here is another Ball's Bluff affair.[2]
But we were determined to fight till the last. For we could not retreat for
it would take us 2 hours to get in to the Gun Boat. But it appears that they
had been wrong informed about our numbers & we was informed that they
had sent scouting parties out to find out our numbers. After we got on the
Gun Boat they comenced to throw shells into some woods on the left & then
landed some men the second time & set fire to them. The Gun Boat Freeborn
was to be their to help us but she run up the river in the night & when she

---

2   On October 21, Union forces crossed the Potomac near Ball's Bluff, VA. The Federals
were ambushed while retreating and suffered almost 900 casualties. It was the largest
Union disaster since Bull Run.

went to come down the Batteries opened on her & she could not pass down to us. If the Rebels had been awair of our arrival soon enough their would have been few of us left to give an account of themselves. We would not care for 2 or 3 rigiments of them for the gunboat could have covered us & I am sure we could have whipt them. We captured a lot of horses 3 was caveldry horses, a fine bull, 2 cows & a calf numerous chickens & in fact anything that was fit to carry off. We could only bring 5 horses across the river. I could not tell you how many contrabrand niggars for their is good many in our camp. Their was about 30 or 40 came to us in a large barge they had been rowing for 12 hours & had a flag of truce was flying wich was nothing else but an old shirt tail. You should have seen them when we caught a hold of their line & pulled them along side of the gun boats. Their was wild with joy, such a looking set. If Barnum could have got just as they landed on the Gun Boat he could have made a good deal of Money. I had forgot to tell you their is no permanent Battery at the Point it is nothing but fields peices wich they move about as a make believe. The Captain of the gun boat was very much pleased with us & he informed us that we had acomplished what the Government was going to do at the expense of a Million & half of dollars. For Matthias Point has always been a dread to them. The Government was going to send 4,000 men & 15 Gun Boats to do what 400 of us & one gun boat had accomplished & we can say that we had advanced further & in fact the first that as advanced in this Part of Virginia. For they say themselves that no troops shall return that attempts to land at the Point. We saw the graves whare the union troops was buried that landed from the Freeborn. They did get more than 30 yards before they were attacked & killed. You can think what kind of fire the Barn and 18 stacks of wheat made When the Boys that was left in camp saw the fire & it was about 18 miles away from them. They could only get 2 prisonars & had to give them a shot before they would stop running they was armed with revolvers. When we returned to the Maryland side their was a good many people from Port Tobbaco waiting to see us & you could tell by their countanance that they did not like to see us return the way we did. they have often toled us that we could never cross the river & return & when we tolled them that we had not seen any troops they were supprised. I just herd a yelling & went out to see what was the Matter and there was a man hunting for a runaway niggar & they hooted him out of camp. Well I must conclude for I think I have sent all the news I know.

And I remain your affectionate son,
Alfred K. Oates

P.S. I sent you a paper called the Port Tobaco times

The chosen men of the Excelsior Brigade, soot covered and sleep deprived as they entered camp, were glad to have performed so well on Matthias Point. They had volunteered to serve their country and that day they did, saving their government millions of dollars, possibly saving countrymen's lives who would have been part of a later assault, and opening up the Potomac to traffic again. They had burned stacks of wheat that had been intended for rebellious stomachs, and they had shown up the traitorous townspeople. The patriotic soldiers of the Excelsior Brigade, from Oates to Guerney, were proud to have won a victory for the Union.

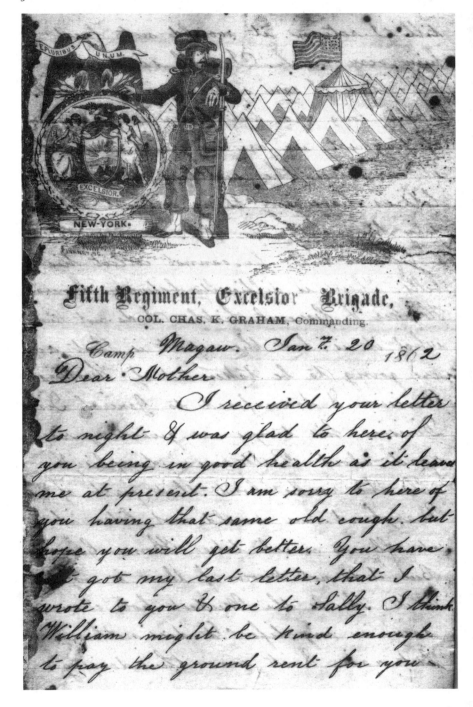

Fifth Regiment, Excelsior Brigade,
COL. CHAS. K. GRAHAM, Commanding.

Camp Magaw. Jan 7. 20 1862

Dear Mother

I received your letter
to night & was glad to here of
you being in good health as it leaves
me at present. I am sorry to here of
you having that same old cough but
hope you will get better. You have
got my last letter that I
wrote to you & one to Sally. I think
William might be kind enough
to pay the ground rent for you

Chapter Four

Personal Business

Camp Magaw, Maryland

January, 1862

Oates was almost asleep when he heard movement near the door of his hut. He barely stirred, assuming it was the corporal come to fetch a sentry for that night. One of the other men roused himself from his makeshift mattress and answered the knock. A young fellow poked his head in to announce that he was going to Pittsburgh in the morning, and he would take any letters the boys in Company A might want to send home.

All of the men in the hut, Oates included, scrambled out of bed. It was better to have letters go direct through a courier than risk them with the Postal Service. Many of the soldiers believed that the army kept letters in Washington out of fear the soldiers were writing the movements of the army home. The few candles the hut possessed were lit, and the low light flickered on the wooden walls and earthen floor. The crackle of the pine logs burning low in the mud fireplace mixed with the scratching of iron- tipped pens against paper as the hut was silently busy with men huddled over their own affairs.

Camp Magaw, Jany 20, 1862

Dear Mother,

I received your letter to night & was glad to here of you being in good health as it leaves me at present. I am sorry to here of you having that same old cough, but hope you will get better. You have not got my last letter that I wrote to you & one to Sally. I think William might be kind enough to pay the ground rent for you till I return. It would not hurt him very much. I will send you all that I can spare. our two months is due long ago but their is no sign of pay yet. we are in grait need of it ourselves. The suttlers will not let us have any thing without we pay him cash. for the congress passed a bill so that he cannot collect his bills.

Oates sat thinking of how to solve this problem. The men of the brigade perpetually waited for the "Fat Pay Master" to come to camp and finally give them their salary.[12] It seemed that no sooner had he finally made an appearance than another two months' pay was due. Oates needed his pay for himself to buy supplies, but more importantly his family needed the money. A twenty-five year old with no wife or children to support, Oates was the main breadwinner for his parents and unmarried sister Nelly, and before the war they had depended on his earnings. Both his parents worked, his father as a carpet weaver and his mother as a midwife, but they had been unusually old when Alfred was born and now were in their seventies and so worked only occasionally. Now that Oates was in the army the rest of the family relied on what Alfred could send back out of his pay. Without it, they couldn't cover their rent and had in fact already fallen behind because of the tardiness of Oates' paymaster.

Smoking and looking over the letter he was writing to his mother and the letter he had received from her that night, Oates hoped his friends back home could help his family. Certainly they would not let his parents be evicted if they knew of their troubles, but Oates was forced to wait for weeks between sending letters and receiving replies, possibly too long for his parents and sister. He hoped that his brother-in-law William could cover the rent until Oates' pay came. If he couldn't, he expected William would ask someone else. In any event, Oates thought, he would probably be home this summer once the war ended when he could again take up the mantle as provider for the family and receive his pay regularly.

> . . . We have a good deal of confidence in General McClelland & hope he will be the second Washington of America. Their is one thing I want you to ask William & that is in regard to the $100 bounty if we ever get it or not. some say we will get it & 160 acres of land. But we might get the bounty but do not think we will get the land. if we do get the land. I will settle on it for I can use the axe & build houses but to tell the truth after we are discharged we can do any thing. When Nelly comes home tell her to write to me as soon as she can and tell me the feeling of the people in Weeling[3]. if it is union or Secech. Judging from the part of Slavedom we have seen that it is only the fear of the troops that keeps them down. And she must let me know how Charley is getting along in business. Tell Sally I

---

3   Wheeling, town in northern panhandle of what is now West Virginia, where at the time a convention had established a "restored" Virginia government that was pro-Union and lobbying to create new state.

will write to her some time this week. Captain Glass has not yet returned.
I must conclude & remain
    your affectionate son
    Alfred K Oates

Oates folded the letter, and sealed it. He handed it to the courier and put out his candle. Oates went back to bed, wishing that his family's problems could be solved and that the home Oates had left to defend would not change hands in his absence.

The expedition to Matthias Point the past November had been a great success — a source of pride for those who participated in it and dismay and disappointment for the rebel sympathizing townspeople. After the expedition, the Excelsior Brigade remained in the area to prevent the locals from turning their leanings into actions. Before the expedition, Oates and a few others from the Fifth Regiment had been called on to keep the peace at a county election in the hamlet of Allen's Fresh, about 10 miles below Port Tobacco. Oates was woken at 1 A.M., and marched through the night; one that was, *"dark as dungeon and ruining like 40,"* to reach the voting place. It was, *"a regular county election every one of them was tight and very insulting. One of them began to dam the Northerners but he had to take leg bail."*[10] The day progressed without any major incident, and Oates returned to camp, wetter and more knowledgeable about Maryland politics.

While back at camp Oates got a chance to look around the mud and rain and see what the United States of America could assemble when incensed to war. To this out-of-the-way spot on the Chesapeake, a tiny hamlet of fifty voters, ancient wooden houses, and tough farmland scratched out of the woods, it seemed that the entire North had descended at once. Nemo, the New York *Times* correspondent, wrote on November 1st that, "'Today from Washington to Port Tobacco the bayonets of Union troops glisten in the sunshine . . . their artillery rumbles over many a dilapidated bridge, while the steeds of the cavalry are prancing on many a military road."[13] Oates could look around and see the machinations of war manifested in the numberless bodies and accents that flourished on the banks of the Potomac.

The Fifth Regiment itself would not stay in the town of Port Tobacco for much longer after the expedition. The men watched for secech (their term for secessionists or Confederates) while on picket, inspected houses for contraband goods, and guarded the area, the left flank of Washington, against a Confederate advance. Of the three, inspecting houses and confiscating Rebel property was by far the most enjoyable for the men. Oates was lucky enough to do this once and wrote *"You would laugh to have seen us. One with a sugar bowl under his arm, another with a basket of eggs. And everything we could lay our hands on."*[10] While stealing civilian property was looked down on by the Union authorities, eager to cultivate good standing with those who were nominally on their side, they would have a hard time persuading Oates and his friends who were risking their lives to protect these people and who hadn't been paid in months of this. If a treat like fresh eggs were available, they would take it.

By December, though, they would no longer be out scouting for sugar bowls. The Fifth Regiment's main reason for being in Port Tobacco was to counter the Rebel batteries at Matthias Point. After the expedition and discovery of the true Rebel strength on the Point, it was apparent they were no longer needed there. The Fifth Regiment prepared to settle into winter quarters, and since the other four regiments of the brigade were farther up in Charles County, Maryland, with Sickles' headquarters there as well, the Fifth left Port Tobacco to join the brigade for the winter. The regiment quickly reached Camp Magaw, named after the commander of the Union flotilla on the Lower Potomac, and the soldiers pitched their tents and began work on the log huts that would house them until the spring.

Camp Magaw, Jan. 28

Dear Mother,

I received your kind & welcome letter last evening & was glad to hear you being in good health as it leaves me at present & also very glad to here that Nelly is home again. We have very bad weather the roads are almost impassible, it takes from 4 to 6 horses to draw an empty wagon. The whole division is buisey repairing the roads, but we fix them & again 4 wagons passes over, it is as bad as ever. Talk about mooving an army this time of the year. we could not march 1 mile a day & it is just the same across the river.

Oates paused to think of what little other news there was at camp.

It is raining now, it rains every day & the coldest rain I ever felt. It snow's Rains Hails, sleet & Thunder & Lightning all in one day. I do not know what I would have done if I had not got them boots. Their is lots of Men in the regament that wares shoes
that never have dry feet only at night. We moove in on our winter quarters to Morrow. But we would rather stay in our tents. For we have them fitted up first rate. And I am afraid 24 of us in one hut cannot agree so well as 8 of us in one tent.

Even though winter quarters was not complete until late January Oates had not suffered under simple canvas since the first of December, when the regiment moved to Camp Magaw. While in the summer or on the march the soldiers slept in open-air A-frame tents, which would fit two soldiers comfortably; in the winter they had larger ones that could hold up to 8 soldiers. Almost immediately after arriving at Camp Magaw, Oates and his tentmates went to work in their spare time fortifying their flimsy home. As Cedma, the New York *Times*' new correspondent to the brigade reported, "Canvass is a poor substitute for a brick wall or weatherboarding, but necessity is an ingenuity, and if a soldier lives uncomfortably it is his own fault. The country is well wooded with a thick growth of pines. The soil is a tenacious clay. With logs and clay, huts are built and covered with a tent, (to give light, and at the same time a roof,) and furnished with a chimney, and a floor of hewn logs make an elegant residence."

"Some dig down a few feet, and then build a log hut over the cellar, or else simply pitch the tent over it. Others simply line their tent with logs, but all of the tents, arranged however they may be, have chimneys. All these chimneys are composed of the same materials — logs and clay — yet there is the greatest difference in them imaginable. A soldier who can build a good chimney that will 'draw' without smoking, is considered 'a regular trump'."[14]

One of Oates' tentmates, at least, was a regular trump. Their tent was a fine example of what soldiers could do with basic materials. Lined with logs, with a working chimney, it served as a warm escape from what Oates called, *"the Muddiest hole I ever saw in my life."*[15] After a day of futilely laboring to repair the roads through camp, Oates would at least be able to warm up near the fire in his tent. In the long months of winter, when there was little to do, and that which there was to do was tedious, cold, and backbreaking, working on one's tent gave a soldier some little activity to occupy his mind and lighten his day.

Some, like Victor Cironx, a Private in Company B, worked on heating their tents properly. Cironx developed what he called a "Caloriere," a furnace made out of clay covered stone. It retained its heat much better than the usual wood and clay chimneys, and required less wood to achieve a comfortable level. Having to go out into the cold less often to fetch firewood was popular with the men, and so the Caloriere was adopted by most of the regiment.

With his caloriere burning near him and Oates having little to do than kill time for the next few months, he finished his letter to home. His mind was still full of what he had seen and enjoyed on his recent trip to Pittsburgh not more than two weeks ago. Not needing to keep all the men in camp during the dead of winter and not wishing to feed all of them, the army had issued furloughs to many of the soldiers. A group of men would go home for two weeks, return, and then another group would leave for home. Allegheny City always had some Company A men there that January, checking in with the families of the soldiers still in Maryland to share with them the latest news and the embarrassing stories the men had opted not to include in their letters.

I suppose John Vernes has been to see you he is one of our Mess, the life of it, Father should see him take one of his hearty laughs. It would do him good. His Brother is coming in a few days. he will also call & see you. I spoke to John, in regards to some stockings if you get them you can send them over by his Brother Jim. I will write to you as soon as I get the Box. So I must conclude & remain,

  Your Affectionate son,
  Alfred K. Oates

Oates sealed the letter and put it aside to send in the next mail. Some other men were going outside to gather more materials for their tent and Oates put on his coat and joined them, his affairs all in order.

Tugging on his gloves and pulling himself into the saddle, Daniel Sickles prepared to leave camp once again for the comfortable hotels of Washington. Sickles had problems in the capital he needed to attend. All appointments to a rank of general needed to be approved by the Senate and while most were passed without any debate, Sickles' had been delayed. The Republican dominated body was not keen to give a star to a Democrat, especially one who had blocked Republican measures in the past, and whose own past was so questionable. The Senate had therefore not yet confirmed him as brigadier-general, and the ambitious Sickles was getting anxious for that star. As he prepared to leave he heard the final reports from his second-in-command, Col. Hall of the Second Regiment, who ran the brigade in Sickle's absence. He told him that since the Fifth Regiment carried the largest burden of the picketing and scouting, it had earned the soubriquet of "The Grand Guard." Hall believed that to be a title of honor (although it only needed to be said with the right amount of sneer to be one of derision) and the men's spirits seemed to reflect Hall's opinion. Companies from other regiments were also on picket surrounding the camp, and he felt the Excelsior Brigade secure from enemy attack or internal strife. Sickles left Magaw with his brigade safe, and he now focused on his problems in Washington.

The aspiring general tramped along the wooden planks leading over the expanses of mud that had become Washington's roads in the wet winter of 1861-62. Slowly, taking pains not to splatter his uniform, he climbed into the carriage that would take him to the White House. Sickles had lived in Willard's Hotel in Washington ever since coming down from Camp Scott the previous summer, making only occasional trips to his men in camp. Most of the time he traveled in the same social and political circles as he had two years before, only this time looking in from the outside. The man who once was yielded the floor of the House of Representatives was now in desperate need of political friends.

In the early days of the war, the appointment of a general's stars to politicians was based on influence in the Senate and recruitment. An aspiring Napoleon could wheedle Senators in hopes of being given existing regiments to command, or he could raise a large body of troops and assume to be placed at its head. Sickles met the second requirement; no one could doubt that he had brought 5,000 men into the arms of the Union. However, the Senate held a Republican majority at the time, and enough of those present had served in the same Congresses as Sickles and could remember when he had delivered speeches denouncing their party's measures. There was also caution at giving a hothead the responsibility of a brigade, and there existed a real fear that he might defect with his troops to the Confederacy. With so many former Southern Democrats in Congress resigning to fight for the Confederacy, the Republicans had to wonder if the rebellion was regional or party based. Did the scurrilous inclination for treason infect even the Northern Democratic ranks of which Sickles was a proud part? The Senators were not willing to risk 5,000 soldiers to a second Benedict Arnold. Therefore, with many of his friends seceded from the Senate, a scandalous history behind him, and a wary Senate blocking his path to a generalcy, Sickles worked the only path to command left open to him.

Sickles already enjoyed a direct link to President Lincoln, and from Gov. Morgan's attempted disbanding of the Excelsior Brigade, Sickles had seen that such a link to the President came in handy. Now angling to build the majority of Senators needed for his confirmation, he worked a connection to another White House persona, the President's wife, Mary Todd Lincoln.

Mrs. Lincoln was somewhat out of place in the fine society of Washington. Although of privileged background, she had lived in the frontier states of Kentucky and Illinois, a world away from the fineries of the East. Wracked by rapid mood swings, she tried to surround herself with those who exemplified the chivalric ideal she thought was proper for a lady of high Victorian society to associate with. Luckily for Sickles, he, the suave cosmopolitan, fit such a type. Sickles came into contact with Mrs. Lincoln through a friend of his, the "Chevalier" Henry Wikoff, the image of a sophisticated Victorian European. Wikoff had served in the diplomatic corps of both England and France, written a bestseller about his imprisonment in Italy after chasing a girl there, and now lived as a socialite in Washington. Such a worldly life had endeared him quickly to the rustic Mrs. Lincoln, and he was one of the circle of friends who shielded her from the realities of the country, allowing her to escape into redecoration of the White House.

Sickles was old friends with Wikoff. They had met when Sickles was a Congressman and Wikoff's stories of adventure earned Sickles' respect and Teresa's admiration. The Chavalier soon became one of Sickles' closest confidants. Wikoff frequently escorted Teresa to parties when Dan was unavailable; a duty Phillip Barton Key performed as well. Wikoff did not make the mistake of having an affair with Teresa — or at least one was never known — and he stayed by Sickles throughout the trial and even afterwards when Sickles was shunned by all other friends. The ex-Congressman would always be grateful to Wikoff for sticking with him when adverse winds of fortune blew so hard. Now in the early weeks of 1862 Sickles asked Wikoff for help in his quest for a general's star. Sickles solicited Wikoff, who also happened to be a secret reporter for the New York *Herald*, to request the paper's editor for an editorial favoring Sickles' confirmation. Sickles also asked that he appeal to Mrs. Lincoln to lobby certain Senators for their votes on the confirmation, assuming that the White House might have something they wanted.

The carriage clattered down the road away from Willard's Hotel while Sickles pondered his next move. Things had not been progressing smoothly for him so far this winter. His divisional commander was irritated that his subordinate could go over his head and speak with the Commander-in-Chief seemingly at will. To help New York fill its quota of volunteers, the Excelsior Brigade lost its status of United States Volunteers and became state regiments. They had been designated the 70th through 74th New York State Volunteers (1st Excelsior becoming 70th New York, 2nd Excelsior becoming 71st New York and so on), and they were therefore under the control of Governor Edwin Morgan. Although Morgan would not interfere with the brigade again during the war, Sickles had no way of knowing that, and feared an order of disbandment. The Senate had not yet acted on Sickles' confirmation as a general, and further, there was a crisis with Wikoff. The Chevalier had submitted to the *Herald* extracts of a speech Lincoln was intending to present to Congress. The House Judiciary Committee was investigating him for transmitting possible government secrets and Wikoff had chosen Sickles as his legal counsel.

Sickles arrived at the Old Capital Prison where Wikoff was being held. He had to be brief for he had much to do that day to save his friends. Not only was Wikoff's reputation at stake, but also the reputation of one of Sickles' other associates, Mrs. Lincoln. It was widely assumed that Wikoff had obtained the speech from her since she was the only person with access to both the President and Wikoff. If she was found to be passing confidential information to friends — and she was already rumored to be a Southern sympathizer because her brothers were serving in the Confederate army — her reputation and that of President Lincoln would be badly damaged. She had privately begged Sickles to find a way out of this mess and he was scrambling for an answer.

Sickles finally found a way. He told Wikoff to keep quiet and agree to whatever Sickles did. The Excelsior then went to the White House where he forced Mrs. Lincoln's gardener, who was a conspirator of hers in a scheme to divert money into the White House's decoration budget, to testify to the Judiciary Committee that he had seen the document on a table, memorized it fully, and recited it word for word later to Wikoff. It was a highly implausible story and no one really believed it. However, it completely separated Mrs. Lincoln from the affair, and the President wrote to the committee asking them to accept that story and drop this embarrassing inquiry. The Committee bowed to their Commander in Chief and accepted the outlandish story. The scandal disappeared.

Later, Sickles met with the President and his wife, who were thoroughly grateful for his services. The end result of the matter was the dismissal of the gardener and the ostracism of Wikoff. Sickles found his stature raised at the White

House because of his help, but lowered in the Senate because of his association with the ever more unpopular Mrs. Lincoln. That winter, he measured everything by how much it helped him get his general's star. He had become so obsessed about becoming a soldier, a general and leader of thousands of men on the battlefield, that all else was left behind in that quest: his wife, his friends, his brigade. By that criterion, the inquiry was a setback, quicksand that could not be avoided without reneging on his friendship and debt to Wikoff. However ambitious and self-centered Sickles may have been, he did manage to show true devotion to his friends. Or at least it seemed that way. Mark Twain once remarked that Sickles had the ability to talk about nothing but himself, yet somehow manage to seem modest at the same time.[1]

The water slapped the side of the *Elm City* as it sat off the shore of Liverpool Point, Maryland. The transport ship was loaded up with the soldiers of the Excelsior Brigade, who had left their cozy cabins in Camp Magaw for the deck of the steamship floating in the middle of the Potomac. Sickles strode the deck observing his men. They had been largely inactive for months and were now ready for the upcoming campaign. As winter moved into spring, and with the Senate inactive on his confirmation, Sickles finally returned to his brigade, his overt politicking having backfired on him.

Since the Wikoff affair, articles had begun appearing in the New York newspapers pointedly wondering why the general of the Excelsior Brigade was not stationed with the brigade. The *Times* wrote that, "we know there is no rule, exceedingly proper in itself, more rigidly enforced than that officers who absent themselves from their posts and haunt Washington, expose themselves to a forfeiture of their commission." The article concluded wondering if the Excelsior Brigade would lose their commander through, "his unfortunate devotion to Wikoff and other attractions of Washington society."[15a]

The *Times* piece called the public's attention to an excellent question. If Sickles was to be trusted with the lives of 5,000 of their sons and husbands, not to mention wielding a tool of war costing the government $60,000 a month in salary alone, why wasn't he training and preparing with these men? Why was someone who was attempting to convince the United States Senate that he was worthy of a general's star spending his time acting as counsel to a European scoundrel? Why was Sickles shirking his responsibility to his men and to his country? In short, was this enigmatic figure, selfish at points, patriotic at others, showing through his place of residence his true colors?

Sickles, teetering on the loss of his one ally, public opinion, was forced to leave Washington, counting on his friends in the White House to see his confirmation through. Frustrated by a slow moving and hostile Senate, and further irritated by the torpor of winter quarters, Sickles was at a low point in late winter. He had a "restless energy" that always drove him on to bigger and better things. That spirit had propelled him quickly up the ranks of Tammany Hall and into Congress. That spirit had kept him moving even after Key sunk to the ground with two bullets inside. That spirit had inspired 5,000 young men of the North to make their mark on the Excelsior's muster rolls. But now that spirit was constrained. No matter how much scheming, gladhanding, dealmaking, speech-giving or petition-seeking he did, he could not move the Senate or the brigade into action. Restless energy like his had driven Julius Caesar from political obscurity to the top of the Roman world two thousand years before, and Dan Sickles craved to prove himself another Caesar.

Sickles, although frustrated, did not lose hope. He could not prod the Senate into action, could not even stay in Washington, but maybe he could do something with the Excelsior Brigade to prove his ability. One night he personally crossed the Potomac to examine the enemy defenses there. Finding the opposite shore lightly guarded, he requested permission from Joseph Hooker, his divisional commander, to make a reconnaissance in force across the river, a thousand man force strong enough to destroy whatever it might encounter on Confederate soil, but with orders only to scout the land and return immediately. Sickles made three such reconnaissances: March 10 — 13, 1862 towards Manassas, Virginia; March 18 to Fredericksburg; and April 4 to Stafford Court House. Sickles returned to Camp Magaw from each triumphantly. He had taken his men into enemy territory and carried out his orders perfectly. He may not have his general's star yet, but he was still in command of the Excelsior Brigade, and as the campaign season approached, Sickles anticipated the time when he could ride at the head of his personal legions and lead his valiant Excelsiors to glorious victory.

Reading over the paper he had just been handed, Sickles was shocked. He couldn't believe the desk generals in Washington would do something like this, on the eve of the greatest military operation the American continent had ever witnessed. Standing on board the transport *Elm City* in the waters of the Potomac, surrounded by the masses of Excelsior soldiers, Sickles held in his hand the worst defeat he could imagine - a few short lines from General Hooker titled Special Orders No. 132. It stated, in plain and simple language, that, since the Senate had recently voted against the confirmation of the rank of Brigadier-General to Daniel Edgar Sickles on March 17, 1862, Sickles was removed from command of the Excelsior Brigade. Hooker had chosen Col. Nelson Taylor, commander of the 72nd New York, Third Excelsior, to lead the Excelsior Brigade. Sickles was advised to depart from this transport, as he no longer was part of the brigade.

Sickles was crushed. The last year had been consumed by his desire for the general's star. First he had needed to raise the required number of troops to form a brigade. With incredible exertion and sharp dealing he had accomplished that. Then he only needed the confirmation of the Senate. This should have been the easy part after enlisting 5,000 men and saving them from the grasping hands of Gov. Morgan, yet in this he failed. The brigade he created, his brigade, was taken from him.

But Sickles had been fighting for command of his brigade for a year, and he was not going to stop now. He still had a few avenues of advance left. President Lincoln owed him a favor from the Wikoff scandal, so he could count on his support. He had been appointed Colonel of the First Excelsior when he had raised the initial 8 companies, and therefore even if he was not a general he was still the senior officer in the brigade and by rights in command of the brigade. There was still a chance for him to lead his Excelsiors in battle, and he was determined to head to Washington and regain his honor and brigade.

In his cabin of the *Elm City*, surrounded by the worn books of military tactics read many times since the past year and the various ledgers and rosters that cling to a commander, Sickles wrote a farewell address to his men, bidding adieu to those who had served through the fires of training in the previous year. The address was printed and circulated to the soldiers of the Excelsior Brigade and also given to the newspaper correspondents to be published for the public of the country.

Headquarters, Excelsior Brigade
Second Hooker's Brigade On Board Transport "Elm City,"
April 6, 1862

General Orders, No. 6

Soldiers: Special Orders No. 132 will announce to you that I am relieved from further duty in the Brigade, by order of the Brigadier General commanding this division.

My last act of duty is to bid you farewell. After a year of service with you, it is hard to yield to the necessity which separates me from so many brave and devoted companions-in-arms, endeared to me by more than ordinary ties.

While protesting that it is unlawful and unjust, I obey this command, because obedience to superior authority is the first duty of a soldier.

It is my earnest hope that a prompt appeal for redress, to the General commanding the army, will permit me to share with you the honors of the campaign now so auspiciously begun.

Whether we are separated for a day or forever, the fervent wishes of my heart will follow your fortunes on every field. You have waited patiently for the hour now at hand, when the Army of the Potomac will move upon the stronghold of the enemy.

Your discipline, courage and bearing will place you among the foremost of our legions. The glory which surely awaits you will help to reconcile me to the pain it costs me to say again — Farewell![15b]

Sickles stepped onto the dock and began the long road back to Washington. Behind him was his brigade, on board the transports, headed off to the great campaign of the war. He had made it so close to battle, the field where men could be valorous and honors be won. There could be no greater loss to him than this loss of five thousand of his own who had become so tied to his heart and sense of worth. As he rode away from his men and further and further from the battlefield, Sickles knew the war had not unfolded as he had desired. Now separated from his beloved brigade perhaps forever, he was off to do battle in the halls of Congress — not for his country or his men — but for himself. It was the kind of battle he was best at.

The soldiers watched their commander leave them. They had always admired the man and always would. He had brought them together, from villages and cities across the country, to serve and fight and leave the indelible mark of their bravery on their nation's history. He had equipped and fed them in New York out of his own pocket, they had heard. The papers reported that old Dan was half a million dollars in debt from supplying them before their enlistment by the Federal Government. He had done so much for them, and now, when the thousands of young faces were looking at a campaign and a start of real war, he was headed to Washington to atone for his political sins. He had held the futures of his men and the fears of their families in his hands for almost a year, and now when his leadership would have a larger effect on them than merely the arrival of the paymaster, he was called away. Sickles promised himself he would return to his men. However, his men now had to forget about him and look to their own futures, and the great campaign upon which they were about to embark.

The "Coffee Mill Gun," an early predecessor of the machine gun. Cartridges were placed in the square compartment at the top and a crank was turned to load and fire rapidly. The Fifth Regiment tested some of them at Camp Magaw and had plans to bring a battery to the Peninsula which were never fulfilled. Courtesy Peninsulacampaign.org.

Chapter Five

Confidence

Yorktown, Virginia

April, 1862

he transport ship rose on a swell, throwing soldiers stumbling across the deck. They had been afloat for nearly four days, but many of the men, accustomed to the stable platform of land, had not yet gained their sea legs. Soon enough they would be on land, on the "Sacred Soil of Virginia," and it would be there that they would do the job they were paid thirteen dollars a month to perform - fight the enemy.

Oates stood at the side of his transport, looking out over the ocean. The Atlantic was thronged with the naval power of the North. The Union had launched a fleet of warships, transports, gunboats, and every other vessel that Washington could scrounge for the campaign. Out of the water Oates could see his destination. The men leaned against the side of the boat, gazing out to the landmass on the horizon — Old Point Comfort, a narrow strip of land crowned by Fortress Monroe, one of the most important forts in America.

The transport docked at the busy port, really just a few quays used to service the fort. The area teemed with ships carrying the entire body of the Army of the Potomac, 100,000 men strong, and it seemed almost possible to travel all the way from Fort Monroe to Washington just by walking across decks.

Oates followed his company down the gangplank onto the land near the fort. Monroe's importance lay in its location. Situated on the outer part of Hampton Roads, one of the largest natural harbors in the world where the James, Nansemond and Elizabeth rivers flow into the Chesapeake Bay, Monroe defended the naval shipyard of Norfolk, Virginia, and the entrance to the James River, which passes through Richmond thirty miles inland. At the start of the war, the United States government, realizing how important it was to block the exit from the shipyards, reinforced Monroe and maintained control of the fort while others along the southern coastline were falling to state seccessionist forces. Now Fort Monroe would be the jump-off point for the first campaign of 1862 and hopefully the last of the war. The Army of the Potomac would disembark at Fort Monroe and march up the peninsula between the York and the James rivers to Richmond. They would capture the Confederate capital and crush the rebellion.

All this was evident to Oates as he marched up the Peninsula. The army was here, Richmond was there, and everyone could fill in the rest. What amazed him most was not how General McClellan, commander of the Army of the Potomac, had circumvented multiple rivers by transporting troops to the Peninsula rather than advancing on the Rebel capital overland, or how the Rebels might be able to establish a strong line of defense on this narrow strip of land, but seeing the full Army of the Potomac and the bulk of the Chesapeake fleet in one place and working perfectly.

Oates marched among sights of peach trees in blossom and sounds of soldiers' shouts. Exiting of Fort Monroe, he heard from another column, "Quickly, boys, over to the left." Oates turned his head and could see four Rebel steamers gliding out of Norfolk, among them the C.S.S. *Virginia*, formerly the U.S.S. *Merrimac*, the Confederate ironclad. Oates was hoping to see a sea fight, but at the same time nervous should one develop. The near-impermeable *Merrimac* could cause incredible havoc among the wooden Union ships as it had a month earlier before it was confronted by the *U.S.S. Monitor*, the Union ironclad. Nothing happened, and Oates saw the *Monitor* farther out in the harbor, waiting for the Confederates to leave the protection of their own guns on land.

Oates and the regiment marched onwards to the new camp, a few miles outside the Peninsula. The Confederates had dug in at Yorktown, and had extended a line of fortifications across the peninsula. The army was currently preparing for the assault on Yorktown that would break the Rebel lines and open up a road to Richmond. Unpacking at camp Oates was awed. There was more artillery on this little piece of Virginia soil than he had ever seen in his life. *"They say that there is 100 batteries of it here,"* he wrote home.[16] Each battery contained 4 to 6 guns, 100 soldiers and 50 horses. The numbers of the men with red piping on their blue uniforms (the colors of the artillery branch in the Union armies) running around camp was extremely comforting to the Excelsiors. The cannoneers were telling anyone who would listen that they could blast the Rebs out of Yorktown with big guns alone. Dropping his equipment on the ground beside his newly pitched tent, surrounded by a hundred thousand countrymen in arms, and under the protection of the Union observing balloon to which the Confederates had no response, Oates felt optimistic. Such a concentration of military force would certainly triumph and end the war soon.

"Quietly, now. Get moving." Oates and the others on duty crept through the darkness to the end of the current trench line.

"Go to work and work fast."

At this second command from the sergeant the shovels came out and the men started digging. A Rebel shell was thrown overhead, exploding in midair and momentarily throwing light on the scene below. In the open fields between opposing walls of earth a few dozen men crouched hacking away at the ground, lengthening a trench in which their officers scurried back and forth checking their soldiers'

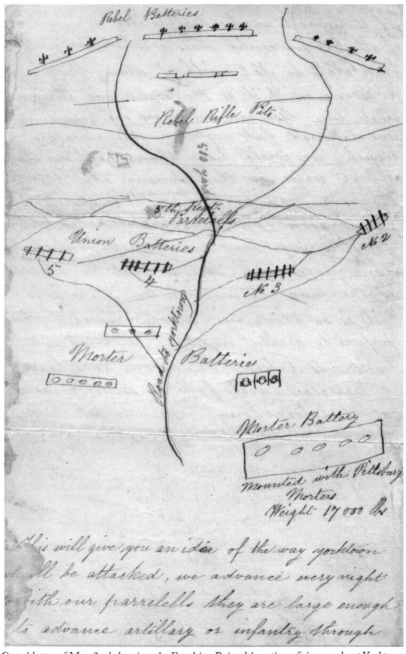

Oates' letter of May 2nd showing the Excelsior Brigade's section of siegeworks at Yorktown.
Author's collection.

progress. The Army of the Potomac was constantly digging: lengthening trenches, starting new ones, and repairing the existing. The men kept their heads down and made no more noise than necessary. In a siege, which was what the battle for Yorktown had developed into, there were thousands of men on the lines at any one time, waiting for an exposed enemy to enter their rifle sights. However, Oates was rarely in any danger. His camp was out of cannon range, and when he did go into range it was only when digging the parallel trenches, which were themselves designed to protect against artillery. His only threat was the Confederate snipers who were always on guard and waiting for a foolish Union soldier. But here too, Oates had protection. In front of the Excelsior Brigade were the famous Berdan's sharpshooters keeping the Rebel snipers at bay.

The men had worked well in the past few weeks. Every day they and all the infantry in the army extended the trenches, guarded from Rebel assault by their own cannon. Each day the Union heavy artillery was moved a few yards further, and before long they would be in range of Yorktown and able to drive the Rebels out of their stronghold.

Oates worked quickly and quietly. The hours of the night passed by as the clods of dirt flew around him and he drew a few feet nearer to the enemy. He knew what his purpose was here; parallel trenches had been a staple of warfare ever since guns became powerful enough to knock down walls. They gave soldiers protection from the enemy's rifles and artillery as the trench was lengthened from within. Parallels were used in the Napoleonic Wars during most sieges and more recently by Oates' home country, the English, during the Crimean War at the siege of Sebastopol. Oates and the men knew that this way of fighting offered easiest way to assault Yorktown — through artillery alone, with the infantry safely sitting back and watching.

Ease of advance was the main reason for the campaign on the Peninsula. The goal of the North throughout the war was to capture Richmond, the Rebel capital of government and industry. At Bull Run the attempt to capture was made by a direct route overland from Washington. McClellan, when he took command of the army shortly after that battle, believed that a straight path was too risky. Virginia was crossed by a number of rivers flowing from the Appalachians to the sea that would stand directly in the Union's way, and behind any of which the Confederates could mount a defense (as they would later in the war). He believed that transporting the army to Fort Monroe and advancing up the Peninsula was the best path to Richmond. There would be no major rivers in the way, all the roads led to Richmond, and the sea would enable Union gunboats to provide additional artillery along the way. Lincoln agreed to the plan, and the next spring McClellan began to execute it.

The sky had changed from the black of night to the misty grey of pre-dawn. The men would be done soon and be able to enjoy the last day of April resting in camp. The sun crept over the horizon, lighting the landscape in front of Yorktown,

fields now crisscrossed by trenches, batteries and long mounds of dirt. Oates slowly poked his head to see behind him, keeping out of sight of the Confederates. He
saw Berdan's sharpshooters in their green uniforms lying behind dirt piles and the
artillerymen perched on their batteries peering out with binoculars, both offering
the forward Excelsiors protection from a Rebel attack.

The sergeant shouted for the men to stop working and pack their gear. Their
shift on the lines was over and it was time to head back to camp. Oates and his
comrades picked their way through the maze of trenches back to their home,
Camp Winfield Scott. They had worked themselves hard over the night, earning
their wages and moving the United States 50 yards closer to victory.

Oates sat around outside his tent in bare feet and shirt sleeves on May 3rd, enjoying the season's warmth and penning a few lines to his family. It was the company's rest day, and the camp was languid, a pocket of idleness in the fast moving
sea of the Army of the Potomac. Soldiers preferred sleeping to even eating dinner,
banking their slumber in the event of another night spent digging trenches.

To Oates, the camp looked lovely that day. What he at first called the poorest
place on earth, *"nothing but Pine trees swamps and mud,"* had grown on him. The
peach trees were in blossom during the month of April and in places the peninsula
resembled a park more than a battlefield. The men had other trees they admired
as well. Anticipating a long siege at Yorktown, some in the Fifth Regiment had
planted trees along the avenues of the camp, which was luckily placed far away
from the swamps, giving the soldiers some shade on their days of rest. What was
most satisfying for Oates to see, however, was not arboreal in the least. What
pleased him most were the preparations for war whirling around him.

Oates sat outside with his pen and ink, scratching away at his scrap of paper.
He once again urged his family not to worry about his safety. *"Of coarse people are
very ancious about their relations that are here in regard to the upcoming seige,"* he
wrote, *"but I am afraid the Rebels will not stay in Yorktown. If they do I cannot help
but pitty them."*[17] The regiment spent its time near the front lines building batteries, and Oates had spoken with quite a few artillerymen and engineers. Many of
them said that Yorktown would fall quickly. It could be taken with siege guns and
mortars and cannon. The infantry had only to build the trenches and batteries and
then watch as the war was won.

Meanwhile the Rebels seemed disposed to impotence. The Union fortifications and roads were dug into hillsides so that traveling before the most heavily
fortified town in the Confederacy was as, *"safe as walking in Allegheny City."*[18]
Reb artillery clearly could not hurt Union boys; the Excelsiors realized this one
day when the Rebels fired 500 rounds of artillery and did not wound a single
Union soldier. Moreover, Reb infantry couldn't do anything. They saw this every
morning they heard another story of a repulsed Rebel night sortie. The only enemy that could get the men were Confederate sharpshooters. However, the men

that managed to get themselves hit by sharpshooters must have been displaying extraordinary amounts of stupidity. One night a man was brought in wounded. Oates wrote home about him that, *"they tell all the men that goes out not to make any noise. One fellow struck a match to light his pipe & the first thing he knew he had a rifle ball in his thigh."*[19] These casualties were not casualties of war but casualties of the victim's own actions. No more men were being killed at Yorktown than in daily life. Oates and most of those around him who saw this man being rushed to the hospital believed that, as long as they abstained from something as foolish, they would not repeat his fate.

Oates looked around for a few seconds then continued his letter. *"Mother the rebellion is coming to a finall very fast & we will be home before the 4th of July."*[17] Oates was confident in the Union's victory, not just because of blind faith - although he did have faith - but because of what he saw around him. McClellan was the commander every soldier would want. He was careful with his men, careful with his planning, and certain in his abilities. He had saved the Army of the Potomac from disintegration after Bull Run, and spent the next eight months training and molding it into an effective instrument of Lincoln's policies. He had created this entire force and made everything run like clockwork in it. The genius that McClellan showed in administration, the men believed, would translate into genius on the battlefield.

A shadow crossed Oates's letter, and he looked up to see what could be blocking the sun on a cloudless day. It was the Union reconnaissance balloon, sent up to spy on the Rebel works. Oates shifted a little and smiled. Just one more reason the Army of the Potomac was headed towards certain victory. McClellan had a balloon, while the Rebels did not. McClellan also had more artillery than the rebs, better supply lines, and better fortifications. With all the North's forces assembled on that spit of land, Oates was confident that just as during the Revolution, the United States would once again win a war at Yorktown. It was poetic the way the battle had once again come to this spot, and heartening how certain defeat lay for the Rebels in that spot.

Confident of a Union victory at Yorktown, which to the men ensured victory in the war, Oates and his comrades began to plan how they would celebrate the end of the war. Sitting around the campfire during the warm Virginia nights they discussed these topics and came to the conclusion that the one thing they wanted was to march through Richmond to the tune of Dixie. Treason's capital and treason's song would be the background for the Union's glory.

Growing even surer that victory was at hand, Oates finished his letter. The Excelsior Brigade had caught some Reb deserters earlier, and talked about the war with them. The Rebs said that Yorktown could be taken but the Confederate strongholds of Island No. 10 and Fort Donelson could not be. Oates and his friends were overjoyed to hear this, as Island No. 10 and Fort Donelson had fallen to Union armies just days before. Every report of a Confederate city captured —

the latest being New Orleans — increased Oates' confidence. Every stroll around camp, seeing the machinations of war, the fields of interlaced trenches and batteries, increased it even more. With all of that in mind, Oates went to bed certain that before long, *"secesh will fall as sudden as a rocket."*[20]

Oates ducked as the shells exploded overhead. His company had been sent out on picket that day, May 4th, and while they were passing through the trenches to reach the front line, the Rebels began bombarding the Union positions. McClellan's attack was scheduled to begin soon, but as Oates and his fellow Pittsburghers picked their way to the front, it appeared that such an attack would be unnecessary. Poking their heads out of the trenches, they peered into the Rebel fortifications around Yorktown. Whereas days earlier they could hear the Rebel roll calls and the movements of an army, today they heard nothing. Officers were called to investigate, and they called for their superiors. All reached the same conclusion — the Confederates had evacuated Yorktown. On that day Union forces along the line struck camp and loaded up the travel wagons, while advance units cautiously probed the Rebel fortifications. Soon their assumptions proved correct. The big siege guns had done their job without firing a shot. The Rebels were scared out of the town.

While others were still learning that the month-long siege was over, Oates was falling into line with the rest of the Excelsior Brigade. The Third Corps, whose 2nd Division included the Excelsior, was the closest corps to Yorktown. It therefore was the first to head out of camp and began the pursuit of the retreating Rebs. Oates passed by the town that had consumed his efforts for a month. Above the town, where once stood the center of visible Rebel resistance, flew the Stars and Stripes, raised by fellow Excelsiors. Yorktown had fallen. The Rebels were fleeing. Oates could almost hear the strains of Dixie echoing off the buildings of Richmond as he and the brigade marched towards victory.

I am sorry to say that John Verner was wounded, he was shot in the same arm as sam Mc Farland, only his bone is broke. Sargent Fulton as brave a man as ever lived was shot dead, he was next man to me as we advanced, George Bond of Allegheny & Frank Kemaley of Pittsburgh are supposed to be captured for we could not find them William Speith was next to me on the right as we advanced was also shot dead Lewis Shuck of Pittsburgh lost his finger, this is the loss of our company Comp H of our Reg^t went in the fight with 38 men & came out with 21 men Comp, K lost 17 men & 2 officers I do not know the loss of the other companys but they all lost heavey. & their is a good

Chapter Six

The Elephant

Williamsburg, Virginia

May 5, 1862

1 P.M. found Oates wet and miserable and edgy. He was still tired from the day before, when his unit had discovered that the Rebels had abandoned York-town. They had moved through the trenches in the dark hours of early morning, and had immediately returned to camp and set off in pursuit of the Rebels. The Excelsior Brigade marched up the peninsula almost ten miles, slowed enormously by muddy roads. At night after twenty miles on their feet they bivouacked in some woods near the road, sleeping around campfires without the cover of tents. Oates awoke at 5 A.M. The Rebels had left a rearguard at Williamsburg, two miles up the road, and were making a stand there.

The brigade (minus the Second Regiment, which had been delayed and was still at Yorktown) lumbered to their weary feet and packed their gear. The rain had continued overnight and the roads, *"bad enough before,"* as Oates described them, were simply awful.[21] The final two miles to Williamsburg were torturous and it was not until 9 A.M. that the brigade reached the ground. They were placed in reserve to gather strength and wait for orders.

When the Excelsiors arrived they found the fight already some hours old, and sitting back in the wet woods they heard how it had developed. The Confederate commander on the Peninsula, General "Prince" John Magruder had anticipated a Union victory at Yorktown, seeing his Rebs outnumbered in men and artillery. He therefore planned a second line of resistance for when Yorktown fell, designed to hold up McClellan for another month or so while the Confederates regrouped. Magruder chose for his anchor of this second line Williamsburg, the colonial capital of Virginia located in one of the narrowest points on the Peninsula, a point further narrowed by two creeks running perpendicular to the Union line of advance. Magruder built an earthen fortification, Fort Magruder, and several redoubts, fortified artillery batteries. His men had littered the ground with abatis, interlocking fallen trees to hinder infantry movement. When Yorktown did fall, a complete line had not been built and the Confederates could not hold at Williamsburg indefinitely. The main Confederate force therefore withdrew further, and left a rearguard to use what had been built so far for a delaying action to keep the pursuing Federals from falling on the retreating Rebel columns.

Almost immediately upon arriving at the scene, the Third Excelsior Regiment was called to join the battle. The First Massachusetts Infantry regiment, one of the regiments in the First Brigade of Hooker's Division, had expended its ammunition and needed to be relieved. Oates stood in the rain and mud as he watched the first of his comrades hustle off to real war. This would not be an expedition or a skirmish or anything the Excelsior Brigade had seen before. From the sound of the Union artillery dueling with Fort Magruder, and the sight of the ambulance trains carrying the wounded to the horrible field hospitals, Oates and everyone around him knew that this would be a real battle with real combat.

The men had boasted of how they would whip the Rebels the first time they met them on the field of battle. Almost all of them were new to war. Some maybe had served in militia units before the war, their only duties parading on the village green. None had "seen the elephant," the term of the day for experiencing the horrors of combat. Only the emigrant Europeans that had served in one of that continent's many wars knew what battle truly was. But they were too few among the companies, not enough for a band of hardened veterans around which the green Americans could rally.

Now with some of their own already in battle, those boasts of the campfires were worlds away. Oates stood ankle-deep in mud on the side of the road, watching the wagons cart off the bodies of those who had died and those who were soon to die. There could be no excuse for these deaths, no lit match that might explain it away and give comfort to those who might have been in the poor soul's place. Oates was no longer in the picnic days of Yorktown with the peach trees in bloom and the war just a spectacle. He now knew how far he was from the Manchester of his youth or the clean and open commons of Allegheny City he lived by just a year before. He was in war, where farmers' fields were axes of advance, men had flanks, and the Virginia countryside was a chessboard. The green troops that had marched gloriously out of Washington, returned gloriously from Matthias Point and planted trees gloriously at Yorktown had entered a world where glory had vanished and they found themselves to be little more than pawns.

Oates and his comrades stood in the reserve, half-joking at times, silent in introspection at others, ready to enter battle with a depleted officer corps. Their brigade commander, Sickles, was in Washington fighting senators. Their regiment commander, Col. Graham, had resigned in protest against Sickles' removal and was also in Washington. Oates' company commander, Capt. John Glass, had been promoted to acting-Lieutenant Colonel, leaving a lieutenant in charge of the Pittsburghers.

But Oates had his own problems to ponder: how would he act when faced with combat, bravely or cowardly, what were his chances of survival, how would his family survive without his paycheck, how the East Commons outside his house looked now that spring had arrived, the trip he had been planning to England after the war, whether he would see his sister married, whether he would see himself married. All things that accompany hours of inaction in the face of certain danger and uncertain ends. He had always known that men died in battle, but now he was at a battle seeing those men only yards away.

Around 1 P.M. Lt. Col. Charles Burtis, in command of the regiment in the absence of Col. Graham, motioned to his captains to get their companies up and ready. The boys fell into groups and quietly discussed what they thought that might mean — retreat or advance. That issue was quickly laid to rest when the sergeants came charging into the wet congregations, yelling at them to throw down their knapsacks and move forward. Oates was headed into battle.

Oates swallowed his heart and fell into line with the rest of the Fourth and Fifth Excelsior Regiments. They moved forward into the hail of cannon fire from Fort Magruder, just as their own artillery was falling back around them. Quickly moving behind the cover of the First and Third Regiments, Oates and his comrades reached their positions and turned left to face the Rebels on the west side of the road. They formed a line of battle and moved forward. Fort Magruder was blazing away with enfilading fire of grapeshot, fist sized cannon shot loaded 9 at a time, designed to spread out upon firing and blast holes in infantry lines. The men were also hit with canister, sacks filled with minié bullets, jagged pieces of metal, or whatever could injure a man when shot out of a cannon. The Rebs fired shell as well, cannonballs timed to explode and throw shrapnel across the field. All these were tools of war designed to kill as many infantry as possible. Felled trees interlocked to block the Excelsiors' path, forcing them to climb over and under the timber to advance. The enemy infantry sat behind strong breastworks, and firing away with muskets at the Sickles' determined soldiers.

Oates crossed the road and threw himself into the abatis with the rest of the Fifth. While struggling to make headway through the trees, the units the Fifth and Fourth Regiments were advancing to relieve began to pull back from the fight. The smoke of battle gave way in patches and Oates could sense through the thick veil of gunpowder and fear that his baptism of fire was about to descend with the hammer stroke of combat. The men in front were retreating pell mell. Rebels were charging close behind them and directly at the Fifth shouting "Bull Run." The shot from Fort Magruder was raining down like hail. The men were all hungry and wet through, mud from head to foot. They did not know what to make of it at first, all order in the world seemed to have been lost and the line grew unsettled and wavered. The officers spoke up, and the order rang down the line: "Stand fast, Fifth." The men regained their focus. Nobody moved. The guns were all loaded. Then the order was given. "Charge!"

Oates and his old friends from home charged through the abatis into battle. The fallen trees broke up the tight formation of the regiments, and it soon became slow going, each man finding his own route through the obstacles, dodging under the timber for cover whenever Magruder erupted.

Advancing forward, Oates tried his best to keep down. The men advanced in a line, firing and moving while dodging enemy bullets. Oates heard a thud, and then a crash of broken branches. Next to him, Private William Speitto had been shot dead. Oates stared at his friend, lifeless on the ground. The body looked the same, except for the blank eyes that focused beyond Oates into the infinite. Abruptly from above, Oates was grabbed. It was Sergeant John Fulton, who shouted to Oates to keep moving. Fulton smashed through the trees and Oates followed his rampaging superior into the smoke of the abyss.

Oates did as he had been trained, load the gun, aim the gun, fire the gun, load the gun. He hugged the trees, the only cover on the otherwise open ground. Bark flew through the air and trees crashed down cut in two by Rebel cannon fire. But Oates kept loading and firing and loading. Lt. Col. Burtis would write in his official repot later that his men performed their duties, "with a coolness and intrepidity worthy of the highest commendation."[22] Oates just tried to keep his head down and keep firing at whatever target presented itself. He and his comrades did just that and, *"every gray jacket or cap came in sight down he went."*[23]

There was little movement by the Union men after the initial charge. The Rebels were caught in the crossfire of the First and Third Regiments on the left and the Fourth and Fifth on the right. Eventually the Rebs would have to retreat if they could not break the Union lines first. The Excelsiors only had to keep their ground in the face of Rebel attacks and they would outlast the enemy.

Oates kept moving. Load the powder, load the bullet, prime the gun, cock the trigger, aim, fire. It became as a dream to him, the unrealness of it all. The smoke from the muskets, instead of drifting upwards and being carried off the battlefield, was kept down by the rain. In the acrid fog, Oates kept fighting. He lost his gun at one point, whether because it became too clogged with expended powder or because it was hit by a bullet or shrapnel, he did not mention in his letters home. He would not have wanted his mother to know that his rifle had taken a bullet that could have taken him. To their backs, Magruder and the other redoubts kept belching shot without response. To their front, the ghostly Confederate infantry kept attacking.

The Rebels used the fallen trees to their advantage. They could not run through the obstacles, so they crawled under them. It was difficult for Oates and the Excelsiors to see them until they chose to pop up and fire, often at extremely close ranges. When the Rebs were noticed, crowds of soldiers set upon them and they were easily captured. When they were not noticed, they would stick their heads up like Indians and whoop at the officers before unloading their guns. If the officers in the Fifth were lucky, the Reb missed or was hit before he had a chance to fire. If not, they had to hope the men carried them to the rear before they were too far gone. The Excelsior also had to contend with the bulk of the Rebel infantry that stayed in their own line of battle and tried to overwhelm the Northerners with raw firepower.

Oates kept his head down and his eyes open. While watching for Rebs, he saw anecdotes of combat unfold on the field before him. A Fire Zouave of the Fourth Regiment, a young boy, captured a Rebel six feet tall. Another man lost control of himself; he dropped his gun, charged ahead, grabbed a Rebel by the neck and started pounding him like the dickens. Across the field, in the ranks of the First Regiment, fought Lieutenant Frank Howard Nelson, aged nineteen. Lt. Nelson had written home just a month earlier, in a vein similar to Winfield Scott Guerney that, "If God sees fit to spare my life, he can. If not, I die in a holy cause."[24] Now that unbridled optimism was pushing him forward into the maelstrom of miniés. The boy was wounded first in the hand. He bound the wound with a handkerchief and returned to the battle. He was then struck above the elbow, and, immediately afterwards, below the elbow. Bleeding profusely, he was forced to have these wounds dressed. The doctor pleaded with him to return to the rear and wait out the rest of the fight in the hospital tents. He refused, replying that he could lead and take care of his men yet. Bound with bandages and bleeding, Frank Nelson ran back into the field to his men. He called for a charge to rout the enemy, and placed himself at the front. Full of life and energy, Frank Nelson surged forward over the abatis. A bullet soon struck him, passing through both lungs. He fell to the ground while his men continued past him. Nelson had a few days before his holy cause would take him.

For three hours Oates fought. He worked through his forty rounds of ammunition soon enough, and was forced to scrounge through the wounded and dead for fresh cartridges. It was a tough fight, and neither side gave an inch. It looked as if the Rebels were constantly receiving reinforcements, and the Excelsiors fired away at those as well. Gradually the enemy fell back just as the Excelsiors were running out of ammunition. Laying his sight, Oates heard the order to pull back. He pressed the trigger and then worked his way back to the main road, loading and firing as he withdrew. Shells whistled over his head, Union ones from the artillery that only now was joining the fight. Each company was withdrawing on its own and the field was alive with movement of men crawling and scraping over trees, staying high enough to move and low enough to survive.

Oates clawed his way to the road, and was told to head further to the rear to make way for the reinforcements from Kearney's Division of the Third Corps. The battle was still raging and the Rebels were still pouring in troops and shot.

The Fifth Regiment was kept in reserve to relieve any unit that might need help. Oates was handed new ammunition and told to wait for further orders. The rain still came down, and the smoke from the battlefield had wafted towards the woods, enveloping the soldiers in a haze of choking battle. Oates, with powder stains on his mouth where he bit into the cartridges, wet and covered in mud, hungry and with a new rifle, was a sight to see. All the men with him were the same — warriors who had spent three hours without boasting, without rhetoric, without promises. During the battle they looked directly into the elephant and had acted as best they could. They stayed alive and stayed fighting. Looking around themselves, they could tell that their ranks were smaller, although they would not know until the next day that the three hours under the cannon fire had cost them a quarter of their number. Once again in the reserve, ready for another call to battle, they stood and waited. As day faded imperceptibly to night, no such call came, and there were reports that the Rebels were retreating. Apparently the battle had been won. Alongside his companions, Oates celebrated his victory by dropping down in the mud. The boys fell asleep, finally resting after a long two days.

Chapter Seven

The Glorious Return

The Peninsula, Virginia

May, 1862

Dear Mother,

I have tried to describe to you a fight with the rebels but I cannot describe it with my pen. I have often read of the wounded, screaming & hollering so that their voice could be heard above the roar of Musketry. But I must say this for our wounded, I did not hear one man cry out, or complane but as we passed them laying on the ground they incouraged us on, saying go on boys you can whip them.[21]

Oates sat on a log outside his tent, trying to find words to convey what he had witnessed in the past week. He had quickly sent off a letter to his family the day after the Battle of Williamsburg, to let them know he was alive and well, but he had not had the time nor the ability to fully paint a picture of the smoke-filled nightmare.

After the battle, Oates slept on the field, soaked by the showers that fell through the night. When dawn appeared the next day on May 6th, Oates struggled to his feet and gazed around at the mud-caked faces of his companions. Many were missing. Lt. Col. Burtis called the regiment to assembly for roll-call to find the exact number of casualties. The Fifth Regiment had lost, according to the surgeon's report, 37 killed, 54 wounded, and 53 missing for a total of 144 casualties. Reports trickled into the ranks about the losses of the other regiments in the brigade. The Fourth Regiment lost 104, the Third 195, and the First Regiment, who had fought for seven hours, 331. Their first fight had cost the Excelsior Brigade 774 men.

The Confederates continued to fall back to Richmond with the Army of the Potomac in pursuit. The Excelsior Brigade, however, did not continue the advance. Chewed up from Williamsburg, they stayed in the area as a provost guard. Immediately they began tending to the wounded and dead from the battle. Oates was assigned to search the field for wounded who could still be helped in the overflowing tent hospitals nearby. Walking over the bodies of Southerner and Northerner alike, he could not help but look at the faces to see if he could recognize them. He approached where his company had fought and began to see the faces of men he knew. He found William Speitto, hands still around his rifle, and to his despair, the body of John Fulton, Oates' angel in chevrons during the battle. Yet they could not be helped this day. Oates had to keep moving and keep prodding the bodies, checking for those for whom there was still some hope.

The men around him took what little advantage their job offered. Most of the Confederates had whiskey in their canteens. The men may have at first shivered a little to drink what belonged to a corpse, but soon they downed the liquid courage. Few could walk through the entanglement of tree and human limbs without the whiskey to help them along.

The Excelsiors found whom they could and left the rest for the burial parties. Oates was assigned to help ship the wounded from Queen's Creek, which emptied into the York River. Those who had been treated at the field hospital were sent by transport to Washington, to recover, hopefully, and even more hopefully, rejoin their unit. For two days Oates labored, carting stretchers and lifting bodies. He saw the great amount that bullets and cannon could do to a man, and the little that army doctors could do to repair him. At the end of the shift, when the wounded were gone and the number of men on the peninsula less, all Oates could say was that it was, *"not a very nice job."*[23] Anything more would have frightened his family.

Sitting back in camp, with the 21 men of the company left out of the 38 who entered the abatis on May 5th, the soldiers talked. They talked in soft tones of John Verner, shot in the arm, of Sam McFarland, also shot in the arm. They talked of Lewis Shuck who lost a finger, of George Bond and Frank Remalay, who were just lost and presumed captured. They talked of Private Speitto and of Sergeant Fulton, whom they called, *"as brave a man who ever lived."* Both were dead on the field.[25]

The men talked in louder tones about the newspaper coverage of the battle. The papers shouted of how a brigade of the Sixth Corps under the command of Brigadier-General Winfield Hancock overran the Rebels' left flank on the other side of Williamsburg towards the end of the day. The papers were calling that the crucial blow of the day and naming Hancock a hero. The men talked of Hooker's division standing its ground for hours in the face of Rebel musket and artillery fire. They talked of the First Regiment's flag shot to pieces, but still receiving little recognition. They wished that if the papers could not do justice to the good old brigade they ought not mention them at all. They knew they had done their duty and it was their stand against the charging Rebels that won the battle.

The men also talked in optimistic terms. They were still confident of Union victory, even more so after personally whipping the Rebs. They were angry at McClellan for giving so much prestige to Hancock, but still felt he was the man to lead the Army of the Potomac. They talked in laudatory terms of Lt. James Stewart, the company commander since Capt. Glass had become second in command of the regiment. At first none of the company thought much of him, inexperienced at war and command. But since taking to the peninsula, he had shown himself a true leader and had stuck with his men throughout Williamsburg. Whereas some

James H. Stewart, lieutenant in Company A and commander on the Peninsula.
Courtesy New York State Military Museum

of the officers took refuge in the rear, Stewart stayed in the heart of danger with his men, and they considered him the best officer they had.

In all of these events, Oates took refuge in what had always given him comfort — his family. He wrote letters almost every day, sometimes more than one a day. His company, his friends, and his parents and siblings back on the East Commons in Allegheny gave Oates somewhere to retreat to in his mind after being plunged into the melee of battle, where the man next to him falls and rest from combat is two days hauling bloody bodies. Oates sat writing, falling into the solace of the world of words and sentences, an escape from the physical world that days earlier was shattered by a hail of miniés.

A world away in Washington, Sickles stepped out of the front door of Willard's with an added spring in his step. The Senate was voting that day, May 13, 1862, on his confirmation for the rank of brigadier-general. He was confident he had the votes; he had been working his avenues of influence for the past month to ensure that. While his men were digging in the ground before Yorktown, he was canvassing Capitol Hill to win himself a star. Just a week earlier, reports came streaming into the city of a bloodless Confederate collapse at Yorktown. A few days later came the stories of a slaughterhouse of a fight: a tough scrap including his own Excelsiors. Much of the news centered around "Hancock the Superb," who won the battle in the eyes of McClellan, but the Excelsior Brigade got a share of the front pages and the coat rooms. The extraordinary number of dead and wounded in the brigade gave Sickles his greatest card to use against the Senate. The four regiments suffered well over 25% casualties. For any unit to suffer that much without yielding an inch of ground required true stamina and courage. If the brigade fought that well at Williamsburg without Sickles, imagine its glorious feats under the steady hand of its general. Sickles lobbied to lead his men onwards to Richmond.

Sickles entered a restaurant, being escorted to one of the private tables near the back. The Tammany Hall man, he was used to doing business in the dark recesses of restaurants, and many of his plans, including the one to form the Excelsior Brigade, had been hatched over a meal. Sitting down, the owner congratulated Sickles on his men's performance at Williamsburg and wished him good luck on the Senate vote. He knew how to treat the powerful of the city. Sickles ate and lingered for some time. The first time the Senate voted on him he was busy assembling the men. This time he was waiting around in Washington, with nothing to distract him from the impending decision. Sickles desperately wanted to return to his men. He had built himself up as a general and most of his worth hinged on it. For a man who had spent most of his life with a title of some sort — from Corporate Consul of New York to Congressman — being out of an office was devastating. He had suffered such ignominy before, but this time was even worse. The action was happening. The battle was being fought, the glory was being won, and here he was sitting in the back of some restaurant in Washington, removed from command and removed from opportunity.

The door of the restaurant exploded open with a mud-splattered young man bursting through. Wild-eyed, he scanned the room, then leapt towards the back room where Sickles was sitting. Sickles rose slowly — he had sent this man to watch the Senate proceedings and now he must be returning with the result. The young man shouted it out almost before Sickles had asked: "Confirmed!" By a vote of 19-18, the Senate had approved Sickles' commission.

Sickles was floored. By one vote, he was a general. But that was all he needed. Sickles quickly righted himself. He had won. He was a general. He ordered the young man, who had sprinted all the way from Capitol Hill, to go and find Charles Graham at his hotel. Graham had resigned in protest over Sickles' removal, and Sickles was grateful for the display of loyalty. Now Graham would accompany him back to the brigade so they could take their rightful places at the head of the columns as they marched to Richmond and victory.

A soldier posted along the road saw the group of riders approaching and he let out a shout, "There comes our General!"

A thousand cheers burst forth. On the road just beyond the Excelsior Brigade's encampment near Bottom's Bridge, Virginia, rode Dan Sickles, Brigadier-General of Volunteers. "Clad in a splendid new uniform, with his fine form showing off to the best advantage as he gracefully bestrode his prancing steed, he looked every inch the soldier," wrote Cedma for the New York *Times*.[26]

The men of the brigade were overjoyed to see their commander who had been snatched away as they were being launched into war. Now on May 23 he had returned. They ran out to him on the road, throwing their caps in the air and voices tumbling over each other. The men mobbed Sickles who reveled in the praise. He first visited the camp of the Fifth Regiment, and from there passed through the lines of all his regiments. Officers and men shouted themselves hoarse while singing strains of "Hail to the Chief," and his hand was shaken at every turn of the road. Cedma poetically reported that, "The scene was a picture fit for the pencil of a master . . . There were those swarthy, sunbrowned men, fresh from the battle-field, with the laurels won on the ever-to-be-remembered field of Williamsburgh yet green upon their brows, crowding around the General whom they love."

Sickles made his way to the First Regiment last, the regiment he had first raised. He walked down the ranks noting those who were absent, who had suffered for their patriotism at Williamsburg. The great general who kept his composure at even the most trying moments was finally overcome with emotion, seeing the true devotion of those under his command both to him and to country. With tears running down his cheeks, Sickles galloped towards the regimental flag, grabbed it in his hands, and kissed it. For whatever battles in Congress had occupied his mind for the past year, right now he was committed to his soldiers, those who had entrusted their lives to him, and who deserved his greatest efforts. He was a commander of men now, and would do his duty.

Sickles calmly dictated orders to his aide-de-camp. Skirmishers were to be thrown forward to silence the annoying sharpshooters who were harassing the movements of the brigade. Immediately following, all regiments were to move forward and push back all Rebels they would encounter. The aide nodded in recognition of the orders and was off, galloping to the regimental commanders to relay Sickles' first commands in battle.

By mid-May, after the Confederates' continued retreat had finally ended, the Army of the Potomac crossed the Chickahominy River, a swampy stream that ran lengthwise down the peninsula and was at its closest point only 8 miles from Richmond. McClellan was moving slowly to take up positions, and the troops were confident victory was near. Then, on May 31, reports came flooding into camp of a Confederate attack up the road. Thousands of Confederates had descended upon the Union Fourth Corps under Major-General Erasmus Keyes near the Fair Oaks station of the Richmond and York River Railroad. They were putting the Federals to flight.

Sickles was told that the Union Second Corps was already headed towards the fight from the north, and that he and the rest of the Third Corps should prepare to move in from the east. Sickles got his brigade in motion and moved them out of camp around 3:30 P.M. They bivouacked in the woods and were on the road again at 7 A.M. the next day.

Sickles moved his men quickly and arrayed them in a line of battle in a large field. The Excelsior Brigade was at the extreme left of a curved Union army facing southwest and the Confederate brigades there. Sickles rode just behind the lines waiting for the battle to come to his sector. Rebel sharpshooters were lying in the woods beyond the field, trying to pick off mounted officers, with Sickles as the biggest prize of them all. Still, Sickles did not show any outward displays of emotion, content to wait until orders came to advance. Soon such orders came and Sickles went into action.

The Excelsior regiments stood up and fired a volley as one. The men loaded and fired another, then advanced across the field at the double-quick loading and firing as they went. On the way across the field, however the men, "apparently voted the gait to be decidedly slow. So the order was given to fix bayonets and charge, and they did it, not mincingly at all, but in terrible earnest and with a glorious cheer."[27] The Excelsiors charged into the woods, with Sickles surging behind his men. He plunged into the woods, exhilarated with the thrill of battle.

Sickles had, according to one observer, "not the air or manner of a novice. He was all activity, and thought only of the way to win."[27] He passed the order to all commanders — continue to advance, engage the enemy where possible. The Excelsiors were pushing forward, smashing through all Confederate resistance. Sickles was a whirl of movement. He checked on his various commands constantly, all the while noticing every detail around himself. A wounded Rebel sharpshooter lying at the base of a tree shot at Sickles but just missed. Soldiers moved to "dispatch" the sharpshooter with their bayonets, but he ordered them to take him prisoner. It was better to capture than to kill, since the prisoner might contain some bit of information. Sickles left the scene and galloped forward at the sound of musket fire ahead. The Rebels were retreating with Excelsior bullets biting at their backs and Sickles reported back that his area was secure.

He watched as the battle drew to a close. Stretcher-bearers swarmed the field, carrying off both northern and southern to the field hospitals. Burial parties got started on their own thankless jobs. Sickles patrolled his lines, looking over the men who had performed admirably under his command.

Sickles was pleased that his losses were small — only 72 killed, wounded and missing in the entire brigade. He was also pleased at his own performance. He had shown every bit of courage that could be demanded of a general. He congratulated himself as he looked over his first battle. Here was Capt. Johnson of the Third Regiment who was seriously wounded at Williamsburg but back today to lead his men. There he saw that a few of the 10th Massachusetts boys had snuck into the Rebel camp and stole a ham. They were greeted by choruses from some Excelsiors of "Johnny stole the ham / Sickles killed the man." It was from a popular song alluding to Sickles and Phillip Barton Key, here replacing Key with Johnny Reb. Normally hearing jokes about his personal life would have annoyed Sickles. Today he knew his men sang it out of affection and pride at how their general had acted.

The man who had three weeks earlier been comfortable in a Washington hotel while his men died in the mud was now riding along a battlefield of his own. His soldiers, those who had crawled through the abatis at Williamsburg, loved him. He was their leader, their general, their champion. He had called them together and had always fought for them even when he was fighting for himself. Sickles was satisfied. He was only twelve miles from Richmond, with a star on his shoulder and glory spread out on the field around him. Now was the time to lead the men to whom he had given himself onwards to victory.

Camp near Richmond June 23rd

Dear Mother

I sent you a letter day before
yesterday, & as I wrote to sally this morning
I will send it to you & you can send it
down to them by William, I will send you 5
dollars in this letter, it is a small amount
but better than nothing, you can read
sally's letter, & it contains all the news
sent you in the last letter. a likeness
Bob Whitehead & George Confer you
must take care of them till I come home
I have very little news to tell you all is
quiet here. I hope Nelly is home by this
time, & I hope it will not be long before
we are all home, I am well & in good
health & so is the most of the boys, the
weather as been very fine, for the last
week but very hot, I suppose Daddy takes
his toddy every night, he would go minus
if he was out here. he would do some
ll grumbling if he was out here
would never get done growling

Chapter Eight

The Company

Camp near Fair Oaks, Virginia

June, 1862

Dear Mother, if you do not get letters regular you must not be arlarmed for when we move we move without knapsacks & are sometimes 3 & 4 days without them & the mail is not regular . . .

Oates sat in the old camp of Casey's division of the Fourth Corps. Casey's men had been routed on the first day of Fair Oaks and, after the battle had been won on the second day, were placed in the rear. The Excelsior Brigade was posted in Casey's camp, which on June 5 still bore the signs of the battle. With the first duty of the Excelsior Brigade to begin building defensive works to fend off another Confederate attack, there had been little time to clean up the scattered cans and supplies. The men had finished their work for the day and Oates was using his free time to send reassurances of his good health home.

I expect the mail going out every minuit so I can not write you much news . . . Well I must conclude & remain your affectionate son.[28]

Oates sealed the letter and got up from the crate he had been using as a seat. He walked over to the regimental mailroom to drop off his letter, weaving through his fellow soldiers enjoying their rest. The camp was full of men, some writing home, others too busy to write home but who had plenty of time to play cards. The soldiers were in good spirits after the Battle of Fair Oaks, called the Battle of Seven Pines in the Confederacy. Their army had advanced, albeit slowly, up to the outskirts of Richmond, and the first Rebel attack to dislodge them from their positions had been successfully repulsed. Their brigade had done their job ably in battle and, best of all, had lost very few of their own. Only one man was killed in the entire Fifth Regiment, and not a single one was wounded in Oates' company. After a tough and otherworldly battle like Williamsburg, Fair Oaks was a reprieve.

Oates continued to the mailroom, squelching his way across the roads. The boots his family had sent him were certainly proving their worth now. They had saved him three times their price in ordinary shoes, he estimated. Heavy rain had caused country roads to devolve into ribbons of mud. There was some "splendid" farm and woodland around, similar to the terrain they had already passed through on the lower peninsula but they were near the head of the White Oak Swamp - acres upon acres of watery marshland. During the battle, when the First and Fifth Regiment was deployed to support the artillery battery, they had to push through a swamp in many places as deep as a man's waist. The boots were a boon to Oates as he made his way through the swamps to face the Rebs, and the mud to face the postman.

All of a sudden Oates tripped and fell to the ground in a flurry of squawking. He pulled his head out of the mud to see the other men laughing good-naturedly at his misfortune and a herd of chickens scrambling out of the roadway. The Excelsiors had had guests since the fight: three hens and each with a good many chicks of her own. The chickens must have come from a farm nearby but now lived with the brigade. They had been in the midst of the fight both days, and had hung around the camp afterwards living off the soldiers' crumbs. They were the only things around not attached to the army, and seemed fully able to take care of themselves. Whenever the Rebels threw shells overhead, the hens would hurry off with their chicks in tow for a nearby house to hide under, coming out when the artillery ceased. The chickens, innocent and oblivious to the sufferings of the war, became pets. Although fried chicken was coveted to augment their plain rations, there was not a man among them that would touch the hens for anything.

Oates finally arrived at the mail office, a little muddier, but no dirtier than a soldier usually was. He dropped off the letter, wishing it to arrive home with all speed (not just to comfort his family; he had asked for new steel pens, and couldn't write properly until his family sent him some). The suttlers were stationed nearby, the private commissars licensed to sell goods to the troops. They were hawking copies of the New York *Herald*, the largest-circulation newspaper of the city. Luckily they were down from the high of $1.50 apiece that the papers were going for in late May, but they were still too expensive for Oates. There would certainly be a copy of the latest news in camp, either because a group had chipped in to buy a newspaper, or because someone had been sent a paper from home.

The men of the Excelsior Brigade, like most soldiers in the Union and Confederate armies, had insatiable appetites for the news. The Civil War was fought on multiple fronts, and the men knew that whatever happened in another region of the country might affect them and how much they would have to fight. The men followed every ongoing campaign, and debated the chances of victory in all places. And they had a lot to debate.

In June of 1862, when the Excelsior Brigade was positioned near the Seven

Pines crossroads outside of Richmond, the Union was on the advance throughout the Confederacy. A little over a year after the war started, a large Union force, the 100,000 man strong Army of the Potomac, could see the rooftops of Richmond and appeared to be digging in for a final siege.

As the New York *Herald* reported, "'All Quiet on the Potomac!' the stereotype and succinct report of matters for months in front of Washington, may now be changed to all quiet on the Chickahominy. But the quiet does not promise to be as prolonged in front of the Rebel capital as that before the federal metropolis. The day of the big battle is hastening on, and the preparations on both sides are incessantly active."[29a]

Westward, in the Shenandoah Valley of Virginia, Gen. Thomas "Stonewall" Jackson had sent a Union force into retreat northward. But Oates did not think much of this front. He wrote that it was a daring move Jackson had made, but it might be at the cost of his command, and would not matter if Richmond fell.

Farther west, the Union had captured New Orleans and defeated the Rebels at Shiloh in Tennessee. Now Union armies were pushing on to capture all of the Mississippi River, with Ulysses S. Grant coming from the north and Benjamin Butler from the south. These were the main campaigns of the day, although the press lent considerable time to the lesser but more current events. The Union General Henry Halleck was closing in on Corinth in northwest Mississippi. All along the Confederate coastline the Union was establishing blockades and holding forces, and slowly whittling away at the southern beaches. While the Union attack on Richmond was the main campaign and expected to force the South to terms quickly, Lincoln was nonetheless exerting the North's full strength across the continent. Oates and the men followed these events closely — if the Union succeeded in most of these areas, maybe it would mean an earlier end to the war, and home by the 4th of July.

> *Camp Near Fair Oaks, June 19th*
>
> *Dear Mother,*
>
> *I have been lucky lately in receiving letters, I have had 5 at one mail. I received one from Mrs. Lawton inquiring about John & I answered it & for fear she will not get it I will his directions to you. John Lawton Comp. A, 5th Reg', Exc'r Brigade, U.S. Navy Hospital, Portsmouth, Va. he is sick their but I do not know what is the matter with him,*

Oates stopped briefly to dip his pen into ink. There were a number of men sick like John during June of '62. The swamps that had only been a hindrance during Fair Oaks had turned deadly later when they were found to be mosquito-breeding malarial pits. Given the poor hygiene of the army, large numbers of men were taking ill and falling out of ranks. Oates himself had had a brief bout with malaria around June 10, but had quickly recovered. Oates was finished with the letter's initial pleasantries and got to his real message. Because the large numbers of sick and casualties had struck the Fifth unevenly, some companies were near full strength, whereas some had less than 25 of the usual 90 fit for duty. Oates' Company A had been lucky and had been spared most of the illness and battle-wounds. Now that luck would cost them.

> *Our company is scattered all through the regiment. their has been 28 of us transfered to fill up other companys & I do not care how many more fights we are in. I will never fight in any other company but the one I left in Pittsburgh with. I think Captain Glass has not a partical of a man about him. or else he would never allowed us to be transfered. He promised to stick to us & this is the way he is doing it, Transfering men is not lawfull according to the Secatary of war's order. & mark my words if our regimant does not run the next fight we are in for they have botched up the whole regiment & gave us to much to do.*[29]

Oates ended the letter with a plea to his brother-in-law to look into this transferring business and see if there was a way out. He sealed it and headed off to the mailroom again. But Oates was not making his way through friends, as he had done many times before. He had been transferred to Company C, recruited in Flushing, New York. Oates did not know a single one of his new company-mates.

Oates headed back from the mailroom despondent. *"Taking a man into another company,"* Oates had written, *"is like taking a boy from home to live among strangers."*[30] There had been some talk of transferring since before Fair Oaks, but Oates did not think much of it then. He knew some men in other companies, and thought that one company was as good as another. He expected the war to end soon and everyone to be sent home anyway. But now that he had been sent into those strangers, his opinion changed drastically. He had not realized until he left it how much his company was his home. While walking past the tents of Company A he saw a group of men and ran over to see what was happening with his comrades. He pushed into the crowd and saw that the soldiers were circled around men from home, from Pittsburgh. A Mr. Preston was there, father of Company A's Charles Preston, a Sheriff Graham and others, all whom the men knew from before the war. They had come to see the intrepid Pittsburgh boys of the Excelsior Brigade, of whom the citizens of the Three Rivers had heard so much.

Whenever anyone of Company A saw a Pittsburgher, he immediately asked him for news of home or to transmit news back to families. Soldiers were not given much time or license to visit other camps, and since corps and even divisions were spaced widely apart, Company A had few opportunities to speak with fellow Pittsburghers. The Excelsior Brigade was comprised overwhelmingly of New Yorkers, and there were few fellow Pennsylvanians other than Oates' company in the whole brigade. But when one came to camp, usually only a few days out of the state, he brought more detailed and fresher news of home life than soldiers could achieve through letters. Oates sent off requests for news on this friend or that nephew, but a thirty second conversation with a visiting citizen could provide him more and newer information than a ream of letters ever could.

Oates made his way over to Sheriff Graham. He led with questions on his family, the usual questions Mr. Graham was peppered with. After the standard "good healths" and "looking wells," Oates took out a prize of war for Sheriff Graham to bring back home with him. It was a sharpshooter rifle ball Oates had taken from one of the dead Rebels at Williamsburg. A prize like that would show that he had really been in the action, and possibly elevate his reputation in town. Oates was a young man, and he was interested in looking the hero for those at home, especially for a certain Nancy Robinson.

The community of displaced Allegheny County men was strong in the Army of the Potomac. After the battle of Williamsburg, Oates was visited by a number of old friends, all checking to see that he was still in the land of the living and to hear stories of the great battle he had fought. Most were in Pennsylvania regiments, and brought Oates (whom they almost did not recognize as he had stopped shaving) the gossip they had picked up in their own letters to home.

For a man who was hundreds of miles from home, in the midst of uncertainty for the state of his country and his life, challenged with the most exhausting, frightening, or dull times of his existence, friends and family were greatly appreciated. That was why this transferring business was so cruel. Oates himself went to Col. Graham to try to explain this. It was unusual for a private personally to make a plea to a field officer, but Oates was insistent upon it, and someone in the regimental headquarters was sympathetic. Graham listened and promised that it would be made alright eventually, but he could do little immediately. He cared about his troops, but he also had to exert himself to construct defensive works to protect his camp and prepare for the siege of Richmond. The men were busy that June building forts and redoubts and every other type of fortifications known to the Union armies.

Oates left Graham's office hopeful that some action would be taken, but still angry he had been ripped from his company. If they were left in camp for a long time, maybe some of the sick would recover, as was beginning to happen, and return to their companies, then the Company A men could return to their old tents. Oates comforted himself with the knowledge that should the great battle for Richmond come before the transferring business was corrected, he would simply fall in with his old friends. When the Rebs are pouring down the volleys on the Excelsiors and solid shot is felling trees, what officer is going to care what company Oates is fighting with? Transferring may have been a petty business to officers, but it was incredibly important to the men affected like Oates, and in a struggle, the more passionate ones would prevail. The men who marched to war to defend their old homes would not sit by while bureaucrats snatched them from their new ones.

Chapter Nine

Battle Weary

Seven Days' Battles near Richmond, Virginia.

June 25 — July 1, 1862

In the dark hours of the night, Oates climbed his way up the slopes of Malvern Hill, weighed down by nothing more than rations, his gun, and the clothes on his back. His was among the last Union units to reach the hill where the rest of the army had assembled the day before. Hooker's division was once again the rear guard of the army.

Oates followed the men in front of him to the east side of the hill, where the Excelsior Brigade was assigned to wait and rest for further orders. Oates and the rest of the brigade were dead tired. Once again they had spent the previous day fighting and the previous night marching.

A short night of sleep was ended by the kicks and shouts of their sergeants. By daylight of the first of July, the men found the Confederates were massed nearby and looking for yet another fight.

Oates and the rest of the company hustled out of camp and into line near the road. The men fell into their regiments and the regiments fell into their place in line. McClellan had settled into a siege of Richmond, trying to duplicate the success at Yorktown. Union camps were still out of range of Richmond and Mc-Clellan needed to get closer before mounting the heavy artillery. There was high ground in front of the Union camps at Fair Oaks that would put the "sacred city" of the South under the guns of the North.[27] McClellan had ordered this ground taken, and the Excelsior Brigade was one of three that was called out to seize it.

It was a fine summer morning on June 25th. Surgeon Thomas T. Ellis, a spectator of the fight, wrote that "Never was there a day better fitted for a fight. Two or three tempest-like showers in the few days previous seemed to have washed all that was disagreeable out of Virginia. Nature and the cool, fresh air, filled our Northern lungs with life. It was just cloudy enough, too, so to temper the sun's heat without making it a dull day, and there was just breeze enough to lift the smoke."[27]

And so Sickles sat on his horse in the early hours of daylight examining his men in the line of battle. They were in an open field just outside of the Union fortifications, and had a long line of woods in front of them. Beyond the woods was another open field, and it was this field the Union forces were to take. Soon an orderly rode up to Sickles with a brief message from his divisional commander Joseph Hooker: move out. Sickles passed the word to his regiments, and his 1,400 men began the slow walk into another fight.

"As the line moved across the field . . . it presented a beautiful spectacle; the light-blue of the uniforms contrasted with the brilliant green of the field; the light reflected from the gun-barrels in a silvery sheen; and their glorious standards blown out in the breeze gave the whole scene the gayety and show of a Fourth of July Parade," wrote Surgeon Ellis.[27]

Oates' sergeant grabbed him on the shoulder and told him to get on the road. He struggled through the swamp with his rifle held high to keep it out of water. Running through the morass, he finally made it to the dry road and fell in line with the rest of his regiment. Half of them, like him, were caked in mud and who-knows-what-else from the waist down. After a quick advance through the first field, the regiment had entered the woods only to find much of it was swamp. The men were now ready to advance again and catch up with the rest of the line that had already made it to the second field.

Oates fell into file formation, four across in a long column, back in Company A. When news of the fight had come, he and the rest of the Pittsburghers had fallen in with their old company, and the officers did not have the time to sort them out. Oates could see the light ahead signaling the end of the woods. It would be only a short trip on the road but a dangerous one nonetheless. In column formation, the regiment only provided a front of four rifles as opposed to the three hundred rifles that could fire on the enemy in regular battle formation. A thin enemy skirmish line could hold up the regiment, and a thick enemy battle line might rout it before the regiment had time to deploy and bring all their force to bear on the enemy. Oates kept his eyes in front and moved quickly forward.

Oates burst into the clearing to find the main body of Rebels entrenched in rifle pits that crossed the open field. The regiment deployed into a battle line and sergeants shouted out the orders to aim rifles. Oates laid his Enfield quickly. At the distance of a few hundred yards he could only direct his shot at groups of men. The order to fire came and Oates pulled the trigger. A long volley crashed out of the muzzles of the Fifth, kicking up dirt near the Rebel rifle pits. The Rebels returned fire, and Oates dropped his hand to his cartridge box to reload. The trumpet sounded the order to advance again, and the Fifth moved across the field towards the Rebels. The Fifth discharged a number of volleys, all the while under a heavy fire. With a final volley and charge the Fifth drove the Rebels from their trenches. Oates jumped into one of the pits, reloaded, and trained his gun on the Rebel reinforcements streaming onto the field to reclaim the ground for the Confederacy.

Behind Oates and the main battle line Sickles was riding with Colonel Hall of the Second Excelsior to reconnoiter the right flank of the brigade when a tremendous crash erupted from the trees nearby. A fresh North Carolina regiment had unleashed a volley into the inexperienced Second Regiment. The volley did little damage to the Excelsiors; the North Carolinians were all green as well and had missed their marks. But Sickles heard, after the echoes of the volley died down, someone in the ranks shout: "We are flanked; retreat."[31]

Suddenly the left wing of the Second Regiment turned and fled. Sickles was riding behind the middle of the regiment at the time and was almost swept up in the flood of men. He spurred his horse forward and shouted for the soldiers to hold their ground. Lt. Col. Potter of the Fourth Regiment heard his general and yelled at his men to hold their place — no one was being outflanked and the Fourth was to keep up its fire upon the Rebs. But the Second Regiment was too disorganized to hear, and its commander was riding with Sickles and out of position to communicate with his subordinates.

Sickles, with Colonel Hall and two officers of McClellan's staff, managed to round up some of the fugitives and form them back in line. Many were missing, most noticeably the color sergeant, who had fled back to the original positions, thinking he needed to protect the regimental flags. To have one of his regiments break and flee at almost nothing was "mortifying" to Sickles, to use his own word.[31] It was all the more mortifying because all of this happened under the eyes of Gen. Joseph Hooker, Sickles' superior officer. Sickles had trained and molded these men, and now they had shown their courage by fleeing at the first volley they faced. It was extremely embarrassing for him who had campaigned on the platform of his brigade's supreme fighting ability. He would later take comfort in the fact that his other four regiments had held fast when another regiment had visibly fled. Routs were usually infectious, but those hardened from Williamsburg stayed immune.

Sickles was pressed hard all along his line, but his men were holding tight. An aide on horseback rode towards Sickles quickly to inform him that Hooker had dispatched the 2nd New York Infantry to support Sickles on the right. That was fine, additional help was needed. Since the right looked secure with the reinforcements, Sickles hurried to the left to find that his men had pushed the enemy far back. When he returned to the right, he found the 2nd New York in position. All seemed to be in order, and Sickles told his men to stay down and hold their positions.

Suddenly, Sickles was approached by another aide from Gen. Hooker. Hooker was relaying an order from McClellan himself to pull back to the Union's original defenses. It was a completely irrational order. Sickles and Grover had advanced through the woods and the open field with little loss. They had seized the correct ground and had beaten back three separate Rebel attacks aimed at recapturing it. Now they were receiving reinforcements and were in no danger of being flanked or driven back. Sickles questioned the aide again, until there was no doubt that, yes, McClellan wanted the men back. Sickles passed the word to his regiments. All along the line there were disbelieving shouts — were they really supposed to give up the ground they had just won? Apparently yes, and the men fell back to their original positions behind a screen of skirmishers. The brigade had left the Union lines around 8 A.M., fought for three hours, and now at 11 o'clock were being called back. It did not make any sense, but they were orders, and the men followed them.

Soon thereafter General McClellan himself rode into camp. He had been conducting the battle from a headquarters three miles back, and it was because of him that the battle had been halted. When Hooker had sent reinforcements to Sickles, he had informed his corps commander, Gen. Heitzleman, of the move. Heitzleman passed the move along to McClellan, who had just received word of the Second Excelsior's rout. McClellan thought that his troops must be outnumbered and possibly outflanked. His mind focused on saving the Union men from the imaginary Rebel onslaught, and he hurriedly ordered everyone back behind the defenses. Heitzleman, on the field, knew that there was no need to retreat, but McClellan, farther back and receiving all his news via telegraph, had very little idea of the true situation of the battle. Imperfect intelligence (McClellan's) had caused a massive blunder.

When McClellan arrived on the field he saw the true state of the fight. He ordered the men to repeat their feats of the morning. Sickles got his men into line, just as before, and moved them across the field. They avoided the swamp and followed paths made earlier through the abatis. The resistance was once again difficult, said Sickles, but the overwhelming number of the Union soldiers once again prevailed.

Sickles' troops remained on the line, not pressed much by the Confederates but still on point for another attack, until 7 P.M., when another brigade arrived to relieve the Excelsior Brigade. With Sickles at the head, the Excelsior Brigade returned to their camps after the twelve-hour engagement, later called the Battle of Oak Grove, after a clump of trees on the field. The men had done what they had been ordered to do — advance the picket lines of the Union closer to Richmond - and they had done it twice. Sickles proudly wrote in his report that out of the brigade of 1,400 only 8 were killed, with 116 wounded and 11 missing. It had been a long day for the brigade, but they had performed well.

Oates lumbered out of his tent bleary eyed on the morning of June 26, the day after Oak Grove. The Rebs had thought that they could drive in the Union pickets under the cover of darkness, and Oates and the regiment had been roused twice the night before to stand ready to repulse a general attack. The men talked of the fight they had had yesterday in between their regular duties. Some thought civilians had fought with the Confederates because Excelsiors had come back wounded with bird shot. They heard that Col. Graham had a narrow miss when a musket ball passed through his coat. However, they mostly wondered what the cannon fire they heard coming from the north meant. Beginning around 5 P.M. the roar was continuous and the men thought another battle must be ongoing. They hoped their side was winning and looked around for messengers coming into camp telling them to move out to join the fight. Nothing happened, the sun set, and the men returned to their tents.

The next day passed with the artillery fire continuing but still no word of what it signified. The brigade went to bed hoping for a full night's sleep in case the next day the fight should spread to them. In this they were disappointed. At 3 in the morning, the regiment was called out to stand ready for a Rebel attack. None came, and the brigade spent the rest of that day trying to sleep and wondering if there was a battle going on just outside the limits of their camp. They went to bed that night thinking that maybe nothing important was happening and McClellan had just been continuing the advance to Richmond in the north, as they had done at Oak Grove a few days earlier.

Late at night on June 28th, or very early on the 29th, Oates was woken with new orders. He was to pack what he could carry, load only the most necessary equipment onto the brigade's wagons and then destroy everything else in camp. The artillery fire of the days before must not have been favorable to the Union because the Excelsior Brigade was abandoning its camp and withdrawing at once with the Rebels close on them. The tired and sleepy Oates grabbed his rifle and letter case and assembled with his company to face what orders awaited him.

The men marched two miles east that day to a crossroads near Savage's Station on the Richmond and York River Railroad which lay along the Rebels line of advance. During the fighting of the 26th and 27th, although the Confederates won no stunning victories, their aggressiveness had convinced McClellan that they must have numerical superiority and, instead of focusing on how to take Richmond, focused on how to save the 100,000 man Army of the Potomac from the 60,000 man Confederate Army of Northern Virginia. The slow wagon train which carried the army's supplies and heavy artillery was exceedingly vulnerable when on the move, and McClellan used most of the army to cover the retreat from the Rebels who kept attacking. Savage Station was the ground where the army would make its first delaying battle.

Oates and the Excelsior Brigade were standing in the long line of two corps when they saw the Confederates come into view. The men waited for the fight to spread along the line to them, but little action came. The Second Corps on the left of the line was hit and turned back the Rebels, and the Excelsior Brigade had only a few men hit from stray bullets. At 4 P.M. the order was given to fall back and the brigade, still strung out in a line of battle, marched steadily away from Richmond. The brigade fell into columns and turned south to guard the next standing point. The men marched for miles that evening, and splashed through Brackett's Ford in the White Oak swamp at dusk. They continued southward, and at last were allowed to sleep fitfully under the stars, waiting for the gray enemy to rouse them from their slumbers once more.

The soldiers managed to get some semblance of rest, but were woken the next morning with reports that Rebels were again in the area. The day before the Confederates had traveled parallel to the Army of the Potomac, and were about to try to drive the forces stationed near the Excelsior Brigade across the road on which the wagon train was traveling. The Excelsior Brigade again was called to battle and soon they could hear the crash of cannon and rattle of musketry. Suddenly a wave of men poured over the crest of the hill in front of the Excelsior Brigade. Pennsylvania troops from the Fifth Corps had been smashed and put to flight by oncoming Rebels. Sickles ordered his men to stand ready to take in the fugitives and repulse any pursuing Rebs, when suddenly a volley crashed into his men. The Pennsylvanians had mistaken the Excelsior Brigade for enemy and were firing in unison at them. Sickles raced over to the color guard and ordered him to unfurl the Stars and Stripes. Through the efforts of the First and Third Excelsior Regiments and Berdan's sharpshooters, who were posted in front of the Excelsiors, the mistaken Union boys were driven back into their own line.

The men collected themselves and prepared for a night on the battlefield. Such a night would not come. In the dark they were told they were to fall back once more. The wagon train was almost to the new base McClellan had picked out for the army, on the James River where Union gunboats could cover the Federals from what he thought was a 300,000 man Confederate force. Oates picked himself up once more, and the tired Excelsiors marched through the night with another day of likely battle in front of them.

Oates climbed the slow rise of the place where the Union army had chosen to stand, a large plateau near the James called Malvern Hill. The Union army had drawn up in an inverted U with the Confederates assembling in the woods to the north. The Excelsior Brigade was in the right wing of the army, far from the current positions of the Confederates. The men fell asleep when they reached their station, aware that they might soon be woken and need to be ready to fight at a moment's notice.

Oates was sitting on the ground eating lunch at 11 A.M., the stale hardtack that had been every meal for the past few days. Suddenly the air shook and a clap like thunder rang over the hill. The Confederates had run out batteries to knock out the Union artillery, and the Union gunners were responding in kind. Oates watched as one of the largest artillery duels of the war unfolded before his eyes. Over to the left he saw a Rebel battery charge out of the woods and open up on the Union positions. The guns sounded big, probably 32 pounders, each one hurling a 32-pound ball of shot or shell at the Federal cannoneers every minute. There were five Union batteries on the hill above the Rebs and each gun slowly turned and aimed at the Rebel battery. The Union guns went off quickly in succession and soon the Rebel guns fell silent. The Union batteries immediately focused on other targets, but Oates remembered that short duel he had seen, and he found out later that when Union infantry was sent down to investigate the silenced Confederate guns, they found every horse and man killed, caissons blown up and pieces dismounted. Oates wrote home that, *"that was the way we served them all that day."*[32]

Sickles had been ordered to report to the headquarters of General Fitz John Porter, commander of the Union Fifth Corps, which was being hard pressed by the initial Rebel infantry attacks. No matter that almost all of their artillery had been destroyed by the Union guns, the Confederates still charged up the front of Malvern Hill. Porter, on the left of the Union lines, was bearing the brunt of the attack, and Sickles burst into his headquarters ready to send the gallant Excelsior Brigade into that fight.

Porter was not there, so Sickles reported to General Kearny, commander of the Third Division of the Third Corps and the highest officer present. Kearney advised Sickles to return to his original position, as the Rebels might try to strike there next. Sickles was not satisfied with that suggestion. The fighting on the left was still very "animated," and his brigade could be critical in the battle there. He requested the signal officer at headquarters find out what the state of affairs was along the front lines. Sickles waited impatiently while the officer communicated with various staffs near the fighting. Soon the report came back: Porter's right was weak, several regiments were close to running out of ammunition. To Sickles, it was a perfect opportunity to use his waiting brigade to plug a hole in the line. He turned to Kearney. The General said, "I have no further advice to give; decide for yourself."[33]

That was all Sickles needed to hear. He was off at the head of his column of warriors leading them briskly to the part of the field where the fighting was hottest. Sickles looked in vain for an officer to whom he could report and from whom he could receive orders. He had 1,400 men at hand, but no one to tell him where to position them. He ordered the brigade into a ravine where they would be safe from any artillery fire and with Maj. Steven of the Third Excelsior, rode down the entire line looking for Porter.

Sickles, Stevens, and the one brigade staff officer left fit for duty galloped the mile long line looking for a chance to get into the fight. Finally spotting an officer on Porter's staff, he rode up and told him where his brigade was waiting. The officer sprinted off to find Porter, shouting for Sickles to return to his command and await orders. The band of Excelsior leaders sped across the field back to the ravine and prepared to enter the fight. In a few moments Porter himself arrived, and directed Sickles to move forward to support two batteries that were playing havoc with the advancing Confederates. Porter further instructed Sickles not to pursue the enemy if it retreated but, "to hold [his] position at all hazards."[33]

Sickles assembled his men *en echelon* — the regiments forming in parallel lines so that both the front and the flanks of the brigade were covered. He moved them behind the batteries and waited for calls for replacement regiments. Soon messages came from Generals Couch, Howe and Abercrombie requesting Excelsior regiments to replace those of their own which had run out of ammunition. The Third Excelsior Regiment relieved the 61st Pennsylvania, and was almost immediately engaged by the enemy. The Second Regiment relieved the 1st U.S. Chasseurs and the First and Fourth Regiments were sent to the right to support batteries there. The Fifth was sent forward 100 yards behind and to the right of the Third Regiment to support their fellow Exelsiors.

Oates climbed out of the ravine and hustled forward into the Fifth's position. As he was headed into the battle Sickles passed by him. Oates heard his general shout out to the soldiers, "Men all I ask of you is to do as you have always done."[34] The soldiers continued onward, inspired by their leader.

The men were just arraying themselves, the sergeants running down the line to press the privates into order, the officers scrambling back and forth to report this platoon or this company in place, when Confederate infantry was spotted in the woods to the left. Oates hurriedly loaded his gun, and fired into the trees. The men loaded again, and the line once more erupted in a volley of musket fire. The battery behind the men trained their guns towards the enemy and opened up.

Oates kept firing, biting into the cartridge, dumping the powder down the musket barrel, priming the gun, aiming, and firing. The grapeshot and canister flew over Oates' head and tore into the trees. The Third Regiment soon saw the enemy and poured its own volleys into the Rebels. The fighting continued for some time, possibly a full half hour, and smoke enveloped the lines of the Excelsior Brigade. But then the men noticed something. Amid the booming of the cannon, and the crashing of the canister, grape, and miniés, they could hear no thuds of bullets coming at them, nor could they see any men in their lines falling wounded. The regiment stopped firing, and when the smoke cleared, they saw that the Rebels had retreated. Oates stood, waiting for the next attack to come. Soon a courier ran up to the Fifth's lines. He told Col. Graham that the Rebs were attacking again, but this time farther to the right. Graham was to move his regiment down the line to support a battery.

Oates picked up his gun and made tracks for the new position. The men were ordered in front of Battery B of the Maryland Light Artillery. Oates and the rest laid down so that the canister could pass over their heads, but were ready to stand up to fend off any oncoming Rebs. But here, laying on the soft field on Malvern Hill, the exhaustion delayed by the necessities of battle caught up with the men of the Fifth. Even with shot and shell flying like hail, the incredible cannonfire only yards away booming *"like forty"* and a battle raging around them, soldiers in the regiment fell asleep. The chaos and fatigue of the campaign had become too much for them, and they escaped into slumber.

Sickles ranged behind the lines, checking that the Rebels made no successful advances into his lines. He looked for the First and Fourth Regiments, so decimated that they formed only one battalion under Major Thomas Holt of the First. They could not be found where they were supposed to be, and Sickles later spotted them in the front line, having been sent there in Sickles' name by another general.

Sickles had no time to reprimand the general, for he had just observed that his regiments were running low on ammunition and there was no reserve supply in the area. Racing to the rear, Sickles directed supply soldiers to bring up 20,000 rounds of .58 caliber bullets. Both Col. Taylor of the Third Reg. and Maj. Holt of the First came to the new depot with men of their regiments. They obtained 60 rounds per man and left to return to their men. The Excelsior Brigade was now supplied to last another few hours of hard fighting.

But that hard fighting would not be necessary. The Rebels slowly broke off the fight, with a few final charges that the Third Regiment helped repel at the point of the bayonet. The Rebels were bloodied and disorganized, vulnerable to counter-attack. But much to the dismay of the Union, McClellan opted to retreat further, to his designated base at Harrison's Landing, a few miles off.

The Fifth Regiment was sent out on picket that night and Oates leaned against a tree in the dark, looking for any nocturnal attacks. He could not see anything, but could hear plenty. The shouts of wounded from both sides for water and help rang out across the woods. The Rebels sang out what regiment they were from, and Oates had to listen to strains of, "4th South Carolina, 10th Mississippi," throughout the night not knowing whether they were signals for attack. The cannons continued to fire, and the orange bursts from the guns gave momentary light to Oates. No attack came, and around 2 A.M., July 2nd, a loud whisper called the pickets in. Oates filed in line and assembled with the rest of the Excelsior Brigade on the top of the hill. Covered by various regiments, the Excelsior Brigade left the hill for the new, permanent camp of the Army of the Potomac.

Oates marched through the night, and dawn found the Excelsior Brigade strung out on the road to Harrison's Landing. The soldiers carried almost nothing, many were barefoot, and almost all had dirty and torn clothes on their backs. They were ragged, bearded and tired. They were few, only about 1,200 strong from the 5,000 they had when they left New York, and having lost 54 men killed, wounded and missing since June 25 in the series of operations that would be known as the Seven Days' Battles.

As Oates walked among the column, Sickles rode at the head of it. He had had an even more difficult week than Oates. When the privates were infrequently sleeping or resting, he was still moving - checking on his command and looking for ways to either get them into action or refit them after a fight. His Excelsior Brigade had performed admirably, excepting the one mistake of the Second Regiment at Oak Grove. It was a tough campaign, fighting on four days out of seven. But at Oak Grove, Savage Station, Glendale (sometime called White Oak Swamp or Charles City Crossroads) and Malvern Hill, the men did their duties with, as Sickles himself put it, "fortitude and constancy."[35] The battered and exhausted Excelsior Brigade pulled themselves into the new camp at Harrison's Landing.

Oates and Sickles entered the camp with the early morning light of the first day in recent memory without threat of attack or sounds of cannon fire ringing across the countryside. Both men had performed superbly and they now knew to what limits a war could push its soldiers. The Excelsior Brigade found its place in camp, and the men and officers alike threw down their weary bodies. This was the time to recover from the week of fighting and prepare for whatever would come next.

Chapter Ten

All Their Efforts Gone to Dust

Harrison's Landing, Virginia

July, 1862

ates and others of Company A, all back together after fighting in Company A during the Seven Days' Battles, sat on cracker boxes in late July of 1862 talking about the company moving into a Pennsylvania regiment. Some of the men wanted to join a unit where they could fight alongside other men of the Keystone State and not dockworkers from Brooklyn. Others who looked to have a majority wanted to stay in their home of the last year, the Excelsior Brigade. They had fought with the brigade, they argued, and had made a name with it. They would not leave those with whom they had stood ranks at Williamsburg, Fair Oaks, Oak Grove and Malvern Hill. They would not leave even if at the moment being a soldier in the Excelsior Brigade was difficult.

After the Seven Days' Battles when the exhausted and filthy columns raggedly entered camp, the promised land towards which McClellan had led his army, the soldiers arrived with only what they carried on their backs. The long road from Oak Grove to Malvern Hill had been strewn with the impedimenta of the army. The stores of the Excelsior Brigade that could not fit onto its small wagon train were burned in the early morning of June 29th, and anything that might impede a soldier was thrown away. It was better to lose a knapsack to the Rebels than oneself.

The entire army had done this, and even though they fought at Savage Station, Charles City Crossroads, and Glendale to protect the army's massive wagon train, that train contained little that the ordinary soldier required. The Army of the Potomac, a week earlier the best-equipped fighting force in the world, was by July 2nd merely a mass of men with only a few days' worth of food and ammunition.

Oates and the Excelsior Brigade were no different from the rest of the army, and as Oates claimed his sleeping area in camp (tents had been discarded as well) he carried just his rifle and ammunition, some stale hardtack crackers, two extra shirts he had worn during the battles so as not to lose them, and his letter case. These were all his possessions in the world — no utensils, no blanket, and only a fraction of what he had at Camp Scott. A couple of weeks later, he even had to

Recruiting poster for the Excelsior Brigade from the late summer of 1862. Bounties were bonuses given to recruits upon enlistment, often a significant enough sum to encourage "bounty jumpers," men who would enlist in a unit, collect the bounty, desert, and enlist in another unit to collect the bounty again. Author's Collection.

throw away his hardy boots, which had become ripped and useless after months of drilling, fighting, and marching.

Such was the plight of the Excelsior Brigade, without supplies, still living on the hardtack they had choked down for the past weeks, encamped in once-ripe farmland that had been stripped of all crops and livestock. Furthermore, it looked as though the men would be needed to fight again. They were still within 15 miles of Richmond and it was only the beginning of July. There were months left in the campaigning season. Their immediate duty was to recover from a week without a solid night of sleep and rest until the order came to move once again. Most of the officers claimed that the Excelsior Brigade had been used too hard in the campaign; there were only 1,200 men left in the brigade and only half of those were fit for duty, Oates said. However, the soldiers had become accustomed to hardship after three months in the field.

Yet hardship in the field was more easily tolerable than hardship in camp. After leaving Malvern Hill and arriving at Harrison's Landing, the soldiers had waited for new orders and new supplies. Neither came and July dragged on. Cooped up in camp with the Rebels still holding Richmond, and without new clothes, utensils, or shoes, the Excelsior Brigade's mood soured.

Supplies were the immediate problem. One might say that they were simply unlucky to be at the end of the line of units who needed material, but the men did not think so. Rather, seeing other units, especially Pennsylvania regiments commanded by Pennsylvania officers receive fresh supplies, they placed the blame squarely on the shoulders of their own officers, who were responsible for outfitting the common soldier. In fact, it seemed there were few officers around. After the Seven Days' Battles, a good many of the officers wanted to resign, and a good many did. Company A lost its last commissioned officer on July 5, Lt. Robert Brewster, who returned home to New York. All others had been wounded, killed, or tired out.

The young Orderly Sergeant Charley Preston was promoted to lieutenant and given command of the company. The men all like him first rate and considered him as good an officer as any.[36, 37] He had enlisted as a sergeant at the age of 18 and had earned the men's respect commanding those older than himself courageously in battle. Nevertheless, it remained that when the times were difficult, and the men needed their commanders to help them find the basic necessities to relieve them from tattered clothes and one tin cup in a mess, they felt deserted.

Some of the officers had good reasons to be absent from their men. Sickles was sent north to raise recruits for the depleted brigade, Graham was excused because of illness, and five lower officers had become casualties while fighting. Not all of the officers had left, the Lt. Colonel and Major of the regiment were still present, other companies still had at least one officer, but what was noticed and what affected the minds of the men, were all those who had returned North while the soldiers were bound to the battlefield. To Oates, these officers had received their commission through political connections and then turned tail when their men were more in need of their commanders than ever. These officers had shirked their responsibility to their men, as bad as deserting them in the midst of battle.

The one who really angered the Pittsburgh boys was John P. Glass, captain of Company A until he resigned after the Seven Days'. He was the first captain of the company, the one who raised it and brought it to the Excelsior Brigade. When passed up for promotion he departed, and although he would never serve with them again, promised to do all he could for his fellow Pittsburghers. Oates was disheartened to see a good man who had led them for a year leave the ranks. However, his attitude, and the attitude of most of the company changed when a couple of weeks later an article about Glass appeared in one of the Pittsburgh papers.

Glass had told the reporter that the Pittsburgh company was badly treated and that no one in the company stood any chance of promotion because of the higher officers' prejudice towards New Yorkers. This, Oates said, was a, *"false and base lie."*[38] The company had burned out seven commissioned officers, six sergeants, and had men from the company as clerks to Generals Heintzleman and Hooker and as the assistant ordinance sergeant for the division. If anything, the company had received more than its fair share of promotions. The only man, apparently, who was snubbed was Glass. The boys were outraged as the man they thought they knew disparaged their brigade when fate did not fall his way.

The group concluded that they would not ask for a transfer to a Pennsylvania regiment, but stay with the unit they had fought with and gained fame with. Even should one of their officers disgrace them, they would not heap more upon themselves by leaving when the road became rough.

Light was fading and Oates stood up from the cracker box that was the soldier's all-purpose furniture and headed back to his tent. He had finally received one only a few days before, a conical Sibley Tent, 12 feet tall and 18 feet in diameter. Seventeen men were crammed into the tent, and they had to erect berths to accommodate them all. Oates pulled out his soldier's letter case and began to write to his sister Nelly.

Camp Near Harrison Landing, July 19th, 1862

Dear Sister,

I was very glad to hear from you & I am glad to hear that you arrived home safe for I would rather you would stay home with Mother & Father for they are getting old & need someone to help them. The weather is been very nice for the last 3 days, we have had a shower every day, but before the weather was awfull hot. I never saw the like of it in all my life. We are getting new clothing & cooking utencils, but they are very slow coming. Mother is afraid that my health will not hold out. But no person need be afraid that as gone through what we have & still has good health. I never was in better health in all my life. We like to go out on Picket here. plenty of Blackberries & Huckleberries & we some times get a chance to get a stray Porker.

With a soldier's resourcefulness, Oates coped with the problems at hand. With the army slow to provide him with the necessities, and the officers who might be prodding the quartermasters returning to their parlors at home, he found his own way to get what he needed.

Captain Glass starts for Pittsburgh to day. If you send a box, he will tell you how to send it. He lives at 429 Penn Street, get him to write down on a peice of paper the directions, send me a small sawing machine, as we soldiers call it, with a lot of pins in it. Canned fruit & some tobics & smoking tobaco, also put one quart can with some brandy or any kind of licquor in it. let it be sealed up like fruit & mark it peaches or tomatoes. It will be very usefull to me & will last me a long time.

Soldiers often asked their family to send packages containing fruit, liquor (often disguised so that mail clerks would not steal it) or small luxuries that were easily available at home and only in the hands of the money-grasping suttlers at the front. But Oates needed not just sweets. As with the sewing kit, he was trying to build up his personal supplies on his own. It was just one small action to prepare himself for the next time he needed to break down the Sibley tent and throw himself into the war again.

Tell Nancy Robinson that I will write to her as soon as I can. Tell sam Williamson to buy a Wig & come out as captain. their is an awfull lot of officars resighning, it shows their patriotism, when their is fighting, it sinks down in their boots. But their is one good thing, the army does not miss or need them. It was the almighty dollar & not the country that them kind of men came for. Well you give my respects to all inquiring friends & my love to Father & Mother. William & Eliza & family & remain
    your affectionate brother,
    Alfred K. Oates

P.S. I wrote a letter to Lilly & one to Eliza. I hope they will get them.[39]

Strains of Taps could be heard lingering over the camp, and Oates put away his letter, pen and ink, and climbed into his berth, feeling more like a sailor than a soldier in his cramped tent. He did not fall asleep immediately, but lay awake in bed staring at the canvas above him thinking about the reason why all his letters from the time sounded tired and almost resigned. It was not the lack of supplies or lack of officers; that was merely the insult to the injury. It was the army's current location, miles further from Richmond than they were in June, miles further from their objective.

What Oates mulled over, probably what every man thought about in the thousands of tents covering the wheat fields of Harrison's Landing, was the fate of the Peninsula Campaign. The North had been stunned by their defeat at First Battle of Bull Run the previous year, but they eventually wrote it off as the failing of the army's commander, General Irwin McDowell. The command of the Union forces near Washington was handed to McClellan, whom had been called a "Young Napoleon" by his supporters. He had built up the strength and discipline of the men, gave them their name of the Army of the Potomac, and instilled in every man the supreme confidence in their abilities. Throughout the fall and winter of 1861, and the spring of 1862, Oates had constantly written home in glowing terms of his commander and given sunny predictions for the army.

McClellan brought the army to the Peninsula, led them into Yorktown and to victory at Williamsburg and Fair Oaks, and marched them to the gates of Richmond. For almost all of June there was no doubt in Oates' mind or in the minds of the thousands on his side of the flag that Little Mac would see them into that capital of treason. It was victory all the way under McClellan.

But then the army fell back. The boys in blue beat back every Confederate attack during the retreat: at Savage Station, Glendale, and especially at Malvern Hill. Oates spoke of the opinion of the army when he wrote, *"We all think the retreat was a master affair and well conducted; if it had not been we would all have been killed or captured."*[37] McClellan had succeeded again.

However, the fact that McClellan proclaimed the retreat a success did not mask the fact to anyone in either the North or South that the Army of the Potomac had somehow been defeated. It was obvious to anyone who looked. The army's goal was to capture Richmond. They had been close to the city and were preparing to besiege it. Now they were farther away and looked only after their own safety. It was clear that somewhere among the many victories at Yorktown, Williamsburg, Fair Oaks, Oak Grove, and Malvern Hill was a Confederate victory that made the entire campaign a failure.

Oates and his comrades did not know that the failure of the army was the failure of its commander. What he knew was that his confident general, who had previously delivered nothing but victory, he thought, had been forced to retreat. Oates could not dream that it was McClellan's fault, and he believed what McClellan reported to the newspapers. Oates, who had weeks earlier made optimistic predictions of marching to the tune of Dixie through Richmond, changed his story saying, *"Mother, I expected this long ago, we never had enough men in front of Richmond."*

The soldier maintained confidence in McClellan, and heaped the blame on the usual targets — the politicians and desk generals in Washington. Oates wrote that, *"our congressmen have too much to say in regards the war"* and, *"the Jackass of a Stanton [Secretary of War] has to be cautious about every move."* Oates proposed that Washington should, *"let McClelland carry out his plan at first."*[32]

Oates did not know as he sat around camp with his messmates killing time and talking of the retreat, that the plan had been McClellan's all the way, and besides one refusal of reinforcements during June, everything had been done as he wanted. But they did not know the failure was a result of McClellan's extreme hesitation and paranoia. They only knew that there was a failure on someone's part, and they heaped blame on the politicians and desk generals in Washington. "A great many of us have come to the conclusion they [politicians] had turned the war into one great grand speculating humbug. And the longer they kept it going the more money they could make."[32]

All of this was untrue, and while it maintained the men's confidence in their general, it shattered their confidence in their government - what they were fighting to preserve. The men felt abandoned by their country, pawns used by the "big men." To Oates and all those who were living on stale, wormy hardtack, sleeping in crowded tents on humid Virginia nights among an ever dwindling number of friends, the war brought only malaria and death.

Oates had already sacrificed a year of his life for his country; only luck had prevented this from being his last. He now believed that his contribution was squandered because of the mismanagement of selfish politicians. He looked to the South, where everyone joined together to defeat the North's plans, and saw how the war should be run. It did not matter that Oates' convictions were false. At that moment, laying in his tent on Harrison's Landing, with no supplies to ease his daily chores, no officers to lead his company, and thinking his government did not care for him, Oates believed his brave brigade abandoned and its soldiers alone.

Near Alexander Sep. 8th

Dear Mother

        I received a letter from
you the other day & was glad to hear
from home. I sent a letter home
on the 5th but do not know if you
received it or not. We have seen some
very hard times the last month; we have
traveled over a good deal of country,
& our division is compleatly run down
They say we are going to stay here for
a long time, but could not say for
sure, it is time we got some rest
after having been in 13 or 14 battles
On the 15th of August we left Harrison's
Landing & took up our line of march for
yorktown our Corpse had to march about
the center of the peninsular while the
rest of the troops took the river road, so
if their had been any fighting we would
have had to do it, We arrived at yorktown
all safe & our regiment was put on board

Chapter Eleven

Veterans

Second Bull Run Campaign, Northern Virginia.

Late August, 1862

A loud shout jerked Oates out of sleep. The sergeants were walking through the companies pulling their men together and telling them to prepare for action. Oates climbed bleary-eyed out of his tent to find the campground fast disappearing. Tents were being broken down, haversacks had been thrown in piles on the ground to be picked up by wagons, and men were filling their cartridge boxes with ammunition. Oates quickly readied himself. The regiment fell in and soon the Excelsior Brigade, with much of the division behind them, were marching northwards along the railroad towards the Rebels.

By August, action at Harrison's Landing had lessened. McClellan had not only given up his offensive on Richmond during the Seven Days' Battles, but he had shown no signs of willingness to attack the Confederates again. He sent out a few scouting missions — the Excelsior Brigade marched to Malvern Hill on August 7th and found that it was extremely lightly defended — but McClellan made no real advance. Robert E. Lee, the Confederate commander, counting on McClellan's inaction, left Richmond and turned north to face the other major Union army in the area. Lee faced Union Major-General John Pope's Army of Virginia across the Rapidan River in central Virginia, each side drawing up plans to crush the other. Lincoln, frustrated with McClellan's timidity, authorized the Army of the Potomac to be withdrawn from the Peninsula and sent to reinforce Pope's army.

Oates and the brigade marched back to Fort Monroe and boarded a ship to take them to Alexandria, Virginia. All they had fought for during the Peninsula campaign was now completely given back, and the first campaign of 1862 was over. Oates debarked at Alexandria, hoping his brigade would be given a rest after being worked so hard on the Peninsula. The rest was not to be. After waiting two days for the brigade to receive its equipment, the men were packed into rail cars and they rolled south on the Orange & Alexandria Railroad. They would soon start on their second campaign of the year, to be fought under the command of Gen. Pope.

The Excelsior Brigade debarked from their rail cars and pitched camp for the night just as events were beginning to go into action. Lee, not wanting Pope to receive the arriving reinforcements from the Army of the Potomac, had struck at once, sending half of his force under Stonewall Jackson around the rear of Union army to cut the Orange & Alexandria, Pope's supply line. Lee would then join Jackson and together they would bring Pope to battle. The Excelsior Brigade had been the last units to travel on the railroad. As they were clattering south to meet up with Pope the Confederates were only a few miles away intent on destroying every piece of United States property in their path. Mere hours after the Excelsior Brigade passed, Stonewall's troops struck. Reports worked their way to Pope who ordered a complete about face of the army to march north and clear this rebel threat from their rear. The Excelsior Brigade, that day the rearmost unit of the army, found themselves by night the most advanced with orders to march forward and clear out whatever Rebels they found. By the morning of August 27th Oates was moving into battle once more.

By midday, most of Hooker's division and all of the Excelsior Brigade had closed in on the railroad at Bristoe Station when a shell whizzed over their heads. They had found the Confederates and deployed into lines of battle, First Brigade on the right, the two regiments of the Third on the left and the Excelsior Brigade in the reserve. Oates was not able to see much of the fighting, but he kept pushing forward and heard ahead scattered pops of musket fire. Someone must have run into the rebel skirmishers. Oates looked up and saw the Third Brigade disappear quickly into the woods, the men moving forward at the double. He could not see them anymore, but only a few seconds after they left his sight he could hear a sustained roar of musket fire. The Third Brigade must have run into the main Confederate line.

Oates kept moving through the woods when he saw Colonel Taylor, commander of the Excelsior Brigade while Sickles recruited in New York, gallop back to the lines. He talked to some of the regimental commanders briefly. Oates could not hear the conversations, but at once the Second, Fourth, and Fifth Excelsior Regiments were ordered to move forward at the double quick. Oates crashed through the woods to find the two regiments of the Third Brigade, their right flank anchored on the graded railroad track and their left flank in the air (not anchored on a natural barrier), lying down in the middle of a field dueling with rebel infantry drawn up in a skirt of woods. The Excelsior Regiments marched through the miniés to the Third Brigade's left and began exchanging shots with the Rebs.

It was, *"as hot a fight as we want to see,"* as Oates later described it.[40] The three regiments of the Excelsior Brigade and the two of the Third Brigade were exposed in the field and facing heavy fire. They could do nothing but seek whatever cover the folds of the ground had to offer and try to keep the rebels heads down. Oates could not see what was happening behind him - he had enough to deal with in front - but the officers were scrambling trying to pull men into position to join the fight. There was little chance that the five regiments in the field could hold out for long; their ammunition was running low, and unless something dramatic happened, there was little chance that they alone could dislodge the enemy from its positions. Hooker was leading unengaged regiments from the Third Brigade far around the left flank, while the Confederates were doing the same. Shortly after the fight had begun, when Oates looked up from the ground long enough to aim and fire his weapon, he saw a new rebel force. A column of enemy infantry was filing down the hill in front of the Excelsior troops on the other side of the railroad. Between loading and discharging his Enfield, Oates could see the rebels march down the hill and deploy in a line of battle parallel to the railroad and on the other side of it behind the Excelsiors' line. The Confederates opened up and sprayed the line with rear and enfilading fire. The soldiers of the Excelsior and Third Brigades, already dealing with the rebels in front, were now being assaulted with unanswered volleys from their right and from behind.

Two days after their fight at Bristoe Station, Oates and the rest of the brigade sat on the ground waiting for orders. They had won that battle after the First and Fifth Excelsior Regiments had charged over the railroad embankment on the flanking Rebels and driven them back, just as Stonewall Jackson had issued orders to his soldiers to break off the engagement and fall back. It had been a tough fight, conducted during the hottest part of the day, and the Excelsior Brigade had taken and given harshly. However, there was no time to rest. That had been only the opening fight of this new campaign and there would likely be another battle soon to come.

Oates looked out across the little valley that lay in between the Union positions on Henry House Hill and the Confederate line on an unfinished railroad line along an opposing ridge. Stonewall Jackson and his corps, half the Confederate Army of Northern Virginia, waited there for the Union attacks, which had been coming piecemeal through the day. The battle at Bristoe Station occurred on August 27th. On the 28th Oates marched north with the rest of Pope's 70,000 man army in pursuit of Jackson's forces. Stonewall pulled back to a pre-selected position, an unfinished railroad whose alternating cuttings and raised embankments provided the rebels with a solid line of defensive earthworks. This line was also placed between the Orange & Alexandria, along which the Union army was marching, and Thoroughfare Gap in the Bull Run Mountains to the west, through which the remainder of the Confederate army would be marching. Jackson was to hold until Lee and the rest of the rebels arrived and they together could spring a trap on the unsuspecting Pope.

At 2 P.M. on August 29th, Oates and the brigade had finally arrived at what would become the battleground. The Confederates were in place along the railway and Pope had been conducting only small attacks against the lines; more probes than any real assault. The brigade halted and the men sat down to conserve their strength while Col. Taylor awaited orders. Before long, orders came and word spread down the line that the Excelsiors were to support the First Brigade of the division. The brigade had broken through the Confederate line near its center, and if the Excelsior Brigade arrived quickly to buttress the attack, the rebel line might be broken and the day end in victory.

The men climbed to their feet and assembled themselves in a line, the first action they had learned in the army. Sergeants and officers ran down the line dressing it — checking that the line was solid and straight. Then the order from the sergeants rang out, "Advance in line of battle!" Oates checked his rifle. All was oiled and working, the powder in the barrel was secure and percussion cap neatly waiting for the hammer. His right hand clutched the stock of the gun as it rested on his shoulder, and Oates took a breath as a thousand feet started down the hill.

Oates continued marching across the little valley, now moving uphill towards the ridgeline and railroad cutting in which Stonewall Jackson had stationed his men. The brigade maintained its speed, disciplined after a year in the army and five months under the watch of enemy guns. Close to the enemy positions, Col. Taylor halted the line just outside a patch of trees the brigade would have to cross to reach the rebels, and he dressed the line again. With everything in readiness, he gave the order to advance for the final leg and, "the little band of heroes moved forward into the woods."[41]

Oates clutched his Enfield a little tighter, anticipating that firing was only minutes away. The line advanced a few steps when suddenly, on the left, a wave of humanity crashed into the brigade. The Second Regiment, positioned on their left flank, was almost swept away by men that Oates could tell through the chaos were wearing blue. These were the men the Excelsiors were sent to support. They were not holding a gap in the rebel line as Oates had been told, but were crashing through their lines, knocking Oates and the men out of order and throwing the line into utmost confusion.

Oates tried to push and muscle the routed men out of his way when a fearfully rapid storm of bullets flew at the brigade.[41] Following the panicked Union soldiers came the rebels who must have retaken their own lines. They had pushed the Federals out of the railroad embankment and were following their prey into the woods. Col. Taylor and his two aides were near the Second Regiment trying to whip the men into some semblance of order, when the swarms of butternuts enveloped both flanks and spread out into the open field at the rear of the brigade. Rebel infantrymen dragged Taylor's aides off their horses and into captivity, and the brigade's commander only barely escaped.

The Excelsior Brigade was surrounded, the Second Regiment shattered by its own countrymen, and the bullets were flying at the men from all quarters. Oates dropped down and began firing away at whatever target presented itself, and the men around him tried vainly to fight the rebels off. Oates saw his green lieutenant fall wounded, as well as two corporals and two sergeants in the company. There was no way for a strung out line, one-fifth of which was nothing more than a rabble, to defeat a cohesive enemy taking potshots at it. But then Oates and the brigade found some luck. The rebels were too close to the brigade and could not fire their rifles without hitting their own men. Oates saw them drop their guns and pick up clubs and stones. What happened next can only be described as a the worst kind of melee, a confused mash of men clubbing, gouging, stabbing and occasionally shooting enemy at less than an arm's length away.

The rebels immediately went for the colors of each regiment, eager to snatch a prize of war. In the Second Regiment the color-bearer was shot but the colors removed to safety. The rebels descended on the colors of the Fifth Regiment, and shot its color bearer, Sergeant Martin Flanagan. He hobbled towards the main body of the regiment leaning on the broken staff of the flag only to find his way blocked by rebels fighting their way towards him with the butts of their guns. He tore off the flag and handed it to another of the color guard only moments before he was captured. Oates could see from his position in Company A the rest of the color guard, in Company C, fighting desperately to make it back to Union lines with the flag, the pride of the regiment. But the rebels targeted them and assaulted them at every inch of ground. As much as the guard fought, and as many rebels as they killed and maimed, there were simply too many enemy around them; the entire guard fell, killed, wounded, or captured.

There was no way the Excelsior Brigade could fulfill its orders of shoring up the Union attack when that attack had already been repulsed. Remaining near the rebel lines, it was only losing many of its "best and bravest."[41] Col. Taylor ordered a general retreat, and the men pummeled their way through the rebels in the rear. They made it into the open fields and the rebels gradually returned to their own lines. The men were exhausted from the nightmarish street fight in the woods, but Taylor reformed the line and sent out skirmishers. The brigade had survived and needed to act like a military unit once more. They were eventually relieved by another regiment, and the men, torn from the branches and bushes, bruised by rebel stones and fists, and covered in dirt and blood, headed back into the safety of their own lines to sleep in the open air and try to forget the brawl.

The next day saw nothing good for the Union. Pope, after wasting a day in small holding attacks again the Confederates, on the 30th prepared for a grand assault to destroy Stonewall's forces. However, he failed to recognize that the rest of the Confederate army had arrived during the night. As Pope was gearing up to attack, the Rebels struck and routed what little resistance stood in their way. Pope had been beaten and was forced to withdraw back to Washington to prevent the Confederates from sweeping behind him. There was a rearguard action fought on the retreat, during which the Excelsior Brigade was in reserve, but eventually the army made it to the safety of the forts surrounding Washington and the 2nd Bull Run campaign was over.

Word came into the ranks that Lee was taking advantage of his victory and had invaded Maryland. Oates expected to be called upon once more, but this time the brigade received the rest it deserved. The entire Third Corps would camp at Alexandria while the rest of the army, under McClellan again, would pursue Lee into Maryland. Walking wearily on the road to Alexandria Oates looked back on the recent campaign that had hammered away at a brigade that had already seen its share of fights. The Fifth Regiment had lost 98 men at Bristoe Station and Bull Run, and the brigade, as a whole, had lost 319 men. Once again the brigade felt let down, this time by Pope who had been completely "outgeneraled."[40] He had allowed the Confederates to sweep behind him and then at Bull Run sent the Excelsior Brigade into a rout.

Oates wrote that they had lost a good many men since leaving the Peninsula, several in his company that he mentioned to his mother so she could let their families in Pittsburgh know. Sgt. Alexander Black, Sgt. William Dithridge, and Cpl. James Franklin were wounded, and their condition was not known. Pvts. Augustus Beckert, Doctor Edward Martin and John McHenry were missing, either dead or captured by the rebels.[42] The regiment lost officers too, this time not to resignation and the temptations of civilian life but to bullets and bayonets. One lieutenant and two captains were killed. The major in command of the regiment, one captain, and eight lieutenants were wounded. It was a small remnant that marched back into Alexandria. *"Look at Hookers Division when we left Maryland,"* Oates wrote. *"What a fine set of men he had, but look at them now. not enough to make one good brigade."*[40]

When they arrived in the open field that would be its camp, the battle-weary soldiers of the Excelsior Brigade were a strange attraction to the recruits manning the forts around Washington. Oates dropped his gear onto the ground, incredibly light once more after discarding most of it in battle or on the road and placed his worn Enfield close to him.

While setting up his tent Oates was approached by a soldier in the 123rd Pennsylvania, a regiment from Allegheny which had seen no fighting in the war. The soldier buddied up to Oates and jokingly told him that they should put the Excelsior Brigade in front again since they were used to it. Oates stared at this unproven recruit who would have the impudence to say that. The man continued on unphased that his regiment should stay in the forts since they did not know much about fighting. Oates said nothing and the man soon walked away.

That night, while writing home, Oates told his mother about the men who had been lost on the campaign. He told her about the man from the 123rd and how they must go into the field and learn like the Excelsiors did. *"But,"* Oates wrote, *"I hope they will not have the hardships that we have seen."*[40] The entirety of the Peninsula campaign, from the terror of digging in the open in front of Yorktown, to the rain and mud of Williamsburg, to the night marches during the Seven Days' and the sheer power of the artillery on Malvern Hill, introduced Oates to war. The losses at Bristoe, pinned down in an open field by enfilading fire, and the horrendous debacle of Bull Run served to cement in Oates' mind what war entailed. By September of 1862, after more than one year in the army and one long campaigning season, the men of the Excelsior Brigade, those who were left, could truthfully agree with Oates when he wrote home that, *"We have seen so much slaughter that it would sicken the best men in the world."*[40]

Oates had survived two campaigns, one long and hard, the other short and bloody. He had seen what only the most experienced of soldiers in any time had seen, and he knew enough not to wish it on any other soldier. He had become a veteran.

Chapter Twelve

Orating

New York City

August 4th, 1862

ickles entered the crowded hall of the Armory amidst loud cheering. He was accompanied by his friend Stuart Woodward, Assistant U.S. District Attorney and various officers of the brigade, including the Assistant Adjutant-General, the quartermaster, the commander of the First Regiment, and a number of company commanders. The crown of epaulets around Sickles led the way as he moved toward the stand, shaking hands and joking with every man nearby.

The men in the crowd amused themselves by calling for "Howard," "Hotaling," "Music," "Anybody." When Sickles reached the stand some minutes after he entered the building, he shook hands with the men around him and took his seat. The men of importance settled down for the meeting, and so did the men of lesser importance in the crowd. Commissioner Henry Wilson was the first to speak, and he quickly went through the procedural aspects of nominating and electing a presiding officer for the meeting, Mr. William H. Wickham, who raced through the long list of various vice presidents and secretaries of the department. He spoke quickly, and finished before the enthusiasm of the crowd wore off. For such a meeting, enthusiasm was crucial.

The first speaker of the night stood from his seat and began his speech. He said that he was proud to take by the hand his old friend, the Honorable Dan Sickles, at which point he shook Sickles' hand to great applause. He warmed up the crowd with, "The men of the South are traitors, and the men of the North who will not help put them down are cowards!" He spoke briefly and merely served to set fire to the crowd and introduce the main speaker of the night, General Daniel Edgar Sickles.

Sickles stood and came forward to speak while the hall erupted into cheers. Wave after wave of applause poured forth and numerous shouts of "tiger" met him. Sickles stood there reveling in the adoration, his immaculate blue uniform overlapped by the red collar of the fireman's shirt he had worn to endear himself to his audience. Sickles walked about the platform, his hands in the air imploring the men to be quiet so he could speak. When the crowd had settled enough, Sickles took center stage and, summoning all his oratory skill, began to speak.

"It is a distinguished honor to have the opportunity of appearing before the Fire Department on this occasion. When I remember that you are one of the institutions of the City; the high respectability of membership of your organization; the deeds of heroism and daring which has distinguished you; that all your service is voluntary; that winter and summer, day and night, you serve the public, saving life and property at great personal sacrifice; and, not the least of all, your noble charity for those who fall in your ranks. When I remember these things, I believe I have come before the right men and I ask if you would go to the assistance of your overborne and outnumbered colleagues." The applause which had been rising through his speech now erupted at his last sentence.

"And if I should tell you that your comrades were in danger, I know that you would rush to the rescue," he shouted over the wildly clapping and cheering firemen in the seats below. Sickles paused for just a few seconds so that he could be heard, but not long enough for the crowd to completely settle down before he continued.

"I have seen your brethren in the Second Fire Zouave Regiment, which is the Fourth Regiment of my own Excelsior Brigade, and I have led them to battle. They have borne the flags presented to them proudly and slept with those flags on every battlefield.

"For the first six months," Sickles roared over the crowd, "I did not lose a single man. But now the ranks of that decimated regiment need to be filled up. There are men enough here tonight to fill up the ranks, and it is the duty of the Firemen of New York, you men in this hall, to fill them up at once. Is there a man who would volunteer? One man in all the assemblage? Yes! Here is the first man!"

Sickles pointed to one who had stood up, full of the conviction and passion that Sickles' had given him. The man strode to the platform amid wild cheers and put down his name in the registry of the Fourth Excelsior. Sickles shook the man's hand who returned into the crowd with firemen grabbing his hands and slapping his back.

"That was what I came here for, to get men, not to talk. Suppose an alarm of fire were to sound now," Sickles rang out through the mists of tobacco smoke and patriotism. "You would all rush to the rescue of life and property. But a more devastating fire — the fire of rebellion — is burning. It is assailing not only your homes and property, but your government and Constitution. Would you not rush to the subjugation of that rebellion?"

Two more volunteers jumped up onto the platform to enroll their names and Sickles strode over to embrace each one of them. "It is true," he shouted with his hands on their backs, "That wherever even three are gathered together, the spirit of the Lord will descend. This is God's cause," he said as he moved back to the center of the platform and the new recruits headed back to their seats. "Could it be true that all the men of courage and patriotism are gone? I despise the man who would not fight the enemy without a bill in his pocket." Sickles' voice rose over louder and louder applause.

"Would you wait for drafting and be dragged to the battlefield by the collar?! I want no conscripts! I have none! I have all volunteers and I know they will fight. They have fought and had never been whipped. I am sorry that the bounties have been offered. I believe that the bounties have put back recruiting. Many are holding back in the hope of being able to get five hundred or a thousand dollars for going as a substitute for some rich man who would rather bleed in the pocket than anywhere else." Laughter greeted him. Sickles rolled on.

"But, the men who held back, they will be disappointed and sadly taken in. No substitute will be received in my brigade. No man could make his bargain with one who was drafted. No, if they held back they will lose their bounty and be drafted in the bargain!" Amid laughter, Sickles continued, "All the men who join my brigade will receive all the bounties offered to other recruits, and at the same time an additional fifty dollars voted this very afternoon by the Common Council in the City."

Several more recruits stepped up to the platform amid loud cheers and recorded their names. Sickles continued. "Let us remember that glorious chieftain, George B. McClellan." Cheers erupted for the popular general. "With what magnificent silence and scorn he has treated his enemies. Not a word for them — all for his army. Do not let him be overwhelmed. The rebels would rather crush McClellan than any other general. Let it be the pride of the people of the North to sustain General McClellan."

At this point in the meeting a gray haired fellow rose from the audience and came forward and volunteered. Sickles warmly shook his hand and the man began speaking, urging more to join the Excelsior Brigade. Almost immediately another fireman came forward to enlist.

Sickles turned to the old fellow and said, "I wish you would say a few words. You have got one recruit already, as soon as you opened your mouth,"

The old volunteer obliged, to loud cheers. "I have left a good situation at eight hundred dollars a year, and taken one at thirteen dollars a month — and for what? For my country. I am so proud of seeing my old friend Sickles that I could not help signing my name."

"Name, name," came shouts from the audience.

"My name is James Troy, formerly engineer of Astor House. I have served my country once in the Mexican War, and I can do it again. And I hope I will come out as safely as I did before." The audience applauded as Sickles shook Troy's hand once more and Troy left the stage so the speech could continue.

"At Yorktown, the Second Fire Zouaves was the first to enter the enemy's works. In the bloody battle of Williamsburg, it was pursuing the flying foe. In the battle of Fair Oaks I witnessed its noble daring. In all reports that regiment had been mentioned with honor. Nothing could resist its overwhelming power. In the next battle — a battle without a name [Oak Grove] — the Second Fire Zouaves won undying fame. Nearly all the officers were sick, but two of the captains had led the regiment from point to point, and gained all the ground that was required. They were ordered back, and again pressed forward and took the same ground over again. They were in nearly all of the last seven days' fighting on the Chickahominy. Will you leave them there in their present diminished numbers? No. It would be an eternal shame and disgrace if you did. I have not more than a dozen yet. I want to raise another regiment here tonight. Did you come merely to listen? Are you willing to do nothing? Do you lack confidence in the Government? Most of you did not vote for the President, but Mr. Lincoln has done his duty nobly." Here cheers for the President broke from the crowd, and Sickles paused for a moment to catch his breath before hurtling onward.

"Yes, which of his predecessors has been called upon to put a million men into the field, to raise a navy, or put five hundred million dollars into the Treasury? The duties of the President have been enormous. Look where we stood twelve months ago. In that short time McClellan has organized the splendid Army of the Potomac, held the enemy at bay, and driven him to his stronghold. Look at the cities and forts we have taken." Sickles began picking up steam now, building up to his final thrusts into the hearts of the firemen.

"Point out, if possible, in the history of the world such a successful campaign. I hear only murmurs, instead of a due appreciation of these victories. Look at our foreign relations. Only a year ago we feared that we must fight all of Europe, or submit to anything that might be dictated to us. But the President and Secretary [of State] Seward have preserved peace with all the world, and, at the same time, the honor of our flag has been sustained. Will you blame the Government that there are not more men in the field? The remedy is with you. Let you fill up your own regiment. I want more recruits. Should it be said in the morning that out of a thousand firemen of New York only a dozen would volunteer? I have given it as my opinion that the Second Fire Zouaves will be the first regiment filled up. I intend to establish a recruiting office in every engine house in the City. I want four hundred and fifty men, and let each company furnish ten men and you will have the largest regiment in the field. Will you not do as much to sustain the country as the rebels will do to destroy it? If you want victory you must give the men. Gen. McClellan's army must enter Richmond, but shall we do it with but half the men that the rebels have? Alabama has furnished 60,000 men out of 80,000, and New York but 100,000 men out of 600,000 in her population. What a discrepancy! Is the patriotism of New York so much less than the treachery of Alabama? That fact will be handed down to our eternal disgrace. Let us hesitate and we are lost. Let it be known to Europe that the North is divided and we will be in more danger of intervention. Let that but once come and the aristocracies of the Old World will find their long-desired opportunity for extinguishing democratic institutions on the continent."

"Let them come," shouted a voice from the crowd.

"It is easy to say let them come," fired back Sickles, "But why do you hold back when only 600,000 rebels are opposing us? Why don't you volunteer?"

The crowd erupted into cheers for Sickles and there could be heard cries of, "Bring him up," and, "That's the man." The young man who had shouted out stepped onto the stand to voice his concerns to the man who wanted him to sign his life away.

"Gen. Sickles, if you will only get the President of the United States to declare that this is not a war to put down slavery in the states where it exists, you will get 500,000 men in the North." There was some applause for this man's argument. But Sickles was on fire and rolling, and he had prepared his answer to such a question and delivered it will all the passion and zeal the old politician possessed.

"I am not fighting for what the President thinks or what any man thinks," Sickles began, "I am fighting to put down the rebellion!" The audience went wild here, and Sickles charged through the adoration.

"I want to see the flag of my country wave over all of my country!" The applause grew even louder.

"I want to see every rebel disarmed and brought to obey the laws. Then, my friends, I will discuss what we shall do with the negroes. Then we shall find out who was right as to what the war was for. Let us have confidence in the President of the United States, and not listen to half and half Secessionists, who want to create a Southern party here, or the other party, who are at the other extreme."

The young man took the platform again, and declared that he would volunteer but that he was physically disabled. He returned to his seat while Sickles came to his conclusion.

"I now urge you to fill up the ranks. The rebellion is at its zenith. Its utmost efforts are being made. In three months the war will be decided for or against us. If your hearts are in the work, join me and fill up the ranks at once."

The crowd burst into cheers louder than the hall had ever heard before, and Sickles retired to his seat with another speech finished. Stewart Woodford, U.S. District Attorney rose to speak, and gave the night's concluding remarks with an impressive strain, sure not to go on too long and let the fire Sickles ignited in the men's hearts to die out. Sickles sat in his chair, drained by the exertions of such an impassioned speech, but exhilarated by the response he had gotten. His friendly style, immediate connection to his audience, and alternating praise and threats of shame, had won him a dozen volunteers on the spot. As the meeting let out around 10:30 that night, the men pouring out of the small armory full of enthusiasm for the war, it was reported in the papers the next morning that old Dan Sickles had led one of the most successful recruiting meetings ever held in New York City. As he headed to his home on Fifth Avenue shaking hands with firemen along the way, Sickles had a dozen recruits, would probably have more by the next day, and had given an excellent speech. This had been his job for the past month and would continue to be for the near future, wheedling and cajoling halls and town greens across the region for an additional few men. It was a side of the war just as crucial as what happened in Virginia. If the Excelsior Brigade was to remain in service, if it was to continue to fight its country's enemies, it needed more men. Sickles was the one to deliver them, and as long as his soldiers had need of him he would continue to exert himself fully for them.[40a]

Chapter Thirteen

In the Place of Cowards

Alexandria, Virginia

September 1862

ates headed back to camp with his friend and messmate Archy Robinson, guns slung over their shoulders and pockets weighed down by fresh corn and fruit. They had just ended their duties on the picket line, which here, unlike the dangerous work on the Chickahominy, was little more than a picnic. The picket line was on top of a hill outside camp and Oates and Robinson could see down the whole valley all the way towards Mount Vernon, George Washington's estate. They had tried to visit the first president's mansion, but their sergeant wouldn't allow them out of the lines. They would have to wait for another day to sneak off and tour the old home.

So the two Pittsburghers contented themselves with standing guard on the hill, surrounded by cornfields and a ripening orchard. It was a lovely day and soon their stomachs and knapsacks were full of the bounty of the South. Oates was, *"sorry it did not last longer."*[43]

He and Robinson walked leisurely down the hill when their stint on the line was over and they entered the brigade's camp. The entire Third Corps had been detached from the Army of the Potomac and sent to Alexandria, Virginia, after the Second Battle of Bull Run to rest and guard Washington from a rebel attack. But the rebels were miles away, and with the massive guns of Fort Ward close by, Oates knew as well as anyone that there would be no attack here.

Oates dropped his equipment and fruit in his tent and, his load considerably lighter, proceeded to where everyone went these days when they had a bit of free time. As he rounded the turn towards the river in camp he could hear the low rustle of soldiers talking and the murmur of the river as it meandered towards the Chesapeake. Oates climbed onto the crowded bridge and found his friends whiling away the time and occasionally shouting when one got a bite on his line. He pulled out his homemade fishing pole and dropped the line in the water and began chatting away with those around him, stopping only to pull up one of the schools of finger-length fish the men were constantly catching.

Oates saw that one of the men had an old newspaper; a New York one. The soldiers were constantly starved for news. Letters arrived at least a week after they were written and what a man heard at camp might be rumor, so newspapers were the only reliable source of information about what was happening in the outside world. Oates gathered up the newspaper from the man who had finished reading it and glanced through the headlines. Most papers still gave most of the front page to the Union victory at a creek in Maryland named Antietam, with various correspondents jockeying to get their angle of the battle in print. Oates already knew of all this; word of a big fight travels fast in the army. However, there was no mention of Antietam in this issue because the paper was from before the battle. Oates read through the first few outdated articles until he got to page six, which contained reports of military movements in New York City. Most of the time it spoke of various recruiting efforts or some prominent citizen opening a military hospital and did not interest Oates, the Pittsburgher that he was. But today the top story caught his eye. He called his mates around to show them the long headline — "RECRUITING FOR THE FIRE ZOUAVES ---- Large Meeting of Firemen at the Seventh Regiment Armory ---- Spirited Address of General Sickles — Volunteers on the Spot ---- Effective Address of Assisiant District-Attorney Stuart L. Woodford."

The men crowded around to read the thrilling text of Sickles' speech, with his impassioned arguments to the crowd, and firemen like James Troy and John Burns who volunteered for the army there and then. All the men reading had gone through the same line of logic as James Troy was reported as saying there: "I have left a good situation of $800 a year, and taken one at $13 a month — for what? For my country." They read the entire article, a long one that took up almost half a page, commentating as they went. Eventually they reached the end and laughed when the reported urged: "Reader, go and be a Second Fire Zouave."[40a] They had already followed similar advice a year ago and now were in Alexandria waiting for more to do the same.

Oates passed the paper along to the next group of men on the bridge and resumed talking with his messmates. The conversation had drifted from Oates's and Robinson's picket duty to, inspired by the newspaper article, recruiting for the brigade. The men knew that every effort was being made to find the men to fill up the ranks. Sickles was touring the state speaking in the town hall and village greens using his skills as an orator to inspire men to sign up. Their old colonel, Graham, who had been dismissed from the field because of illness, was in charge of the recruiting office in City Hall Park. He had opened up offices in, "all the principal cities of New-York, Pennsylvania, New-Jersey, Massachusetts, Connecticut, and Ohio," and nine engine houses to recruit for the Second Fire Zouaves.[43a]

But even though Sickles and Graham were making tremendous efforts they were only having limited success. Sickles sought to replace all three thousand men the Excelsior Brigade had lost over the past year, but the job was more difficult than his initial round of recruiting, even though he now had definite glory to speak of. The patriotic men of the north were no longer in the north, but had already enlisted in the army. The ones still in the cities and on their farms had resisted the wave of patriotism that had swept the country in 1861.[43]

Oates and the men, subjected to weeks of reading Sickles' speeches or calls by "prominent citizens of the city" for recruits, but without seeing the ranks filling up around them, were discouraged and frustrated. The prominent citizens aided Sickles with monetary contributions to be put towards bounties for the recruits, but they thought too grandly and not towards the problem at hand. Recently an editorial proposed the creation of an "Excelsior Division" by attaching new regiments to the old Excelsior Brigade. The proposition was praised, it being claimed that, "No schooling so quickly converts the raw volunteer into a trusty soldier, as the association in camp, on the march, in picketing, skirmish, and battle, with men whose nerves have been steadied by long custom in the endurance of hardship and facing danger."[43b] The men at Alexandria could not believe this idea. Dan Sickles was unable to replenish a brigade, let alone raise an entire division.

Oates looked around at his fellow Excelsiors, experienced soldiers fishing while enemies invaded their homeland because their shattered regiments had fought until they were too small for the field and his frustration grew. Most of that frustration was not directed at the "prominent citizens" of New York, who were at least *trying* to help the brigade, but at the ordinary citizens of the North, who were hoping the war would end without requiring a sacrifice on their part. *"I suppose you would think it funny if I was to tell you, that all the boys are glad to hear of the Rebels marching into Penn^ia," Oates wrote, "but it is so. every one says that the people have not shown energy enough. While we have been fighting vast numbers of them week after week & month after month, the young men of the north have been laying on their oars & waiting to see if would not give a little more bounty."*[43]

The Excelsiors had joined up and suffered deprivation, separation from home and loved ones, bad food, fetid living conditions, slow fear of dangerous picket duty and the sharp terror of battle. They had done their duty to their country. The men still at home had not suffered at all. All Northerners lived in the same country and would face the same outcome of the war — victory and their ways of life would be safe, defeat and the Union would fracture and the great experiment of republicanism would fall prey to the aristocracies of the Old World from which Americans had fled.[44] To Oates, those at home were disgraceful cowards, and not worth caring for.

Winning the war required more troops, and if enlistments were slow and, *"this Patriotism that was so much talked about as all dissapeared,"* then Oates believed that a draft was necessary. A draft might be unpopular, but those who had fought and suffered had little sympathy for those who hadn't.

The sky grew dark. Autumn was slowly arriving and the air was beginning to chill. Oates and the men on the bridge pulled up their lines, grabbed their catches, and made their way back to their tents. In camp, at Alexandria, there was little of the drilling and training that had defined their earlier days at Camp Scott. In the morning the regiment had roll call as usual, but then in the place of morning drill the men went down to the river for a swim. That and picket duty once every five days, here only a break from fishing, were the only responsibilities the men had. The officers knew the soldiers could march and fight, and they did not need to waste the men's time with such elementary training. It was to a relatively peaceful camp that Oates walked back to, but always with the knowledge that their time there was limited and that Sickles was working to ensure that Oates would be at the front lines as soon as possible.

Oates approached his tent and gave his fish to his messmate who would be the cook for that night. The men were receiving fresh bread, were catching fish, and with the fruit and corn Oates and Archy Robinson had picked that day, they would have a fine meal.

There was a commotion over to Oates' left, and he could see most of the company crowded around something. Leaving the cook to sit and wonder and curse his luck, Oates walked over to the crowd. It was some of his old brothers-in-arms, men who were wounded at Williamsburg and just now returning to camp. The entire company gathered around them to greet the men whom they had lost amid the fog and pine trees. Very few of them appeared fit for service, most still hobbling and barely able to walk after taking bullets to the limbs and then spending weeks in bed.

Oates had had a brief bout of malaria during June, but other than that was unharmed during the war. He constantly wrote home how well he was doing, and how much stronger he had become since joining the army. But there, in camp with his depleted regiment of veterans, seeing his wounded comrades, he saw just how lucky he had been. If some bullet had hit him in one of the battles, he would be either dead, like so many, or broken like those in front of him. Instead of standing with a hot meal before him and a good day behind him, he would be in the hospitals for months, witnessing horrors even worse than what he had faced in battle.

Oates listened as the wounded told their stories. One soldier told how he had been placed between two badly injured North Carolinians. The one on the right had his leg amputated. The one on the left had been struck in the spine but the surgeons thought the bullet was in his leg. They searched for the bullet and gashed his leg poking and fumbling around, while the young boy passed out from pain. The surgeons cut an artery and the boy soon died. Another soldier told of a Confederate casualty in the bed next to his, and how they had become good friends. The southerner told the man about his home, his wife and his family. One day the Excelsior fell asleep during one of the man's reminiscences. When he woke up fifteen minutes later, the former rebel was dead.

These returning men were the luckiest of the wounded. They had been hit in one of the first major battles of the war, so the hospitals were not yet overflowing as they would be later. These men had made it back to their unit, when so many of those around them had died immediately from their wounds or slowly from infection and disease. These men had navigated through five months of the worst places one could imagine, and had survived to be back with their friends.

Oates came away from the encounter badly shaken. He had seen men who had survived combat; he was one of them. He had seen men who died from combat. Now he saw those who fell in between. Oates returned to his tent to find a meal and the prospect of another easy day in front of him. He had suffered and sacrificed for his country but those nights of sleeping in mud, of eating maggoty crackers and having bullets fly past him seemed like mere discomfort compared to what those poor souls endured. He wrote to his mother that he had heard the South might want to negotiate peace.

"I hope to God they will come to terms," he wrote. *"Not only me but every Soldier is of the same mind. We all think there has been enough of Powders wasted, & not to mention the Lives."*[45]

In the year and a half since they enlisted as eager would-be warriors Oates and his companions had given up much and they knew men who had given up even more. They did not want to see the long months of boredom of winter quarters. They did not want to see battle again. But above all they did not want to see an independent South. Therefore, they wanted every able-bodied man in the North in the army by whatever means. They wanted the ranks to be filled, not with wounded cripples unfit for service, but with the unpatriotic bounty hunters of the homefront. They wanted command given to the generals and not the politicians. They wanted action taken quickly. They wanted this war to be over.

"Stand up for Liberty."

Camp near Falmoth Dec
22

Dear Mother

I received your letter of
the 7th & was glad to hear of
you all being in good health. As this
leaves me at presant, I suppose the
Baltle at Fredricksburg, has caused
grait excitement in the North. It
as satisfied all of us. But it was
a hard fight our men fought well.
But it was Murder to make men
advance against them Hills, when
they had fortification from the bottom
to the top. The rebels behaved very
well to our Wounded. & allowed our
Ambulance Corpse, to go inside their
line & pick up our men. I have not
seen any of my Cousins seince the fight
I have not had time to go over to see
them But Andrew Jackson is a

Chapter Fourteen

Out of the Mud

Camp near Falmouth, Virginia.

Winter 1862-1863

ates threw down another heavy log into the muck. All around him were men wading through mud, knee-deep in some places, trying to build roads out of fence rails, logs, brush, or whatever they could lay their hands onto. Nothing seemed to be working. The logs would sink into the mud and it would be just as useless as before. Oates' division was working in a large field strewn with parts of the Army of the Potomac, cold, miserable and stuck in the mud. The men had to fight just to get through the morass. It took twelve mules to pull an empty wagon through the bog, and twenty-four horses could not stir the Pontoon Wagons. Oates looked around at the state of this new campaign the Army had set out on and realized that it was absolutely hopeless.

The Excelsior Brigade left their camp at Alexandria in early November of 1862 to guard the Orange & Alexandria Railroad. McClellan, once again in command of the Army of the Potomac was still in camp near Antietam, Maryland, but was possibly going to advance south into the Shenandoah Valley. The Orange & Alexandria and its branches westward into the Shenandoah would be his main supply lines.

However, McClellan did not carry out this mission. His continued tendency for inaction had reached the limits of Lincoln's patience, and the Commander-in-Chief appointed Major General Ambrose Burnside commander of the Army of the Potomac. Burnside moved at once, pushing the Army of the Potomac, with the Third Corps back in the fold, towards the city of Fredericksburg on the Rappahannock River in Virginia. The city lay open to him, but because of inclement weather that delayed the arrival of his pontoon wagons, he was unable to cross the river for two weeks. By that time, Lee and his Army of Northern Virginia had arrived and established themselves in one of their most strongly defended positions in the war. Burnside crossed the river on December 11th and attacked on December 13th.

The Excelsior Brigade was lucky in this battle. They had been placed in the reserve, never crossing the Rappahannock and never approaching the Confederate lines. Oates could see much of the battle from the Fifth Regiment's position guarding artillery on the north side of the river. He saw the long lines of blue charge up the hills to where the Confederates waited, hesitate for a moment, and then be broken and retreat, leaving the ground covered with Union bodies. This repeated itself many times that day, and almost always the result was the same. Oates summed it up by writing, *"It was a hard fight. Our men fought well. But it was murder to make men advance against them Rebels when they had fortification from bottom to top."*[46] The day ended with the Confederates still firmly in place and having lost only 5,000 men. The Army of the Potomac lost 12,500, and withdrew back across the river. It was a total defeat.

The army went into camp at Falmouth after the battle and the men returned to the dull times of winter quarters. They built cabins, which gave them some relief from the monotony of camp. Oates' mess took special pride on theirs. It was 17 feet long, seven feet wide, with log walls built up five feet high and the floor dug down two feet into the earth. The roof was a sturdy canvas tent and they had their mud fireplace to keep the room warm. Eight men lived there and they called it the Encyclopedia House because, as Oates said, *"their is not a subject in the world but one or another of us is able to argue on it."*[47] The days went by slowly and the men, often confined to the cabin because of inclement weather, passed the hours.

A few days after the new year, the army received news that infuriated most of the Encyclopedia House. Oates wrote, *"That bill that President Lincoln passed has turned our patriotism & If I had my will I would not fire my gun, if by firing it would save the Union. We look on the war with indifferance & do not care one pin."*[48]

The bill was the Emancipation Proclamation which President Lincoln had issued on January 1st, 1863. Oates and the men felt the proclamation had turned the war from a fight to save the Union and punish the treasonous rebels to a crusade to free the slaves. Oates and the rest of the men in the regiment had enlisted to fight the rebellion, not to free the slaves. They had not suffered untold hardships in the service of their country and seen many of the friends killed and wounded to free some blacks in states where they had no concern. They felt that Lincoln had perverted the war and tricked the men into sacrificing their lives for an abolitionist cause.

The war was fought for the cause of freedom but not for the freedom of the slaves. Oates was sympathetic to the plight of slaves, but the men of the North had signed up to protect the liberties they and their families enjoyed. Their freedom, they believed, was only made possible through the Union of all the states and was imperiled if part of the country tried to break that Union. The industrious country Oates fought for was one where a man could raise a family and hold an honest job that allowed him to live in peace and dignity. That political and economic freedom, they believed, did not exist in the South with its aristocracy and slave labor that made it difficult for a regular man to put food on his table. The United States of America was expanding westward, and if the country were to remain free and prosperous in the future it could not allow any more land to fall prey to the South's slave-based feudal system. Therefore it could not compromise with the Confederacy, exchanging peace for more slave lands. Nor could the North continue to enjoy the freedom it currently had if the Confederacy triumphed and a divided America fell prey to the aristocracies of the Old World. That freedom, of his own home and family, was what Oates was fighting for and what he had sacrificed two years of his life for. It was what many of his friends had sacrificed all for. He could not abide that his efforts would be used for other purposes or that Lincoln, who had promised to preserve the Union, now appeared to have other priorities. The soldiers had little patience for anything they saw as squandering or misusing their patriotism. [48, 49]

Oates and the men stewed in their outrage over the Proclamation, but after a few weeks they began to forget about it and some looked at it as the way Lincoln sold it — as a means to undercut the Confederacy's workforce by encouraging Southern slaves to flee to the North. The furor died down and the dull lives of winter quarters took over once more. Yet that would not last for long: Burnside still had one more plan. On January 20, 1863, he moved the army out of camp to try to steal a march on Lee and sweep around the Confederates. This campaign would be an utter failure, although at least it did not cost the army any soldiers.

The Excelsior Brigade left their camp on January 20th with three days' worth of rations. It rained all day and the brigade did not make it even one mile on the road. At 6 P.M. they were ordered back to camp. It rained all night. The next day they tried again and slogged through the continuing rain all day. They encamped in a wood that night as it continued to rain. The next day they were to report for fatigue duty and build roads for the army's baggage to move on. Now they saw the result of the rain and why armies don't usually fight in the winter.

The days of rain had left the ground incredibly soft and wet. Thousands of feet and dozens of wagon wheels had churned the whole countryside into one vast field of mud. It reached over the soldiers' shoetops every step, sometimes reaching up to their knees. The mud almost brought a halt to the marching. The soldiers had to wade through it, pushing and pulling each other upright. Oates and the Excelsior Brigade tried to build roads, but found it was a hopeless job. The entire Army of the Potomac was stuck in mud that extended to any place it went. Disgusted, dejected and wet, the army was told to give up the campaign and return back to camp. The second great battle of the winter did not materialize.

Oates and the brigade slogged through the night. They finally reached camp and the men scrambled for the dry and warm cabins dotting the hillside. Oates entered the Encyclopedia House with relief. It was a warm refuge from the freezing cold that immobilized the limbs and gnawed at the body. He threw off his soaked gear and dropped his heavy equipment. The army appeared to be in camp for a long time and Oates huddled by the fire trying to dry off before spring.

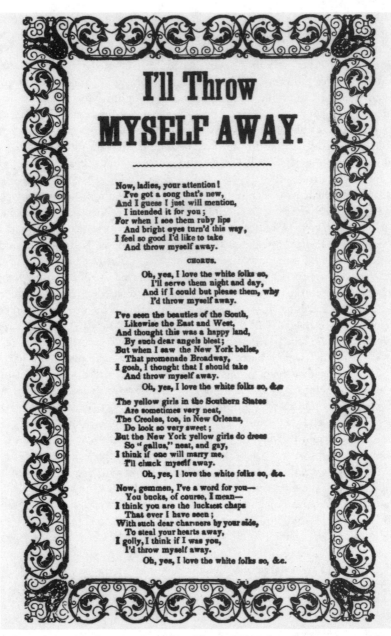

I'll Throw
MYSELF AWAY.

Now, ladies, your attention!
 I've got a song that's new,
And I guess I just will mention,
 I intended it for you;
For when I see them ruby lips
 And bright eyes turn'd this way,
I feel so good I'd like to take
 And throw myself away.

CHORUS.

Oh, yes, I love the white folks so,
 I'll serve them night and day,
And if I could but please them, why
 I'd throw myself away.

I've seen the beauties of the South,
 Likewise the East and West,
And thought this was a happy land,
 By such dear angels blest;
But when I saw the New York belles,
 That promenade Broadway,
I gosh, I thought that I should take
 And throw myself away.
 Oh, yes, I love the white folks so, &c.

The yellow girls in the Southern States
 Are sometimes very neat,
The Creoles, too, in New Orleans,
 Do look so very sweet;
But the New York yellow girls do dress
 So "gallus," neat, and gay,
I think if one will marry me,
 I'll chuck myself away.
 Oh, yes, I love the white folks so, &c.

Now, gemmen, I've a word for you—
 You bucks, of course, I mean—
I think you are the luckiest chaps
 That ever I have seen;
With such dear charmers by your side,
 To steal your hearts away,
I golly, I think if I was you,
 I'd throw myself away.
 Oh, yes, I love the white folks so, &c.

*Songsheet requested by Oates in a letter from March of 1863. Songsheets were one of the main
ways new songs (often new lyrics set to previously known melodies) became known in the days
before radio. In the musical armies of the Civil War they were in great demand.*
Courtesy Library of Congress.

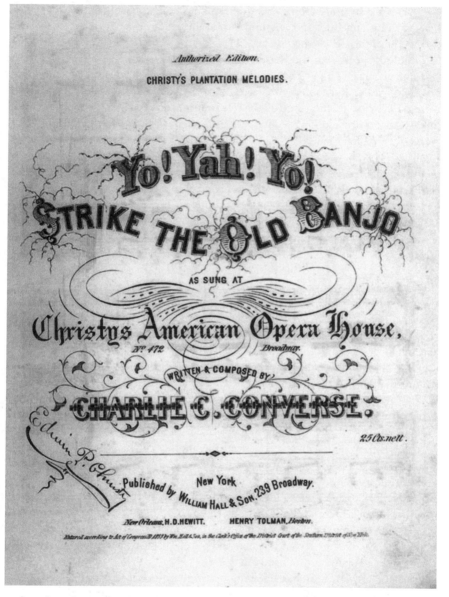

Songsheet also requested by Oates. Edwin Christy was one of the originators of blackface, musical shows where white singers wore dark makeup and acted as slaves, often singing songs supposedly from the plantations. He created his Christy's Minstrel troupe in Buffalo, New York in 1842 and opened in New York City in 1846, quickly becoming a sensation. They remained popular even through Christy's mental illness and suicide in 1862.
Courtesy Library of Congress.

Oates was by himself on picket duty walking along the bank of the Rappahannock with his gun stuck in the ground, the same as the Rebel pickets across from
them. One of the Rebels shouted out, "Why don't you speak?" Oates responded that
they did not speak with the Rebels when there were officers around; fraternizing
with the enemy was a punishable offense. The Rebels stopped speaking, and Oates
saw them gather and confer with each other. They shouted back that Oates should
meet them two miles higher up on the river outside the picket line so that they could
talk without officers lurking around. Oates thought about the idea for a minute. It
was against military law, but he was unlikely to be caught and more unlikely to be
punished. He checked for officers, and when the area was clear, shouted that he
would do that tomorrow. He told a few of his mess and the men he was on picket
duty with, and they all liked the idea and wanted to accompany him.

The next day Oates and his companions walked out of camp and past the
picket line. True, that was not permitted, but the officers in the company had
been with these men through a great deal and gave them more freedom than was
customary, and the privates on the picket line did not care if someone was talking
with a Rebel.[5] Oates and his group approached the designated spot and found
the Rebels already waiting. The men exchanged greetings, where they were from,
where they had fought, what they thought of the war. The Rebels, who were from
Alabama, said that if the war was left to the privates of both armies it would be
over soon. That got a laugh out of the Union men, who had witnessed more than
their share of incompetent generals.

The soldiers talked about where they had fought. Both sides were amazed
to find that they had all been at Williamsburg and Fair Oaks, and to find they
were genially chatting with men they had once sighted along their rifle barrels.
Remembering how difficult those battles were, Pennsylvanians and Alabamans
exchanged respect for the other's bravery and fell to reminiscing about the fights.

While they were conversing, Oates and another of the group were making a
little boat so the two enemy groups could send each other things. It was a miniature Monitor, with a whittled piece of wood for the bottom and an overturned
tin cup for the turret. Oates put some coffee inside the cup and sent it across. No
doubt the rebels were eagerly wishing the boat across to them. Coffee was an
import from South America, and had been cut off from the Confederacy by the
Union blockade. Most Rebel privates had to suffer burnt bread crumbs in boiled
water as their version of the drink.

Both sides were united in cheering on the little boat in its struggle against the
Rappahannock. But a great groan went up, and both sides cursed fortune, when
the Monitor hit a rock and overturned, sending the coffee downstream. Oates
and his friends made another boat and put a letter and a Pittsburgh *Dispatch* in
it and this made it to the rebels. The Alabamans filled the boat with tobacco, one
of the few goods the Confederacy possessed in abundance, and sent it back to the
Excelsiors. They continued talking, but the clouds began to gather above them,

and it seemed time they should end their pleasant encounter. With a final wave Oates and his friends left the river and headed back to camp, laughing and joking and in good spirits after such a pleasant encounter with the *"perfect gentlemen"* of Alabama.[5] As it started to rain Oates wondered whether any of the men he knew from Allegheny who had joined the Confederate army were in those ranks. If they were, it was good to know they were with such fine fellows. The rain started to come down even heavier, and the men scrambled back to their tents and cabins. Oates sprinted through the Fifth's camp and slipped and slid his way to the door of the Encyclopedia House. Drenched, he came into the cabin, glad to see the fire roaring. It had been another day in the army, one of the better ones he had seen.[5]

Oates woke to hear that the canvas above him was silent, and that the rain had stopped during the night. He slowly pulled himself out of bed to the sound of the bugle, and the seven men around him did the same. He pulled on his old socks and new boots, recently arrived from home, and tramped outside while pulling on his shirt and coat. All the men, all the army around him were going to extra lengths in preparing their toilet that morning. The President had come down from Washington to review the army, and the Army of the Potomac's commander, General Joseph Hooker, was preparing a grand spectacle.

The men around him were pulling on their boots, finishing shaving, and the like while someone passed around a few newspapers. Oates, who had stopped shaving a while ago, grabbed the nearest paper and flipped through its pages. The men around him were talking about the report of the Congressional Committee on the Conduct of the War, the committee which oversaw the military affairs of the country. They had just finished reviewing the Peninsular Campaign, and the report they had issued was scathing towards McClellan. Oates and the men had seen it a few days ago, and it caused a revolution in the ranks. The men, who the past summer had looked to McClellan as their leader and a young Napoleon, now saw him as a hesitating incompetent. Oates wrote that, *"I was a strong McClellan man, but I must say, I never want to be in any command that he is commander of. All that supprises me is that we was not all killed or captured on the Peninsular."*[50]

The men were still somewhat talking about the report, although the initial outrage had died down, and began to discuss what would be happening that day. Oates continued to flip through the paper until he stopped at a picture of a man he recognized. He scanned the page for the article, and found what he was looking for. The Prince of Wales, the future King Edward VII of England, had wed Princess Alexandra of Denmark. The Englishman in Oates took a fair deal of interest in the pomp and splendor of the royal family that used to rule him. Oates found another Englishman, one of twenty young Londoners who had recently come to America to win glory with the Excelsior Brigade and toasted the health of the new couple over their morning coffee and biscuits. Even if Oates was now an American and fighting for the government at Washington, he had grown up in a household where stories almost always occurred in Manchester or Yorkshire and he still retained a good deal of affection for his birthplace and former Prince.

The company commander walked by and brought Oates' thoughts back to the business of the day, April 8, 1863, and to his current ruler. Oates finished preparing himself and grabbed his rifle and bayonet, specially cleaned for the event. The company assembled and they fell in line with the regiment, which fell in line with the brigade, and marched off for the reviewing grounds. Oates took note that the roads over which he was walking were becoming sturdier and more solid every day. The winter had turned the roads into morasses of mud, and the spring was beginning to dry them out. When the roads became capable of carrying the army and its wagon train, the campaigning season would start, and Oates and the Excelsior Brigade would be thrown into another six months of fighting.

The brigade halted, and for the next few minutes the men were busy organizing themselves into the proper formation for the grand review. To his mother Oates wrote, *"I have seen a good many grand sights scince I have been in the Army, but yesterday beat any thing I ever saw."*[50] An enormous field, almost three miles long, was one huge mass of troops. Then, to Oates' amazement, someone told him that only four corps were being reviewed that day, the Second, Third, Fifth and Sixth. With half the army they had this giant assemblage of manpower. Suddenly the soldiers started yelling and twisting their heads around. Oates turned to see what they were looking at and saw a group of figures on horseback, one of which was taller than the others and wearing a suit instead of a uniform. It was the President, Abraham Lincoln.

The review would take the form of a massive parade of the army marching before the President so that he could see them in their finest form. The Excelsior Brigade's men were clean and looked as good as they ever did, and Oates thought as he scanned the field that there were none as good as the Old Third Corps. Oates and the men stood around for several hours while most of the infantry, cavalry, and artillery had passed before the President until it was the Excelsior Brigade's turn. As Oates marched by he got a good look at Lincoln, and saw that the *"poor fellow"* looked much older than he did the last time he reviewed the army, over a year ago.[50] Lincoln's weathered face was enough to endear him to the army, who saw that their President, at least, was not just sitting and enjoying life in Washington, but had suffered like his countrymen.

Oates also saw Major General Joseph Hooker, his former divisional commander, on horseback alongside Lincoln. Hooker had rapidly climbed the ranks, leading a corps at Antietam and a "grand division," a Burnside invention comprising two corps, at Fredericksburg. After the dismal Mud March, Lincoln was forced by public outcry to remove Burnside, and Hooker was one of the only viable candidates to replace him. He took command of the Army of the Potomac at a time when morale was low and the soldiers were settling into winter quarters, after a year of three defeats and one draw in their fight against Lee's Confederates.

The army that marched that day before Lincoln was not the same one that had returned to his camp defeated by the rain a few months earlier. Hooker had turned the army around. He granted furloughs freely, thereby combating desertion. He increased rations, giving the men some small luxuries. He clamped down on inaccurate newspaper reporting, which had done much to hurt the spirit of the literate army. And simply by acting the part of a victorious leader, he brought out the naturally optimistic attitudes of the common soldiers like Oates.

The Excelsior Brigade had paraded and were discharged back to their camp. The weather was good that day and as soon as the soldiers got back to camp the usual fun and games started up. Men fell into sides of nine to play a few innings of baseball, probably the New York version that developed into the modern game. Larger teams picked up a ball to start a game of football, at that time an early form of rugby and not yet developed into the line of scrimmage style of American football, nor the hands-less play of European football.[4] Two men put on the boxing gloves while spectators gathered around to cheer on their favorites.

Some men were circulating through the ranks appealing for donations for the Irish Relief Fund to which the Excelsior Brigade contributed $1,744.[51] Others were returning to camp after visiting friends in other units. The benefit of a vast camp that held practically the entire Army of the Potomac was that a soldier could visit any man he knew in the army. Many traveled outside their regiments during their free time.

Oates saw in the distance a play being performed by a group of soldiers. There were often plays in camp, mostly Shakespearean comedies in which the ability to ad lib was a main requirement for actors. The regimental band and men with instruments struck up tunes and played some of the day's favorite ditties. Christy's Plantation Melodies were among the songs demanded, as well as the limitless other patriotic songs the publishing houses of the North printed out during the war.

Oates was on the sidelines, moving from event to event and cheering on his friends from the company. He stopped by a group of men listening to a joke that always found a receptive audience in soldiers. It was a conversation between two soldiers, and when the New York *Herald* printed it a year later, the correspondent gave them New York accents and the names of Mose and Sykesy.

MOSE- Saay, Sykesy, what you goin' to do when yer three years is up? Going to be a vet? Saay?

SYKESY- Not if I know myself I ain, no! I goin' to be a citizen, I am. I goin' back to New York and am goin' to lay off and take comfort, bum around the engine house and run wid der machine.

MOSE- Well, I tell yer what I a goin' to do. I jest been thinkin' the matter all over, and got the whole thing fixed. In the first place, I goin' home to New York, and as soon as I get my discharge I goin' to take a good bath and get this Virginia sacred soil off me. The I goin' to have my head shampood, my hair combed forward

---

4   For a detailed example of this form of the game, read The Firm of Girdlestone by Sir Arthur Conan Doyle, Ch. 7, in which the game is played in Britain in the 1870s

and 'iled, and then I goin' to some up-town clothing store and buy me a suit of togs. I a goin' to get a gallus suit, too — black breeches, red shirt, black silk choker, stovepipe hat, with black bombazine around it, and a pair of them shiny leather butes. The I goin' up to Delmonico's place and am goin' to have all he has on his dinner ticket, you bet. What? No! I guess I won' have a gay old dinner, much: for I be a citizens then, and won' have to break my teeth of gnawing hard tack. After I had my dinner I will call for wine and a segar and al the New York papers, and then I just set down, perch my feet up on the table, drink my wine, smoke my segar, read the news, and wonder why the devil the Army of the Potomac don' move.[52]

The men anticipated the punch line and laughed along with it. Oates moved on through the camp that at night turned into a truly fun place. Oates wrote home that no person could get lonesome in camp, there was so much going on.[50] Their camp was a far cry from what they had been used to experiencing: lonesome, far from home, bored, with bad food and bad times. The spring weather had gotten them out of their cabins and the lack of military activity had freed them to pass their time with sports and singing. However, the roads were improving, which meant that the campaigning season was fast approaching. But even this did not daunt the men. Hooker had worked so many reforms in the army, and pulled it out of the mud and into the bright sunshine of the reviewing fields, that he enjoyed the full confidence of his men. Oates said that, *"The Men's Faith is improving every day towards General Hooker. He is getting very popular, every time I see him I like him better."*[50]

Oates walked past the boxing stage and peered over the mass of blue kepis with white cloth diamonds sewn upon them. The diamond was the badge of the Third Corps, the insignia a system instituted by Hooker to mark the various units. The soldiers had taken a liking to them, and they had become the emblems of the units and worn on nearly every man's uniform or cap. Oates found some of his mess also watching the sparring and they fell to talking about the army's future. Everyone present agreed in loud shouts that the Rebs were going to get a thrashing this spring, and that 1862 had been one long string of blunders that were over. Oates chimed in that if they fail again they had better retire in disgust, but he did not think that would happen. Their generals were not fools like before, but fighting men who had already proven themselves. Hooker was in charge of the army, and the Excelsiors' own Sickles commanded the Third Corps. In those hands, and with a newly revitalized army and optimistic outlook, Oates and his fellows knew that the coming spring would deliver great victories for the Union and the Army of the Potomac.

Chapter Fifteen

Courage and Fire

Chancellorsville, Virginia

May, 1862

Oates sat eating biscuits and salt beef in the woods behind the large brick Chancellor's house that gave its name to the area. The men anticipated action or a move soon. He had heard rumors from the others that the rebels were withdrawing from the area, and that the other two divisions of the Third Corps had marched out of the lines to attack the rebel column. Oates and the men around him knew the latter to be true — they had witnessed it — but the Rebels' retreat was just one of the many speculations that flew around an army camp on campaign.

The Army of the Potomac had left winter quarters on April 28th, and embarked on the first campaign of what they hoped would be a better year than last. They marched and counter-marched for four days, part of Hooker's plan to outfox Lee. On May 1st, five corps had crossed the Rappahannock and assembled near the Chancellor House. The soldiers could hear skirmishing between picket lines that night, and the men slept on the field anticipating battle or another move the next day.

The afternoon of May 2nd wore on. Oates watched what he could of the activity in the field in front of him, where the Chancellor house and Hooker's headquarters were. He could see aides and staff officers galloping back and forth as usual. Suddenly one charged up to the woods where Oates and his division were lying. The courier jumped off and spoke to Major General Hiram Berry, Oates' divisional commander. Berry turned and said something to his own staff officers, who bolted off to the three brigade commanders. Shortly Oates heard the order ring through the crowd of men: Drop packs, pick up rifles, off at the double-quick.

Oates fell in with the rest of the brigade, and they set off at the head of the division up the Orange Turnpike. The brigade was charging along when they saw a mass of blue uniforms rush towards them. Oates saw crescents — red, white and blue — on the hats and coats of the men swarming around him. The crescent was the emblem of the Eleventh Corps, and this appeared to be the entire corps around them. The amount of men fleeing was incredible. Thousands upon thousands, mostly immigrants shouting to each other in German, their units and cohesion completely shattered. The road and fields were one great mass of confusion; infantry, artillery, cavalry jostling each other to get as far to the rear as possible.

The order came down the line that the Excelsiors were to ignore the fleeing Germans and press onward. The Eleventh Corps was lost, a shattered body of panicked men who would not be ready to fight for hours. Gen. Berry needed to push through them and reach those who had set the Eleventh to flight. All the men in the column knew what had happened, especially those who had seen this before at Bull Run. Behind every fleeing band of Union troops was a band of charging Confederates. Oates figured that it must be an awful amount of Confederates to have routed an entire corps, and this was what his small division was being sent to stop.

Gen. Berry led the division up the road, and Oates and his cohorts dodged the ambulance wagons, artillery caissons and overturned horses to follow him. With a great yell rising from every throat, Hooker's old division charged up the road and into the thick of it again. *My heart was in my mouth,* Oates wrote home, *"For I knew what was before us and I thought it was all up with our army."*[53] The depleted Fifth Regiment, numbering only 194 men fit for duty, had to go forth into the chaos to stop whatever came at it.

"Few people appreciate the steadiness and courage required," General Abner Doubleday wrote after the war, "When all around is flight and confusion, for a force to make its way through crowds of fugitives, advance steadily to the post of danger in front, and meet the exulting enemy, while others are seeking safety in the rear. Such men are heroes, and far more worthy of honor than those who fight in the full blaze of successful warfare."[54]

The brigade was ordered to cover both sides of the Plank road, and half a mile from the Chancellorsville crossroads, the men turned off the road and crashed through the thick undergrowth to take their positions. These woods were nothing they had ever seen. They were dense second-growth forests called the Wilderness, full of tangled brush that hindered movement and thick trees that broke up formations. It was a struggle for each soldier to get to his position, and even more of a struggle for the officers to work their way down the line to communicate with their men. The regiments slowly deployed, acting not like rectangles or lines or anything geometric envisioned in military science books, but small groups of men, clothes worn down through weeks of use and bodies built up through months of surviving hardship, smashing through the brush into battle. All this was done with the knowledge that only a few hundred yards away were thousands of Rebels, jubilant from destroying the Eleventh Corps and pressing the attack.

Dark fell and the Excelsiors laid low constructing earthworks. They took anything — logs, brush, dirt — that would stop bullets and piled them up in front of them. Three times during the night the Rebels charged their lines. The men could not see the Rebels, only hear them snapping branches and softly moving through the woods and the only light came from the flashes of muzzles. Oates wrote that it was the most nerve-wracking and tense situation they had ever experienced. All were on edge peering into the inky night seeing and imagining enemies. It was the first night fight any of them had been in, and they wanted it to be their last.[53] Many stayed up all night watching for an enemy they could see only at a few paces. Some of the veterans hoped the earthworks would stop the first volley of bullets and took the chance to sleep.

Light appeared in the sky behind them and the men roused themselves after an uncomfortable night awake or sleeping with their rifles. They talked quietly about what was happening in the battle. They had no idea of events behind them, only that as of yesterday afternoon a large number of Rebels had attacked the right wing of the Army of the Potomac and destroyed it. The men had been in thick woods for the last twelve hours and had had almost no communication with the rest of the army. From what they could see, they and the shadowy enemy in front of them might be the only soldiers on the entire battlefield.

Oates tried to stretch and prepare his body to fight, a difficult task when one cannot stand up above the log and dirt breastwork for fear of sharpshooters. He heard noise over his shoulder and saw four bodies crawling through the brush. They were Sgt. Maj. Eugene Jacobson and Privates Felix Brannigan, Joseph Gion and Gotlieb Lutz of Company A. The four had volunteered to scout the Rebel positions the night before, and they had willingly crawled into the unknown to put their lives in further jeopardy for a little information. They immediately went to report to Lt. Col. Lounsbury, in command of the regiment. They brought important news: the Rebels were close, numerous, and looked ready to attack. Also, a Rebel picket had accidentally shot Gen. Stonewall Jackson during the dark hours. If Jackson was present his entire corps was probably also nearby, almost 25,000 Rebel soldiers. If he was wounded and unable to command, the Confederates were without one of their best generals that day, but the thousands of enemy nearby were still a threat ready to extinguish the Excelsior Brigade. The four men returned to their lines and tried to grab a little sleep after the night of scouting, for which they would receive the Congressional Medal of Honor.

As the sun rose on May 3rd, the time until battle began to tick down for the Excelsiors. The Rebels had felt these lines the night before. Now they were going to hit it with every man. Oates looked around at the little force that stood between the enemy and their army's headquarters. No more than two thousand men trying to become as small as possible behind their paltry fortifications. Soon the enemy would attack and Oates said a prayer that his unit would not be routed as the Eleventh Corps had been the day before and that he would survive the day. He loaded his rifle and waited.

With the sun the Rebels emerged. They were in heavy force, covering the entire Union front. Oates and the line of diamond-decked Union boys stayed low behind their earthworks waiting for the command to fire. The officers held the men for a long time. The Rebels kept coming, possibly not knowing the Union line was hidden in the dense undergrowth. The Rebels came within 80 paces of the Union line, less than 400 feet away, when the officers shouted out "Fire." The volley issued from over two thousand rifles ripped through the still air and slammed into the Rebel lines. The men were ordered to fire at will, and the steady pounding of miniés stopped the Confederate advance cold.

A ferocious firefight ensued. Each side was pinned down along much of the line. The Excelsiors and company were under orders to hold their ground, and the Rebels were stopped by the thick woods and thick musket fire. General Berry had chosen the ground well. The men were in a hollow, and the Confederate cannon fire, grape and solid shot that might have ripped through the breastworks passed overhead.

Oates stayed low, loading and priming his rifle behind the earthworks, and poking his head above the logs only long enough to aim and fire. The Rebels had made it to a patch of spruce pine woods about 30 yards from the Excelsiors and the long line of Union rifles was *"giving them fits."*[53] The Union boys aimed especially at the sharpshooters running forward to get a better shot and they rarely missed. The Excelsiors, *"knocked them over like sheep."*[55]

Both sides were keeping up a heavy fire on the other, and both sides were fighting like devils. Many times the Confederates advanced screeching the Rebel yell and many times the Excelsiors responded with a volley of bullets and a *"hearty cheer."*[56] Oates dropped back down to load his rifle and looked up and down the line while tearing open the powder cartridge. He saw the officers of all the regiments standing low, encouraging the men to keep up their firing. Suddenly he caught movement out of the corner of his eye and he saw Lt. Col. Lounsbury on the ground with blood streaming down his face. Oates forgot about his cartridge and watched as aides and officers rushed to the commander. Lounsbury sat up and was alive, but the blood rendered him incapable of command. Capt. Henry Alles, acting-major of the regiment, took charge and moved down the line lending his voice to the noise of battle.

Oates redirected his attention to the battle and kept firing. The next time he turned around he saw Capt. Alles being carried off the field, wounded but still alive. Command of the regiment devolved upon Capt. Tyler of Company E. The firing kept up, and Capt. Tyler moved along the lines to keep his men in order.

Not long after Oates had seen the prostrate body of Capt. Alles carried away from the action, a sergeant came up to him and shouted in his ear to fall back. Oates turned and looked at him in bewilderment, as did the rest of the men around him. They had lost almost no men, not counting officers, the breastworks provided perfect protection, and the Rebels had not even approached the lines. Oates and the rest of the men ignored the sergeant, and shouted back to him that they would not leave such a safe situation. They would not take the chance to stand up and move. The sergeant sprinted back to where he had come from and the men kept firing.

The sergeant came back again to order the men to fall back. Again he was ignored. A third time he returned, lucky to be alive after dodging so many bullets, telling the soldiers in the most urgent and vocal tones that the order from the regimental commander was to fall back. The men finally did as commanded. They did not know why they had to leave a fight they thought they were winning, but after three direct orders from Capt. Tyler, they obeyed. The men would find out later that the left of the line had given way and that the Rebels were coming up on them from behind. If they had refused the order for much longer, all of them might have been dead or captured.[53]

The men maintained a suppressing fire on the Rebels, and then sprang up and fought their way backwards through the brush. Soon the Rebel bullets which had been hitting earth and wood started hitting flesh. Men dropped all along the line. Oates crouched as low as possible to avoid the bullets, but without any sort of breastworks in front of him he could only pray and hope. An infantryman on the move in the Civil War was one of the most exposed and defenseless units on the battlefield, and Oates had to hope that he would live for another few minutes until the regiment made it to a secure location.

The Excelsiors made one last push through the brush and left the woods. Capt. Tyler directed the men into a line of earthworks near the center of an open field near the Chancellor House. The regiment turned and formed a line as the pursuing Rebels emerged from the woods. The Confederates were met with an eruption of artillery power. The Fifth Regiment lay down as the Union grape and canister screamed overhead and into the Rebels. For about fifteen minutes the Confederates tried to form up to attack, but the cannon fire continually broke them and they fell back.[53]

Oates and the men were lying prone in the field waiting for the next assault, when they started to see smoke rise from the woods. This was not the acrid smoke of gunpowder rising from thousands of muskets and cannon, but dark smoke that billowed and rose. Oates saw orange flames shoot up and there was no doubt about it. The woods, full of the wounded and dead of both sides, had caught fire. Oates could only give thanks that he was not in there and hoped that as many men as possible were able to make it out alive.

By this time it was late morning and the brigade had assembled in the field near Chancellor House, ready to fend off the next Rebel attack. Then Oates heard the order from the officers to stand up and get ready to march. The entire brigade rose and began walking, but for some reason they were going away from the battle. Gen. Revere, the Excelsior Brigade's commander, was leading the men not to the front lines, not to replenish their ammunition at a supply depot, but towards the rear and towards the river. Oates could not believe this. Something had to be wrong. The Excelsior Brigade had never before retreated in the face of an enemy and now it looked like it was running away.[53a]

Oates saw men from other brigades in the division marching with them, also wondering where they were headed. Oates heard that Gen. Berry had had his head blown off by a Rebel sharpshooter, and that Gen. Revere had taken command of the division, even though he was not the senior brigade commander. The men kept marching north away from the battle as they were directed, although they could not understand why; they were still able to fight and help their countrymen.

Finally, as morning turned into afternoon, an aide on horseback rode up to Revere and the brigade turned around and marched back to the front. Oates watched as Revere approached Sickles and spoke with him. The men looked on as Col. J. Egbert Farnum, the former Slave Watch Wanderer, commander of the First Regiment, rode up to the men and began giving orders as commander of the brigade. Revere turned north with an aide at his side. He was arrested for his cowardly march to the rear, and the Excelsiors were furious that Revere might jeopardize their fighting reputation.

Sickles ordered the men into position north of the Chancellorsville crossroads, Confederate artillery had made the old field untenable, and the men flew into action digging trenches, and lines of earthworks. Before nightfall they had constructed seven lines of trenches and Oates was praying for the rebels to come and try to drive them out of these impermeable fortifications. They would give them such a fight that would make up for Revere's march. By nightfall on May 3rd, the Army of the Potomac was connected and in a strong position with each flank on a bend in the Rappahannock and no opening showing for the rebels to attack. It started to rain and the men's ragged clothing was soaked in no time. Darkness fell and Oates saw Sickles ride along the lines checking on the men who had fought for him for the past two years and he ordered a big drink of whiskey for his exhausted boys.

The next morning around 3 A.M., Oates was awoken and ordered to fall back towards the river. Hooker had given up on his plan of offensive operations south of the Rappahannock, and the entire army was falling back across United States Ford. Hooker had been dazed when an artillery shell struck a column he had been leaning against at Chancellor House, and he probably suffered a concussion. Whatever was his state of mind, the army was ordered back to the old camp at Falmouth. As Oates re-crossed the pontoon bridge on May 5th and reached his old camp that evening, he realized had survived yet another campaign and his brigade, and although suffering the indignity of a cowardly commander, had fought well. They were old hands and had been through battles before. They would not give in to the fears that might cripple a recruit. They had shown their courage before and at Chancellorsville they had shown it again. They had marched into a rout, fended off night attacks, and fought in the brush until ordered to withdraw three times. They might have been cursed with a cowardly commander, but as the four soldiers who earned a Medal of Honor could show, the shortcomings of Revere did not exist in his men.

Chapter Sixteen

Thoughts of the North

Camp near Falmouth, Virginia

May, 1862

Oates looked down at the river from his post on the picket line and wished he could be there. It was a hot day, the hottest Oates had experienced since he had joined the army, he thought, even too hot for marching. He had never known heat like this in late May, and standing on picket duty did not give him any relief from it. The Rappahannock was alive with soldiers of the Brigade sharing the cool waters with a number of Rebels. Such a day was a fight between man and the elements, and disputes among men were forgotten.

Oates stood and sweated through his shift on picket, and when his relief finally came, he gladly turned and headed back for camp, the swimming party having broken up already. The new campgrounds for the brigade were at the top of a hill, luckily, and picked up the small breeze that drifted through central Virginia. Oates arrived at his tent to find his messmates cooking dinner. The Encyclopedia House had been dismantled when the army moved from winter to summer quarters and now the men were in lightweight canvas tents that allowed fresh air through and provided shade.

There was good food tonight. One of the mess had received a box from home, and in their habit the men shared it. Another had gone into the country and bought milk from a local farmer, only 50 cents a quart, much less than the suttlers around the camp had marked it up to. Oates sat down, loosened his shirt, and gulped some milk, thankful his long and unrelenting job was finished.

He had walked in on a conversation in progress - there was always one in progress in camp. The men were discussing a New York *Herald* article they had been reading. This issue was a couple of weeks old, but it was appreciated nonetheless.

"Valor of the Excelsior Brigade," the one with the newspaper read aloud. "The Excelsior Brigade was among the most efficient corps in the army."

"Concerning the fighting at Chancellorsville, they mean," another interjected.

"Of course," the others responded.

"They fought like tigers wherever placed," the reader continued, "and never wavered. They were deserted by their commanding officer (who, I understand has been placed under arrest), but remained steadfast at the post of duty and danger. Among the trophies taken by them are nearly a dozen stands of colors, the regiments to which they belonged having been annihilated by the steadiness and bravery of this little band."[57]

The men clapped and applauded the good sense of the reporter, and cheered themselves on having made the papers in such a positive light. The *Herald* and other papers the men had read had all made note of Gen. Revere's cowardice in battle, but all had made a point to say that the men of the Excelsior Brigade in no way shared their commander's weakness.

The public image of the brigade was important to the soldiers. They had fought well at Chancellorsville and ought to receive credit for what they did. More importantly, and more personally, the newspapers were how friends and family at home knew how they acted under fire. Letters traveled slowly and a soldier could not send messages boasting of his unit's actions to everyone he knew back home; he had to rely on the papers to do that for him. It was because of this fierce fixation on public image that practically the only people the men detested more than those who wouldn't fight were those who didn't, but took credit for doing so. The object of much of Oates' animosity, and the animosity of all those in Company A, was the 123rd Pennsylvania infantry.

The 123rd, the same regiment that the Excelsior Brigade had met on the march from Second Bull Run a year earlier, was recruited mostly from the Pittsburgh area, with a number of men from Allegheny City. The soldiers in Company A had a number of friends in the 123rd but held no affection for the unit. The 123rd had spent much of 1862 in forts, getting their first real taste of battle when they charged the Confederate lines at Fredericksburg. They had fought well, but it seemed that their performance had gone to some of the men's heads, and Oates constantly wrote home about the 123rd acting as if they were the bravest band of heroes in this hemisphere. Their Colonel, the Reverend John Clark, had outfitted the regiment with white gloves during the reviews before Lincoln that spring. The 123rd, to Oates and his friends, played soldiering while the Excelsiors lived it. A letter in a Harrisburg newspaper stated that after Chancellorsville the 123rd was, "black with the smoke of battle & the Powder marks was still on their hands," yet the 123rd was in the 3rd division of the Fifth Corps, which had been in the reserve the whole time.[55] It made Oates furious to read such things. *"They never fired a shot at the rebels,"* he wrote, *"& most of them was awfully afraid they would have to do it."*[55]

Another man brought up a newspaper article he had read, saying that the people of Pittsburgh presented the Rev. Col. Clark with a gold medal. Oates had to shake his head. *"I wonder when the people will learn some sense,"* he wrote.[58] Oates had at least a little something to put the men in better spirits. He heard that the people back home were beginning to "hoot" [mock] the men who left the ranks in time of action. These included deserters and those who had signed up only for nine months' term of service. Many regiments formed the previous fall for nine months had disbanded almost immediately after Chancellorsville, and the Excelsiors mercilessly made fun of the poor patriots who were so devoted to their country they were willing to give up a whole three-fourths of a year. Oates had already given more than twice that and still had another year to go.

The men laughed that deserters were being ostracized back home, and they wished it had happened years ago. One of their favorite newspaper articles had appeared in the New York *Times* the year before in which the Excelsior Brigade's correspondent Cedma wrote:

"One other thing the army feels bad about. The officers and men who have borne the brunt of the various battles on the Peninsula, who have stood picket at night and dug trenches by day, who have braved death from the enemy's bullets, and the no less dangerous, though more silent, swamp malaria, feel incensed when they see both press and people lavishing honors on those who on one pretence or the other have skulked away, and are now being fêted as heroes or promoted to high stations. Such instances are more common than are imagined. Many are the men who have shot of [sic] their fingers who are now loudly vaunting their 'valorous' deeds. Many the officer who skulked off under pretence of sickness who now claims honors for gallantry in battles he never saw.

"There is but one way to stop this crying evil, for as it now stands cowardice is at a premium, and that is a plain, simple and effectual one. Let the Colonel of each regiment publish in the papers, printed in the section where his regiment was raised, the name of each absentee, the ostensible cause for which he went home and length of leave, thus:

"John Smith, ten days' leave — sickness.

"Thomas Brown, skulked away from his company — shot his finger off and went home without leave.

"Capt. Jones, left his company at battle of Fair Oaks — ostensible reason: sunstroke.

"The public would soon find out how severe Capt. Jones' sunstroke was, or how sick John Smith was, while Thomas Brown would be hooted at. As it now is, it pays a man to be a coward, and skulk at the North. Drag forth these skulkers to light — place them in the pillory of public opinion, and there will be fewer marriages of officers on sick furlough — a less number of able-bodied men rehearsing their pretended valor, and less incentive to cowardice. That alone will abate this crying evil."[41]

The men recalled this article, and they were glad that only their brigade commander had skulked off. After the Peninsula the brigade had weeded out the bad and was left with mostly excellent officers who looked after the men and knew their way around the battlefield. They lost some of those superior leaders at Chancellorsville. Lt. Col. Lounsbury, Capt. Alles, and young Lt. Charles Preston, commander of Company A, had all been wounded, but luckily none of the wounds were serious and all were expected to recover within a few months. The regiment received as its colonel Thomas Holt, an original Excelsior, a major in the First Regiment, who occasionally led that regiment when the colonel was absent. The men of the Fifth took a liking to him, glad to have someone who had been with the brigade from the start.

Oates got up from the campfire and dumped out what remained of his meal. He headed into the tent, leaving the men to continue talking about what they thought of Col. Holt or whatever subject came next. Standing picket in the heat had drained the energy out of Oates, and he could no longer expend any more of a fighting man's energy on the 123rd.

Oates poked his head out of his tent, the first time he had done so in a while. The first week of June had been windy and the breeze that a couple of weeks before had been a cool respite from picket now kicked up dust and turned the campgrounds into a sandstorm. Fortunately the wind had subsided for the moment, and the camp was safe for open eyes.

Oates and the rest of his tentmates filed out into the streets of the camp to find most of the company already waiting there. The bugle sounded for assembly and the regiment fell into ranks. Oates looked around at the Fifth Regiment, now little more than a full-strength company. Three enlisted men from the regiment had been killed, nineteen wounded, and fifteen missing at Chancellorsville. By the time Revere took them out of action and the officers could call roll, there were only 137 men present in the ranks. The little band had suffered 40 casualties in the battle, more than one-fourth of its total strength.

Oates ran up to the lines of the regiment and fell in with his company. When he took his place he stood next to a regimental celebrity of late, a sergeant who had been shot in the chest during the battle. The bullet had passed through the sergeant's coat, a memorandum book he carried in his breast pocket, his shirt, came out under his arm and never broke the skin. When the regiment had assembled back in Falmouth, there was a small crowd staring in wonder at the destroyed book and the sergeant was bewilderedly checking himself to make sure he was alive and intact.

The bugle sounded again and the men marched slowly towards the parade ground. The sergeants directed the men as they formed a hollow square, three sides of a square with one side and the middle left open. The men were standing, waiting for the event to start, when they saw a group of men on horseback loping up the hill. The men stood to attention as the riders dismounted and gathered at the open side of the square and the function began.

The night's event was a party to honor the Fifth Regiment. Col. William Brewster, new commander of the Excelsior Brigade, gave a speech about their accomplishments so far in the war. Then came a speech by Charles K. Graham, now a general commanding a brigade in the First Division of the Third Corps. Graham stood up to give a speech. His old regiment still admired him, and when he stood up they cheered wildly for the man who had led them from New York to the front and been with them at Fair Oaks and the Seven Days'. Graham, seeing his men so depleted and worn out from war but still showing him affection, could not give the speech. He broke down and cried like a child.

Graham stood to one side as a man from New York, some official of importance Oates did not recognize, came out and presented the regiment with a new stand of colors to replace the tattered set they were presently carrying. He said they were from the citizens of New York and cost six hundred dollars, a princely sum for flags. The color guard marched up and accepted the flags to cheers from the regiment. It always boosted a unit's morale to be seen with new and expensive colors. Colonel Holt then treated all the men to whiskey punch and the men broke ranks to enjoy the rest of the night.

Oates and his messmates eagerly headed towards the whiskey. The men were normally issued only half a gill of whiskey, two liquid ounces, and then only twice a month.[59] The opportunity to drink something other than poor coffee or water was one the men seized. The monotony of camp life was momentarily disrupted as the men toasted each other with the lemon and fruit flavored punch. The men milled around and saw the officers enjoying themselves as well. Most of their junior officers were men "imported" from New York. The joke in camp at the time was that if a man gets drunk in New York and cannot pay his fine he gets sent to the Excelsior Brigade and considers it a very severe punishment.[60]

The men did not have much contact with their officers, though, and most orders passed through the non-commissioned officers, sergeants and corporals, before reaching the rank and file. The sergeants and corporals were all men promoted from the ranks, and were often those who had shown excellence in battle or had been with the regiment from the start. Oates said he could have easily been promoted if he wanted to, but being a private and able to enjoy himself in camp was preferable to waking up early and looking after others.

Oates was walking around the parade grounds thirsting for another glass of punch when he spotted some of his messmates standing around laughing. He walked up towards them and immediately started laughing as well. The drum corps had been detailed to act as waiters at the event and they were occupying themselves by stealing everything they could get their hands onto. Knives, forks, spoons, lemons, cigars and all manner of things all disappeared into their pockets. Oates even saw one of them take a gold watch and chain off of the drunk quartermaster. The drummers would be tied up by the wrists the next morning, but the officers had no way of getting their supplies back.

The night wore on and eventually the party broke up and the men found their way back to the tents. They were surprised by large piles on the streets of the camp, and in the dark a daring soul ventured up to them to discover that they were all their knapsacks and overcoats. The men had been ordered to send away their impedimenta the week before in preparation for a move. The move hadn't come, and the men got their gear back. It was a good thing too, because it had been cold at night without any covering.

Since their knapsacks had been returned, Oates presumed, that meant there would be no immediate move. The entire army had been waiting for the next campaign. There had been cannon fire below Fredericksburg a couple of nights before, and many of the men thought that they would try to attack Fredericksburg again, their third try for the town. Oates didn't think so seeing their equipment there that night. He said to one of his messmates as they lugged their gear back to the tent that General Hooker probably just wanted to keep the rebels in sight and on their feet so they could not slip away and reinforce Vicksburg, a city on the Mississippi that Union Major General Ulysses S. Grant was currently besieging. Vicksburg was the last rebel stronghold on that river, and all the men were following the reports of that struggle, praying for Union victory.

The men dropped their gear inside their tent and continued to talk about the prospects of the army. One man ventured that Hooker was probably waiting for the drafts to take place and the conscripts to join the army, likely sometime at the end of July. Other disagreed, saying that was too long. Whatever the plans, Oates ventured, he had confidence that Hooker would lead them to victory. This the men agreed with. Even though Chancellorsville had been a Union defeat, the men did not consider themselves beaten. Over four corps had not been involved in the fighting at all, and the only reason they retreated, they said, was because the river was rising and the pontoon bridges threatening to break up. Besides, they said, Hooker had crossed the river to kill rebels. He had certainly accomplished this, even getting lucky when Stonewall Jackson was shot by his own men and died a few days later. *"We all felt sorry for Gen. Stonewall Jackson,"* Oates wrote. *"He was a brave & smart General & the rebels can never get another like him. When ever we was outflanked or our line broken, it was done by him & his troops."*[55]

As the men placed their overcoats and knapsacks under their bed, they were glad that the apparent move had been cancelled and they could continue to have fun times in camp.

Oates charged through the cloud of dust, spitting the bitter grains out of his parched mouth every few steps. The sun blazed and the brigade had already lost a few men to sunstroke. It didn't help that there was no clean water around; in fact the water was worse than on the malarial Peninsula. It made no matter. Oates was glad to be on the road.

The Army of Northern Virginia had slipped out of its encampments in early June and began to move northward to attempt an invasion of the rich heartland of the north. After a delay of a few days that allowed the Confederates to gain a significant head start, the Army of the Potomac broke camp and turned about face to pursue its enemy. On June 12th the Excelsior Brigade left its camp and tents and began some of the hardest marching it had ever endured.[61]

Called up at 5 A.M. on the 12th, it marched a dozen miles that day. The next day the men were on the road by 4:30 A.M., and marched twenty-one miles to Rappahannock Station. Days more of marching with only the smallest of stops to rest led the men past the Virginia towns of Cedar Run, Manassas, Centerville and Gum Springs. The weather was hot, and the thousands of feet kicked up a cloud of dirt that got into everyone's mouths and eyes. It was by far the longest march any of them had ever made, but it made no difference to them, they all wanted to fly as fast as possible.

The Confederates had invaded Pennsylvania, and newspapers the men picked up every day told of the rebels hitting some town or the other. One day it was Chambersburg and Carlisle that had been burned. The next the rebels were marching on Harrisburg and Pittsburgh. Oates had read that John P. Glass, Company A's original captain, had gotten hold of a battery of artillery for the defense of Pittsburgh. All the men knew that a rabble of untrained civilians wouldn't have a chance stop the rebels.[62]

The men realized that this move had been a desperate one by the rebels. They had left their base of supplies and their own states, and could very well be destroyed so far away from friendly territory. The men also knew that with the Rebels so far into Union land the Confederacy would probably win the war if their gamble succeeded.

The invasion had been a well-conducted move by all accounts. No one knew where the rebels were or heading, they could only read what part of Pennsylvania they had recently passed through. But even so, the men were confident that Hooker would make the rebels pay dearly for this campaign.

The men were thankful that they were marching, no matter how arduous the road. The Excelsiors, hardened veterans who had no illusions of the romance of battle, wanted a fight. Even Oates, who rarely wished for a chance to risk his life, wanted to be in Pennsylvania to defend his country on the soil of his home state. The men were crazy to get to there and make the rebels stand and fight.[63]

The brigade still had many more miles to march before they caught up with the rebels. They would pass through Edward's Ferry, Middletown, Frederick City and Emmittsburg. But the group of men marching north on the dust-choked roads of Virginia and Maryland of June, 1863 were a group of maddened soldiers, pushing their bodies to the limit so that they could move a little faster and bring the invading rebels to battle just a little sooner. When the rebels marched on their homes, the Excelsior Brigade showed itself and gladly ran towards battle.

Camp 5 Excelsior

July 13th 1863

Dear Mother

I received a letter
from you about 5 days ago, but
this is the first opportunity I have
had to answer it. We have been
on the move every day since we
left Falmoth, we are now laying
near the Enemy about 5 mile from
Williamsport, Maryland, ware he
has entrenched himself. We are
looking for another big battle every
day. We have been reinforced &
I suppose have more men than
we had before Gettysburg. We
are all tired out, for we have
had nothing but rain every day.
All our wounded out of our Company
are doing well, George Bond's left
arm was amputated close to the
shoulder, he is getting along first

Chapter Seventeen

Victory and Loss

Gettysburg, Pennsylvania

July, 1863

ates pushed onward through the night. They had crossed the Pennsylvania border a few hours ago and the officers were hurrying to move the men as fast as possible. There had been reports that morning that the Union forces ahead of them had run into the rebel army, and it was believed that a battle was being fought. The Army of the Potomac raced forward to take part in this battle that they knew might decide the war.

The Excelsior Brigade slogged up the roads, the men tired from a month of chasing the tails of the Confederates across Virginia and Maryland. But still the men pounded the earth and moved themselves towards into battle, not knowing exactly where they were going, just that it was north, where the rebels waited. Oates saw the men above him in line take a right and he followed suit. It had been a difficult march that night, but it looked like it was over. The men turned off the road and threw down their gear in a field near a farmhouse outside a small town named Gettysburg. It was close to dawn, and the officers told the men to get some sleep. Daylight was about to shine on July 2, 1863, and there would likely be fighting before the sun set. The veterans would need to be rested. Oates found a soft spot of ground to lie on and, putting an extra shirt under his head for a pillow, fell asleep.

The next morning Oates awoke to see the soil of his home state covered with the activity of an entire army. Around 10 A.M. the rest of the Third Corps had arrived and those who were there began to rouse themselves and prepare for battle. Oates looked around at his surroundings, the ground he might die defending.

The land around them was almost the definition of rolling, the gentle hills, valleys, and streams that covered most of central Pennsylvania. It was farmland too; they saw homes behind log rail fences, wheat fields interspersed with orchards. Most of the land was open, unlike Chancellorsville, and Oates would be able to see his enemy coming from hundreds of yards away. There were some patches of woods, but the farmers in the regiment knew that there would be little brush in there. The locals let their livestock graze in the woods. This would eliminate the horrible tangled growth they had faced below the Rappahannock.

It was good ground for the larger Army of the Potomac, which was currently concentrated to the north around Culp's and Cemetery Hills. The Third Corps was stationed about the west side of Cemetery Ridge, near Trostle's Farm, but it looked as if they would not be staying there for long. The Excelsior Brigade was ordered on their feet and they moved a couple hundred yards east, to a low point of land in the shadow of two big hills on their left, the Round Tops and the rising ridgeline to their right. There the corps drew themselves into lines of battle and faced west, awaiting the arrival of new orders or the enemy, and prepared themselves to deal with either one.

Dan Sickles rode up and down his lines, surveying the land he had been ordered to hold. Followed by his staff, the group of horsemen paced back and forth along the three-quarters of a mile that the Third Corps occupied. Sickles halted his horse and looked around, as if making up his mind. Then, giving a few words to his staff, he rode north to the headquarters of General George Meade, who had taken command of the army from Hooker less than a week earlier.

Sickles arrived at headquarters and entered to speak with the general. Sickles wanted Meade to come and see the Third Corps' positions, to confirm what Sickles was beginning to believe. Meade had no time. He anticipated the rebel assault to come from a different sector and was busy strengthening those positions, but he did send the army's chief of artillery, Brig. Gen. Henry Hunt, to go with Sickles and examine the ground.

Sickles and Hunt rode back to the lines and were soon trotting across the fields and woods talking military science. Sickles explained why he had gone to Meade's headquarters and wanted the general to look at the corps' positions. The Third Corps had been ordered to take up positions on the left flank of the Union army, extending south of the Second Corps along Cemetery Ridge until Little Round Top. However, as Sickles found when he inspected this stretch of ground, Cemetery Ridge lost most of its height at that point. In fact, the ground was forty feet higher in elevation a half a mile *in front* of the ridge. At Chancellorsville Sickles had seen his corps pounded by rebel artillery firing from higher ground, and he feared that if the rebels took possession of the high ground here, his corps might again be slaughtered.

Sickles proposed to Hunt that his corps take a new position along this high ground near the Emmitsburg Road. It would offer excellent field of fire to the Third Corps, would cramp the movements of the enemy and would offer a staging ground if Meade wanted to take the offensive. Most importantly, the Third Corps wouldn't have to fear a Confederate bombardment like the one at Chancellorsville that had cost it a quarter of its men.

Hunt said he would report back to Meade for instructions. He left and Sickles waited for a reply. Morning passed to afternoon and there was still no message from headquarters. Sickles received word that the cavalry screen in front of him had been withdrawn, and there was word from forward sharpshooters that rebel infantry was moving to his left. An attack seemed imminent but still there was no word from headquarters. Sickles needed to make the decision himself, it seemed. The politician with no military training except what he had taught himself and what he had seen in the last two years had to decide what to do with an entire army corps, over 10,000 men and 30 cannon. Both positions had their advantages and drawbacks. If he stayed where he was he would occupy three-quarters of a mile, but the ground was low. If he moved forward he would have to stretch his lines to a mile and a half, his flanks would not be connected to the Second Corps or Little Round Top, and his lines would join at a right angle, meaning if broken at the apex the entire corps might be routed. Still, the ground was higher and there was no chance of the corps being battered by artillery as it had been only a couple months before.

At 3 P.M., without orders from headquarters, Sickles made up his mind. With the lives of his men and perhaps the fate of his country in his hands, Sickles called his division commanders together and told them to move their men forward to the Emmittsburg Road. In Sickles' mind it was a better position, and it was his duty to move his men there.[64]

Oates grabbed his rifle as the officers ran down the line telling the men to get up for the move. The brigade lined up and was soon out of the woods and into the fields. The men passed the brigade's supernumeraries, the chaplains and quartermasters and correspondents who did not fight, but at this moment paused and took in the sight in front of them. They saw the veterans pass, "the light of valor in every bronzed face;" a chaplain would say later, "a solid line of manhood; the flag of the world's brightest hope over them, marching with firm, eager step into the open field."[65] As they saw the fighting men go off to battle again, and remembering other times when the brigade performed such a ritual, they said to themselves, "There go the bravest men in this army."[65]

The Third Corps advanced towards the high ground. The First Division arrayed below the Wheatfield Road facing southwest. The Second Division was along Emmitsburg Road, facing northwest. Oates and the brigade took positions as reserve, 200 yards behind the division's First Brigade, which was posted right along the road, and 200 yards in front of the Third Brigade, which was acting as a second reserve. Oates was on the reverse slope of the ridgeline, and couldn't see much other than the men in front of him. The men lay down and waited for the attack.

Oates looked up and around. He saw Sickles on horseback surrounded by his staff and General Meade arrive to inspect the lines. Sickles rode over to confer with Meade. Oates could not make out what the generals were saying, but could tell from Meade's body language that the commander was not happy with the new line. It looked to Oates as if Sickles was offering to withdraw his men to their original positions. Just then a loud rumble rolled across the field, followed by another, then another, then another. It was a rebel battery opening up on the Third Corps. The attack had begun. It was too late to withdraw now, the rebels would hit and destroy the corps as it was exposed on the move, and so Meade turned back to his headquarters. He promised Sickles the support of the Second and Fifth Corps as well as the army's artillery reserve, but with rebel artillery blasting and rebel infantry approaching, the fighting would begin, at least, as the Third Corps' and Sickles' own battle.

Oates grabbed his gun as the Fifth Regiment charged forward. The rebel infantry had struck first at the apex of the Third Corps' salient. The attacks then spread, and the corps found itself hard pressed to hold its ground. The Excelsior Regiments were called to plug gaps in the line. The Second and Third Regiment had been ordered to the left flank of the First Brigade. The Fourth to the left to support the First Division. Now the Fifth was ordered to the right flank of the First Brigade. Oates scrambled into position. With the cracks of muskets and roar of cannon ringing in his ears, the men began to break down the rail fence in front of them to make a breastwork. The men piled up the wooden rails, rocks, and whatever they could lay their hands onto with amazing speed. Fortifications had stopped many bullets intended for them at Chancellorsville and they labored to build similar protection here.[66]

Oates lay behind the breastworks, craning his head to the left to catch sight of the fighting. Rebel infantry was approaching the Union batteries in the Peach Orchard at the apex of the line. Oates watched as regiments of infantry fired volleys into Union artillery companies, and the artillery responded with point-blank rounds of canister. The fighting was intense, and the sounds of battle rang in Oates' ears as he stayed low and avoided the artillery fire that was flying around the field.

Oates looked to General Sickles for encouragement and to see what their old general was doing on that field. He saw Sickles, easily distinguished by the staff surrounding him, riding along the lines urging the men to keep fighting, not to let up. Oates turned away to check that there were no Confederates in front of the regiment. He piled a few more rocks in front of him and scraped a little ditch for himself. Suddenly he heard shouts to his left and quickly turned to see what had happened. He saw the line intact, things as they were just a few seconds ago. But then he spotted Sickles' staff. They had circled their horses around something and a few of their horses were riderless. Oates looked closer and found that he could not see Sickles. Word streamed down the line that Sickles had been hit. The general who had looked out for them throughout most of the two years, who had recruited them and made them into a hardened fighting force was down.[67]

The men couldn't believe it. Oates watched and saw a pair of stretcher bearers and a chaplain rush over to the fallen general. It looked like Sickles was dead or mortally wounded. The men either fell silent or talked feverishly as they saw the body hoisted onto the stretcher with a small army of staff members crowded around him. It looked as if their general had finally run out of luck.[61] But then Oates saw some movement. Sickles' stretcher was being carried along the lines, and there was the general, smoking a cigar and waving to his men. The soldiers cheered as their old general passed by. Not even a cannonball to the leg could dampen Dan's spirits.

The men returned to the battle at hand. The rebels were still coming on hard and the attacks were expanding to almost the entire line. Brightly colored Zouaves rushed forward to save a battery of guns, teams of horses carrying replacement batteries charging to the line and suddenly Confederate flags, surrounded by Confederate soldiers, were behind the Second Division's line. The rebels had broken the salient and were now trying to roll up the Third Corps' line. Regiments left the reserve and threw themselves into the fighting to stem the rushing flow of Rebels. Oates watched the flags of the different forces approach and disappear into the clouds of gunpowder smoke.

Men started shouting and Oates looked in front of him. The attack had spread to the Fifth Regiment's sector and rebel infantry were approaching their positions. The men stayed low behind their breastworks and took aim. The men waited until the rebels were in range. Then, at the signal of the officers, they fired as one and sent a volley of miniés into the lines of the Rebels. The men now fired at will and Oates rapidly loaded and fired his gun, staying low to avoid the rebel responses, and checking behind him every so often to see if the rebels were about to descend on the regiment.

The Fifth continued fighting the enemy in front of them, but the order came to fall back. Looking around, Oates saw that the rebels had effectively rolled up the division's flank, and units were falling back before the rebels. With one final volley at the rebels in front, the regiment stood up and double-quicked the half-mile to the relative safety of the woods behind Trostle's farm. No sooner had Oates started running with his regiment than the shot and shell began to fall among the Excelsiors' ranks. The rebels who had broken through had turned the Union guns around and were firing them into the retreating Third Corps. The rest of the rebel infantry had gained the crest of the ground and was firing with thousands of muskets into the dense pack of fleeing soldiers. Oates kept moving, trying to stay in line with his regiment which was becoming increasingly disorganized as rebel bullets gave some men additional speed. Soldiers fell; some were left behind, other grabbed by comrades and pulled towards safety. It was a shooting gallery for the rebels. They had acres of enemy, almost all with their back turned and unable to return fire. It was a harrowing retreat for the Second Division of the corps. As Oates made it to the original line he turned and saw the slope covered with bodies of his countrymen, and he was thankful he had survived the sprint.

But this would not be an end to the division's fighting that day. The rebel brigades surged forward, tracing the retreating northerners' steps. The regiments had become entangled and confused. The retreat before the enemy had broken their cohesion. With the rebels charging into them, the officers rode through the men, trying to rally them and beat them into some fighting order.

Oates halted and fell in with the makeshift battle line. He saw Col. Brewster, commanding the brigade, riding through the men ordering them into position.[67] Officers of every regiment were shoving and shouting those around them into a line. The veteran soldiers quickly recovered, and the line of battle soon filled up with determined faces loading their guns. The rebels kept charging forward, seeking to overrun the new line and sweep into the Union's rear. As the rebels passed the Trostle House the order to charge rang out down the line. The men poised with rifles ready. The officers waited for the bugles to sound. Then, the thousands of men of the division who had rallied moved out and marched towards the surging rebels. The pace picked up and the men started jogging forward. The two sides neared each other and as the rebels unleashed a volley the Union line ran forward. Another round of fighting erupted. This time, neither side had any fortifications. Neither side had any real advantage. Both sides were disorganized, the Federals by their retreat, the Confederates by their advance. The fighting was brutal, and distinguished by small moments of bravery on either side. Oates watched as a sergeant from the Third Regiment captured the colors of a Confederate regiment. He saw bands of Union troops surround and capture huge numbers of rebels, as many as were in the division's ranks. He fought forward through the melee, occasionally hand to hand, occasionally finding enough room to fire his weapon. It was as horrible as Bull Run, Chancellorsville, or any other battle he had fought in. The two masses of infantry went at each other's throats in an open field with nothing to stop the fighting but one sides' withdrawal or annihilation.[68]

Eventually the rebels fell back to the road, and the rallied Union units were called back. They returned to the original line carrying stands of rebel colors and recovered Union cannon as prizes. They had lost many winning them, however. The ground was covered with bodies, most to be scavenged over by barefoot rebels. The men tried to find their officers, and regiments slowly began to form again. These regimental collection points, however, resembled hospitals as much as military units. The officers counted the men and found that they had lost approximately a third of their soldiers. The sun set and the battle ended, in that sector at least, and the brigade was relieved and headed to the rear to reassemble. As dark enclosed the army the company commanders made their report to the regimental commanders. The story was the same throughout the Excelsior Brigade. The First Regiment had suffered 117 casualties; the Second, 91; the Third, 114; the Fourth, 162; the 120th New York, attached to the brigade over the winter had suffered 203 casualties. The Fifth Regiment, which that morning had numbered around 300 souls, had lost 6 officers wounded, 12 enlisted men killed, 68 wounded, and 3 missing, for a total of 89. In one of the hardest fights of their career, the Excelsior Brigade had been broken and then rallied to stalemate at the cost of 778 men and

Dan Sickles.[67] The men looked over the field and each other, and they could not help thinking that, in Oates' words, *"Our division numbers 2,600 men, and in one more fight like Gettysburg & we will number zero."*[68]

The brigade bivouacked in the woods that night, and on the morning of July 3 the entire corps was put into reserve. The men were to witness Pickett's Charge that day, in which two rebel divisions charged the center of the Union line and were decimated. The rebels retreated, and fighting ended. On the left and right flanks enemies lay only a hundred yards apart, and Oates and the rest of the army went to sleep that night waiting for more combat that might be even worse than before.

The next day was Independence Day, Oates' third in the army. The soldiers were worn out from the battle. On the 2nd they had fought for hours. On the 3rd they had been exposed to the rebel artillery barrage before Pickett's Charge. On the 4th they occupied themselves by burying the dead. At home people were spending the holiday with fireworks and banquets and news that three days' worth of attacks by Lee's army had found the Army of the Potomac unshakable. In Pittsburgh, where the people had heard faint sounds of the cannons firing over 150 miles away on the ridges north of the Round Tops, Oates' family celebrated this great Union victory that Meade had won, which had delivered the north from defeat. At Gettysburg, their son celebrated with a pick and shovel and the bodies of former friends.

In the ranks of the Excelsior Brigade the day was not one of jubilation. Yes, they had performed well, better than could be expected of any unit, and they had won the greatest fight of their lives. However, they had won it at an incredible cost. At Williamsburg the brigade had lost 25% of their number. At Chancellorsville they suffered 33% casualties. At Gettysburg the number was an enormous 45%. Sickles' recruiting efforts were being laid to rest in the rocky soil of Pennsylvania.[67]

For the entire day nothing was done in either army but to send out burial parties. The ground was littered with fallen soldiers, and they were interred rapidly, with the parties digging a shallow ditch and then moving on to the next unlucky soul. Oates did his job and came back to where the brigade was stationed. He threw down his gun and sat near his sleeping roll. The men that day who had not been out burying the dead were back in camp waiting for the next move. Every man in both armies was waiting for the next move.

For three days Lee had thrown himself at Meade. For the last two of those days the Confederates had been repulsed at great cost. It appeared unlikely that after such losses as the Confederates had suffered, especially after Pickett's charge, that Lee had enough strength for more attacks, so the men waited for Meade to go on the offensive.

On July 4th, the Confederate Army of Northern Virginia looked as if it could be destroyed. Oates and the rest of the soldiers in the army saw how Lee had left his base of operations, had cut himself off from reinforcements, had expended his army while in enemy territory. Now his army was tired and scattered. Longstreet's corps, which had attacked the Third Corps on the second day, was near the extreme left of the Union army. Ewell's corps was miles away opposite the extreme Union right. The Confederate center had been virtually eliminated during Pickett's Charge. Furthermore, Longstreet's and Ewell's men were only a hundred yards from the Union lines in some places, close enough for the Federals to keep an eye on the rebels. Oates knew enough about the fight that the numerically superior Union had the advantage, and he waited for Meade to push his tired army to fight and finally destroy this enemy army that had kept them from ending the war for two years now. It looked like the war would soon be over and Oates would return home.

Oates woke on the morning of July 5th expecting at any moment for the order to march out to fight. But instead burial parties were sent out again. On the 6th Oates woke again waiting to hear reports of Lee's army destroyed or of an impending move to destroy it. But again, burial parties were sent out. On the morning of the 7th Oates once again expected to fight. He received orders to prepare for a move, but as he looked across the fields as the fog cleared, he saw that the rebels had disappeared, and that the Army of the Potomac was to pursue the retreating enemy. The Army of Northern Virginia had been vulnerable to a killer blow for three days, but nothing happened, and they escaped to fight another day and prolong the war.[67]

Oates' palms were moist with nervous sweat, his heart pounding with fearful force. The order to advance rang out down the line, the bugle sounded, and the Excelsior Brigade, one long line of blue coats and bayonets, moved at the double-quick towards the hill.[69]

The Confederate Army had withdrawn into Virginia in the weeks after Gettysburg. The Army of the Potomac had followed and had now caught up with at least the Rebel rearguard. The Confederates were in place on a series of hills and the Excelsior Brigade had been assigned to dislodge them. Brigadier General Francis Spinola, new commander for the Excelsior Brigade, gave the men a word of encouragement. Oates looked up at him with disdain. Spinola was a New York Democrat, a political general like Sickles but with none of Sickles' abilities. He had not earned his general's star by raising troops or military talent but simply through influence in Congress. He had joined the army in October of 1862, after Oates and the rest of the Excelsiors were already veterans. Spinola did not know anything about commanding men in battle and his men wanted him gone.

They were stuck with him for now and he ordered them forward. The brigade gave, "one of its peculiar cheers, so full of determination and confidence," and moved forward.[70] The brigade charged under fire from rebel infantry. The grade was so steep that the line was not stepping smartly together, but rather the men were scrambling up the rocky slope using their hands to pull themselves up, grabbing onto whatever trees and bushes were available. Panting, puffing, and climbing on all fours, Oates and the brigade forced its way up the 300 foot high incline. As they reached the top the men halted, aimed, and unleashed a volley into the rebels. The rebels responded and Oates saw men fall around him struck by the miniés. The men fixed bayonets and charged forward, passing Gen. Spinola as he lay on the ground wounded. They gave another ferocious shout and sprinted right at the rebels. The Rebels fled with a few of the Excelsiors in pursuit. Col. Farnum of the First Regiment took command and briefly restrained the brigade so the men could fall into an ordered line. The Rebels had fled to a second hill and the Excelsior Brigade needed to dislodge the Rebs from this one as well.[70]

Slightly winded, Oates and the brigade again started to move forward. The Rebels fired down upon them with muskets and artillery, but still the Excelsiors pressed onward. The line began to break up coming up the second crest, not from the fire, but because some men were faster than others and pushed forward more quickly. The Rebels at the top of the hill were pouring on the musket fire, but the Excelsiors charged into them, and in groups or singly, fought them hand to hand and threw the Rebels onto the ground to take them prisoner. Oates was exhausted, but he charged at the front of the attack and acquitted himself well. All around him the fighting was coming to a close as rebels surrendered to breathless Excelsiors. The officers rode through the men telling them to stop here. There would be no charge into the next hill; they had done enough for that day.

Oates looked at the scene around him. There were Excelsiors everywhere, mostly sitting to catch their breath, some of the recruits shaking at the thought of the bold charge they had just made. He saw on the crest of the hill the Fifth's colonel carrying the flag, and coming up the slope behind him the color sergeant who had been too fatigued from the first charge to carry the colors for the second. Oates walked back to his company to inquire as to who had been shot. The casualties had been somewhat light. They would find out later that the brigade suffered only 75 dead and wounded. The men checked who was around, looked back down the slope for bodies, and saw that Lt. Preston was not with them. The man who started the war as a sergeant and earned his commission through hard work and bravery, the man wounded at Chancellorsville and only recently returned to his men, had been killed charging the hills. He was a Pittsburgher, and Oates would have to write something to Preston's parents about him.[69]

Night fell and the Excelsiors assembled for another battle soon. Day broke and scouts reported back to Meade that Lee had been marching south for the entire day before and were now miles away from their pursuers. The Excelsior Brigade's fight, named Wapping Heights after the hills, had not been the start of a great battle, but a diversion and accomplished little for the Union. The men were proud of their fight, and it would play well in the papers, but it did little to destroy the Confederacy.[70]

Oates walked in from picket duty on the banks of the Rappahannock once again. Lee had finished his escape from Gettysburg and was back below the same river he had set out from, twenty or so miles upriver from the old camps near Fredericksburg, but the same river nonetheless. Oates and the men were all despondent that Lee escaped. They had thought that this time, at least, Bobby Lee had made a mistake and they would be able to catch and destroy his army. They did destroy part of it, killing, wounding, or capturing forty percent of the enemy, but the Army of Northern Virginia still blocked the Union's path to Richmond.

As Oates walked back to camp he saw men lying next to their knapsacks completely worn out. For two months they had been marching, stopping only to fight the biggest and bloodiest battle of the war and to charge up two hills into the muzzles of enemy muskets. They had lost over a hundred men during the Gettysburg campaign, which, as Oates looked across the river and saw the Confederates safely encamped with the wide Rappahannock as protection, he was forced to admit was over.

Oates returned to camp, to the increasingly smaller area that his company occupied. Some of the men around him were talking about the prospects for the next battle that summer. Others discussed what type of wild berries would comprise their next non-army meal.

Oates arrived at the little patch of grass he was currently calling home. Men around him were cooking dinner while others were just sat and talked. Oates looked up from his seat and saw someone in civilian clothes. All the boys stirred themselves and approached the middle-aged couple who had come to camp. It was Mr. and Mrs. Preston, the parents of their own Lt. Charles Preston. The men greeted the Prestons and began talking about what a fine man Charley was, and telling them how he had fought and died. The Prestons had come to get their son's body. The men did what they could to comfort them, but they knew that it was unlikely his body would be recovered. At Wapping Heights the dead had been buried on the field in anticipation of another big fight, and it would be extremely difficult to find his unmarked grave. The whole company keenly felt the loss of their 19-year old commander and doubted that they would ever get another like him. There Oates was, talking to a dead friend's parents about a soldier who had been alive the last time Oates was on the Rappahannock. Over the course of the two months' campaign the Excelsior Brigade had lost an excellent man in Charley Preston and dozens like him. All they had to show for it was a blocked rebel offensive and reports that the rebels had lost more. All they had to look forward to were recruits who had been drafted unwillingly into the army and had not the fortitude, strength or experience of their own poor Charley.[71]

Chapter Eighteen

And the War Drags On

Camp near Freeman's Ford, Virginia

August, 1863

ates took a swig of milk from his canteen. It had cost him only 25 cents for the milk, a bargain. Oates' messmate Jake picked up a tin of stewed apples that had been sitting over the fire and took a spoonful. A second later he shouted, jumped up, and began spitting out the food. The men around him fell to laughing as Jake spat out a yellow jacket that had hitched a ride on the apples. He returned to the fire grimacing from the sting and poked and prodded his food for the rest of the meal. That was the only problem about this camp. It was full of yellow jackets, and *"if you kill one there is 10 come to its funeral."*[72]

Oates dug into the feast before him. No longer were the men living off crackers and salt pork. They had fresh meat, fresh and dried fruit, ripe corn, green beans and potatoes. They were living on the top of the pile, as they called it, some of the meals better than ones they had in civilian life.

Oates and the mess finished their food and stored the leftovers away for tomorrow's breakfast. The men sat back and relaxed, some of them smoking pipes and cigars if they had them, the smell of tobacco mingling with the sweet pine scent wafting from the trees around them. Oates looked around and thought how lucky he was to be in this camp. It was in the middle of dense woods and there were many small saplings in between the tents. The trees gave the camp solitude, a park-like feel, and most importantly, provided shade as the Virginia summer lingered on into late August.

A man from another company was walking by and he stopped to talk a while. He had been on picket that day, and was telling men the funny stories of what he had seen standing near the river. It had been a slow day and little of interest had happened, but he had seen a rebel run to the top of the hill on the opposing bank, look around for a second, then run back down and out of sight. The men laughed at this. Probably the rebel was hoping to find the river unguarded. To his disappointment the Excelsior Brigade was still present and blocking the way.

After Lee had escaped back to south of the Rappahannock River, Meade sent detachments of his army to most fords along the river so he could control the gateways for Union offensives south of the river and so that Lee could not slip northwards again. In this capacity the Excelsior Brigade had been sent to Freeman's Ford along the upper stretches of the Rappahannock. The rest of division was back at the army's main camp where the other brigades had drill and inspection every day. The Excelsiors felt sorry their comrades did not have as easy a time as they were having, a strange and pleasant feeling for the veterans. They, in their idyllic camp amid the pines, had nothing but picket duty once every fourth day. The balance of the time was free for the soldiers to do with as they chose.

The man left to return to his own company and the mess stopped talking for a while. The camp was silent except for the buzzing of the yellow jackets and the hum of activity from other companies. The sky grew dark, and one by one the men filed into the tents to turn in for the night, a comfortable sleep in the woods with little chance of disturbance.

The next day the soldiers emerged from their tents late and milled around outside waking up and rubbing their eyes. Over a small meal of bread and meat the mess discussed what they were going to do that day. Most of them were going out foraging, searching for fresh food the army didn't provide. There were several cornfields nearby, the river had plenty of eels and catfish, and occasionally they would shoot some farmer's pig or sheep — always in self-defense, of course. There were vegetables to be confiscated and fruit to be picked, and in fact much of what they ate at that camp did not come from Uncle Sam.

Oates did not feel like foraging that day. He had heard that there was an event in the camp of the Fifth Corps nearby, and he was going to head over there and see it. He arrived there to find the corps all drawn up by division on a slope. Oates pushed through to a spot where he could see all that would be going on. It was a big hill, and if the soldiers of the Fifth Corps noticed the man walking on his own with a diamond on his hat, they did not give him a hard time.

It turned out to be an execution of five deserters that Oates had come to see. Oates heard a solemn dirge carry across the hillside and turned to see the Procession of the Condemned beginning. First came the Provost Guard with a brass band playing the Dead March. Then came soldiers with coffins and prisoners following their coffins. Finally came the doctors, pioneers, and the rear guard. The prisoners were marched along the entire line of spectators so that every soldier could get a good look at the deserters. They passed within a few feet of Oates and he saw the five men.

Their countenances were *"not so good."* They wore military pants, white shirts, black neckties and fatigue hats. The condemned looked frightened, and Oates could only imagine what was going through their minds. All the men there had risked death in battle. None had ever had to face a certain death. The prisoners were marched to where their graves had been dug. They were pushed to sit on their own coffins. The place was silent. 15,000 troops and not a word was spoken. A horn blew from headquarters, and the priests left the men. Their eyes were bandaged, and all was ready for the execution. The shouts of the captain rang across the subdued ranks of the audience. Shoulder arms. Make ready. Take aim. Fire. The muskets of the provost guard exploded and the prisoners slumped into their coffins. The guard did their duty well, and the prisoners' souls passed into eternity immediately, Oates thought. The coffins were closed and lowered into the graves, and the burial detail went to work shoveling the dirt. An officer shouted through the silence to break ranks and head back to camp, and the assembly soberly dispersed back to their tents.

Oates walked with those from the Excelsior Brigade who had also come to see the execution. The terror of the event, even for those who were not the condemned, was felt by all, and none wished ever to have to witness another execution. However, as the men talked, they agreed that it was necessary and that the Government had done perfectly right in shooting them. They had been runaway substitutes, men who volunteered to take the place of draftees for a fee. The men had collected their bounty and pay and then deserted, probably hoping to join up again under a different name and collect another bounty. The execution was nasty work, but if the threat of death was not put into the new troops, they might desert their post, costing the army men and money. None of the old soldiers had much sympathy for those who had not willingly enlisted to serve and even less for those who actively tried to hurt their country's armies. Apparently, there were lots of runaway substitutes in the Third Corps, and Oates expected more to die in the upcoming weeks.

Oates returned to camp as the mail was being distributed and he found he had a letter from an old friend back home. He read it thoroughly, soaking up the latest news from Pittsburgh. Most of the wounded from Gettysburg were home, recovering until they were able to return to the field. It was said that crutches were in great demand in Pittsburgh. If a man had a toothache he needed crutches, which would also get him out of reporting for duty. Oates had also heard that the wounded at home were not well enough to fight, only well enough to go out and dance. Yet unlike the runaways, Oates did not feel angry towards these skulkers.

Perhaps the comfortable camp had softened his outlook, or eating well had changed his disposition, or it was because the men shirking duty were wounded veterans he knew personally. While he had little sympathy for the deserting recruit, he could relate to the soldier who had been in the field for two years and now was only trying to connive another month at home. Oates said that he could not blame those men, "*if I was home I would not come out again until I was forced to.*"[73] Men who had avoided all battle were just poor cowards for whom Oates had little respect. Men who were not in camp because they had taken a bullet were honorable, and deserved a few weeks' relaxation. Oates knew most would be back eventually, and until then he would just stay in his lovely camp, eat fresh food, watch the seasons turn, and once every fourth day, fulfill his duty.

Oates dropped his equipment near his tent. The fireplace was roaring and he was thankful for the heat. It was cold outside, as he could expect for December. The fall of 1863 had been spent waiting for another big battle, the great fight that would do what Chancellorsville and Gettysburg had failed to do and open the way to Richmond. However, no such battle came. The brigade had been on expeditions, the first to Bristoe Station after Lee again moved north across the Rappahannock. Meade responded faster than Hooker had done that spring, though, and the Confederates found the Army of the Potomac in an entrenched position near Manassas. The Rebels fell back below the Rappahannock once more and the Union army followed. There had been one last attempt at a campaign before the snows set in. The Army of the Potomac tried to steal a march on the Lee and smash his flank. The Excelsior Brigade was in this campaign and fought well in a minor engagement, but when the extent of the Confederates' fortifications were seen at a creek named Mine Run, the campaign was called off and the soldiers returned to build winter quarters once more.

After Gettysburg, Oates had thought that the war would be over in six months.[74] Here he was, close to six months later, with the war still dragging on. He had survived another campaigning season, this one even worse than the last. The regiment had lost 150 men since leaving their last winter quarters and the number of men who had seen the inside of Camp Scott was constantly growing smaller.

On the brighter side, the men had survived more than two years in the army, and they could safely wait in their warm cabins for the spring and their terms of service to be complete. Only months remained until all who survived could proudly return home. Oates hoped he would be among those lucky ones.

Chapter Nineteen

Hoping for Home

Camp near Brandy Station, Virginia

Winter, 1863-64

ates pulled back from the pile of logs and kindling paper as the flames took hold. The fire grew and smoke billowed up the makeshift chimney as heat filled the small shanty. The army had been busy for this past week now that they returned from the Mine Run Campaign. The weather was cold, colder than Oates could ever remember for December.[75] The men had built up their tents into cabins and been busy constructing fireplaces with chimneys to draw away the smoke. They did not know if they would stay near Brandy Station for the whole winter but they had constructed their shelters solidly nonetheless.

The fire crackled and threw light across the room. The cabin was emptier than before; one of the mess had been hit during the last campaign, *"a nice wound in the thigh,"* and he was home recovering in a hospital.[75] The remaining men took out what they had to amuse themselves. Some brought out cards, Oates grabbed pen, ink and a piece of paper, one man unfolded an old newspaper he had scrounged.

Camp 5th Excelsior, Near Brandy Station, Dec 11, 1863 . . . Oates began only to be interrupted by a loud noise coming from the man with the newspaper. He was talking animatedly with one next to him about an article he had just read. Oates squinted across the room at the paper and realized what the man had just seen. He was holding the November 9th issue of the New York *Times*, the one reprinting the letter from Col. Brewster, commander of the Excelsior Brigade, to the Adjutant-General of the Army in Washington.

"The officers and men of this command," the man read aloud, "proud of its record, which has never been tarnished, and desirous of perpetuating it by remaining in the service till the close of the war, now offer to reënlist in the service of the Government for an additional term of three years . . ."[75a]

The man continued reading the conditions the Excelsior Brigade had for a mass extension of its service: first, they must be allowed to reorganize as a brigade of mounted infantry, and secondly, that they must be allowed to return to New York to fill their ranks.

One of the mess asked where he had been when the Excelsior Brigade had their big meeting and decided to a man that they wanted to reenlist for another three years. The rest laughed and went back to their own amusements. The men all knew that there was not a chance in the world that what Col. Brewster had proposed would ever go into effect. It was an interesting proposal, and on paper a good one. As the editors of the *Times* pointed out in an editorial, "Each one of these [veteran Excelsior] soldiers is worth three raw recruits; and each recruit introduced into a regiment, which has a skeleton, or cadre, of veterans, is worth twice as much as he would be if he formed part of an organization entirely unversed and inexperienced in the duties of the field."[75b]

Also, mounted infantry would surely help the Union cause. Already the Union had employed similar tactics at Gettysburg and in the west where cavalry occasionally dismounted and fought on the ground. Mounted infantry would have close to the same mobility as the cavalry but would carry more firepower using the infantry's Enfield muskets as opposed to the cavalry's weak carbines. A whole brigade of this, one full of experienced veterans, would do much in the east, perhaps giving the slow Union army the edge it needed when trying to outmaneuver the Confederates. But however perfect this plan was in the heads of editors in New York or Brewster at headquarters, Oates knew it would fail. The entire scheme depended on the entire brigade, or at least a large part of it, reenlisting for another three years. Oates knew that this would not happen.

As the fall and winter of 1863 wore on, the veterans of the Excelsior Brigade slowly shifted their mindset from awaiting the next battle to awaiting the day of their discharge. As they did this, the officials in Washington searched for ways to entice the soldiers to stay in the service. In October the men had been read orders that anyone who wanted to reenlist would receive 450 dollars bounty and be sent home until a new regiment was formed. It was a big offer, three years' soldier's salary at once and the possibility of not having to fight again if the war ended before the new regiment was formed. Plenty of men, especially those who had no families back home and for whom the army was as easy as their civilian jobs, had taken the money and signed up. The offer was good for someone who wanted to take up soldiering for a living, but neither Oates nor anyone else in his company reenlisted.

"*We have seen enough, or will have again our time is up,*" Oates wrote in October, "*We have made up our minds to never serve again, till the rest have been out, I mean the ones that have been fethering their nests scince this war began.*"[76] It was not that the men were soft on continuing the war to its end. All wanted the war to continue until the Confederacy unconditionally surrendered. Sickles, for example, was the most popular man in the army at the time for being, "*down on the rebels & sound on the union*" — but most felt they had done their part and were ready to go home.[75]

Oates finished his letter and looked it over. He had mentioned the visit Charles K. Graham, "*a fine man,*" had made to the brigade en route to his new command in North Carolina. He had mentioned what he thought of the Mine Run Campaign *("The children of Isreal was in the wilderness & Mother so was Mead's army & I seen enough to do me, the wildest & most desolate place I was ever in"*) and he had wished everyone well.[75] The letter looked finished, so he signed it, sealed it, and put it aside to mail in the morning. Oates turned to bed with the fire still roaring and the soldier across the room still baffled by the article. It did not give Oates any uneasiness. He was assured that all he had to do was make it through the coming winter and he would be out of the army and home at last.

Oates guided his horse over the stream swollen from the recent thaw. The horse splashed through the cold water and galloped across the field bright in the winter sun. The cold that had persisted from December through the New Year and into January of 1864 had finally snapped, and the army encamped near Brandy Station was getting a few days of mild weather. Oates had decided to take advantage of the relative warmth. He borrowed a horse and went out riding alone across the Virginia countryside.

Oates had a few more privileges now. A friend of his, George Getsinger, had been wounded at Mine Run and was in the hospital recovering. George had been the Left General Guide of the division and had asked Oates to take his spot until he returned. The guide worked at divisional headquarters and did not have to go on picket duty or carry a gun. George would likely return before the spring, before any action that would require the left general guide to perform its duties, so Oates took the offer. He still lived with his company and stayed with the men he knew, but escaped from the minor responsibilities they endured. That day, as his company went to take their place on the picket line, Oates watched them leave and took a pleasant ride by himself.

Oates slowed his horse down from a trot and slowly made his way across the frozen fields. The empty farmland was quite a change of scenery for him; camps were like small cities, and he was accustomed to living surrounded by thousands of other soldiers. Even when the brigade or regiment was posted away from the main army, the camp still had the population of a small town.

The camp that day had been busier than it had been all winter. There would be a grand ball the next night in the headquarters of Gen. French, commander of the Third Corps and many carriages containing the high society of Washington had been rolling around and discharging their well-dressed occupants. It was said that even Uncle Abe and his wife would be there. But Oates would not be going, even with his new position at the division. *"I suppose not one person will be admitted unless he has shoulder straps and big ones at that,"* he wrote.[77]

However, it was not as if the men had no functions of their own. Just a week ago there had be a fun time in the Fifth Regiment. They had a new flag presented to them by the City Council of New York to replace their tattered old one. This new flag had fifteen battles inscribed on it, with Chancellorsville, Gettysburg, Whapping Heights and Mine Run still to be added. Instead of medals, a soldier of the Civil War would point to his regimental flag, with names of their battles sewn

onto the stripes, to show where he had fought. The occasion of being presented
an updated flag was the source of a holiday in the regiment, and the Fifth had
some nice speeches by Doctor Calorighn, Gen. Prince, the divisional commander,
and Gen. Birney, commander of the first division of the Third Corps. The night
concluded with lots of good singing, and the men were pleased with their night
of merriment.

Yet even as their leaders were lauding them with speeches and civilians were
presenting them with flags, the army officials in Washington were keeping up
pressure for the men to reenlist. The bounties remained and were growing even
larger, and whole companies of the Third Regiment were putting in for another
three years. But Oates and most of the brigade knew what they wanted and would
not be dazzled by the enormity of the money offered. They wanted to go home and
be out of the service where a new flag was the highlight of the month and privacy
could only be found when a friend with a good job was wounded.

Oates finished his ride and led his horse back into its stable. The day had been
peaceful, but it did not change his mind that the army was not where he wanted to
spend the next three years. He would be back to the old routine of sitting around
soon and there was no chance he wanted that to continue for longer than it had
to. He had been in the army for two years and nine months now, and with the
thought of reenlistment completely out of mind, he had only to wait for his date
of muster to come up. Then, finally, he could go home.

Soldiers squatted on cracker boxes looking upwards. Activities that day were
done inefficiently and without attention. The men in camp were busy searching

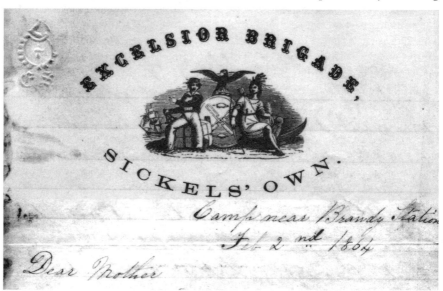

the sky. The shadows began to grow and the men gathered outside their tents for their evening meal, all discussing the news of the day. Some came in saying that while gathering firewood they had met a rebel deserter, and that he brought news of widespread dissatisfaction in the Southern ranks. Those who were on picket came with stories that they had heard musketry and cannon fire coming from the Confederate lines. These were met with knowing nods. They had heard this often themselves on the picket line. Some had put together the alleged rebel dissension and sounds of gunfire, and claimed that the rebels were fighting among themselves. They hoped the Confederacy would soon crumble from within. One man ventured that the day's latest reports were proof that the Confederacy was near an end.

"I hope to God it is so for our Government seems determined to crush them in the Spring," said Oates to nods of agreement.[78]

With the mention of spring the men looked up again at the partly cloudy sky. They began discussing the weather. The sun had been out most of the day and that indicated a late spring, some said. The men relaxed when they heard this. The ones who knew of the predictions had been watching the sun anxiously that day, measuring how much time it spent shining down upon them and how much it spent obscured behind clouds. They decided it was out, and that shadows could be seen by any creature who ventured outside. That meant a late spring, which was what they all wanted. The longer the winter kept the cold in the air and the roads muddy, the smaller the chance the veterans of the Excelsior Brigade would fight another major battle. All of the men sitting around the fire had survived more than two and a half years of war, and none wanted to die with only weeks remaining on their terms. They were set to go home in the spring and there was a chance that one more battle before then that could take all of them. And so, with renewed hope that they would be home before the roads thawed and the campaigning season of 1864 began, the veterans of Williamsburg, Chancellorsville and Gettysburg went into their warm tents to read, write, play cards and pass the remaining few hours of Groundhog Day.[78]

Oates pulled the wet boots off of his weary feet and set them down beside his bed. He had not written home in a few days and he quickly set pen to one of the few pieces of paper that had not yet been destroyed by the rain.

Camp Near Brandy Station, Feb. 13, 1864

Dear Mother,

I received your welcome letter of Feb. 8ᵗʰ and was glad to hear you are all so well as this leaves me at presant. We was out on reconoisance to the Rapidan, our division was reserve for the Second Corps. We lay about 2 days at the river & then turned about & came back to camp. The road's was in

an awfull condition, mudd over shoe tops. Some of our Company took a very
sudden notion for to reinlist & 9 of them as gone for 3 years more. New York
State is giving about One thousand dollars bounty & that is big inducements
for men, that want to follow soldiering for a living. But I am not one of the
number. I am tired of it & the sooner I am out of it the better. The Major is
offering our Company anything if we would only reinlist. But I guess he has
got all, he will get out of our company . . .[79]

Oates heard a noise coming from outside the tent, and he put down the letter to investigate. Wading out into the "terra aqua" Oates heard that some of the brigade had broken into a chorus of their latest favorite song, developed by one of their own:
"Mud to the right of us,
Mud to the left of us,
Mud all in front of us,
Mud in the rear of us,
Through it we flounder,
We sleep in mud at night,
Mud never out of sight;
Mud present day and night,
Everywhere around here."[52]
Oates continued outside to the laughing men. It was, in fact, muddy in camp. The weather had been very moderate recently, and most of the snow that had fallen during the winter had melted. But the men persevered and continued about their business nonetheless. Oates made his way back into the tent where men of his mess were having an animated discussion. The topic was one which the soldiers had been debating for months: when they would be released from the army.

The debate stemmed from the fact that none of the men knew when their service in the army had officially started. Those in the Pittsburgh company had all enlisted in the army on April 22nd, 1861, but had not been sworn into the service of the United States until June 22nd, 1861. They knew that they were not technically in the army until June, but they had been paid by the government starting in April, and why would they be paid if they were not in the army yet? None of them had considered the issue before because they had assumed that the war would end before their three years' term was up. Now that the date of muster out grew closer and there were no signs of the war ending before April, they needed to know. Should they be required to serve until June instead of April, not only would they be away from home for an additional two months, but two months that were in the heart of the campaigning season. During previous Mays and Junes Oates had fought at Williamsburg and Chancellorsville, and in each battle the brigade lost a quarter of its men. Should Oates be forced to endure another spring there might be another battle just as big — one which he might not survive. With the same thoughts in mind, all the men were hoping to be released in April. At that time the campaigning season may not have started — especially if there was a late spring as they hoped — and they might be able to escape the army without risking another battle.

The boys in the company discussed this issue constantly. There was little else to do during that winter, and the specter of another campaigning season loomed large at them. They might be able to get out of it, and having fought the nineteen battles inscribed on their flag, they knew they had done their part in the war. Oates sat back on his bed, heaving off his wet boots and pulling out his letter once more. He had done his fair share of talking, now he was content to let others split hairs over it. There were still over two months before they would find out one way or the other, still another definite two months left in the army. Oates had seen the caprices of army leadership, and he knew only time would tell whether another campaigning season was in store for him.

Oates looked through the boxes of food, oysters 50 cents a half can, salmon 25 cents a pound, haddock 20 cents, mutton 20 cents, venison 25 cents. The men with Oates took out their small bits of money and bought some meat from the suttlers. For a few nights, at least, they would be spared wormy crackers.[80]

The men from Oates' mess had the day off from duties and he had nothing to do for the division, so they went to Brandy Station to pick up civilian food. As they threaded their way through the carloads of Washingtonians coming down to the camp for generals' balls they spotted the suttlers' tables piled with real food. The prices here were high, of course, but the men paid nonetheless. Months of hardtack and salted meats gave fresh food a higher worth to soldiers than to comparatively spoiled civilians. The men bought what they wanted and with their next few meals in their hands began the walk back to the Fifth Regiment's camp at the foot of Pony Mountain.

The camp was buzzing with excitement. Oates put down his food and went outside to hear that the issue of their discharge had been taken up by yet another paper. The Excelsior Brigade was a well-known unit and there were many newspapers in the North that reported on them. This particular paper had agreed with others and stated the company would be discharged on April 22nd, the date of enrollment. The men had been talking of little else recently. There was a review a few days ago of the whole division, and the fifty or so ladies on horseback present had dominated conversation for a little while, but sure enough the issue of when they could go home once more took primacy.

Oates stayed outside for the rest of the day, cleaning up his tent's surroundings for a bit, talking with soldiers about when they would get out, and helping cook dinner in his mess, a regular day's work. He finished his meal and kicked out the fire, ready to head inside and pass the time until taps. It had been an interesting day, out of the ordinary with a trip to Brandy Station, but otherwise the same as usual. The sun set and the camp began to wind down for the night. Pickets were replaced and men took off their uncomfortable brogan shoes and heavy overcoats. The camp grew quiet and slowly the lights seen peeking out of cracks of the countless shanties dotting the hillside went out. Oates turned over in bed and started thinking about how he might pass the time tomorrow. A couple of the men near him were still talking, and he caught a few lines of what they said.

". . . only a few more days till the 22nd and then only two months till we get out . . ."

Oates smiled when he heard that and then something hit him. If it was only a few more days until the 22nd, he reasoned, then . . . He quickly tried to work out what today's date was and it dawned on him. Today had been February 19th, his birthday. He had gone the whole day without remembering it. He was 28. Hopefully, he thought, this would be a good year, and hopefully, he added, one without a battle.[80]

Oates flexed his fingers and continued to write gingerly. He had sprained his right hand a week ago and could barely grip a pen. He looked up from his letter at his cabin, quiet now for the first time in months. The army had increased the incentives for reenlistment again, giving a month long furlough to all who signed up for another three years. Men had to weigh the chance that they would die in those three years against the chance that they would die before their first term was up and never see home again.[81] A large rise in reenlistments ensued, and a number of Excelsiors chose to stay on. Others who had not reenlisted, mostly veterans, had nevertheless managed to receive furloughs during the winter and they were home as well.

Oates was not among those who departed camp. He was still officially working at division headquarters and was not eligible for the furloughs given to the veterans of the regiment. As such, he was stuck at a deserted camp, with nothing to do and no one to talk with. With only a dozen men in the company present, the energy had been sucked out of the whole camp and for most of the day the remaining soldiers sat in their empty shanties trying to pass the time until the others returned. It was difficult for Oates to bear, reading letters carrying news of the veterans having fun in Pittsburgh. Oates had not seen home in more than two years, since his only furlough in January of 1862. All he could do was to sit at the empty camp missing its usual fun and games, look outside at the soggy late winter landscape, and count the days until the boys returned when they could collectively count the days until they were out of the army and back home in Pittsburgh for good.

Oates went back to his bed to take a few moments out of the loud day to write a short letter home telling his family how the situation at camp was progressing.

Camp near Brandy St.
April 17th, 1864

Dear Mother,

I have received the Package you sent me & I am very much obliged to you for it. The Boys have returned to camp & look first rate.

They are Satisfied with their trip home.

I am in good health at presant & hope this will find you enjoying the same blessing.

We have been very buissy making out Muster Out Rolls for the Co. & they will be ready to go to head Quarters on Monday.

I do not know if they will be approved or not. A grait many thinks we will not get out till June. But the company is bound to go home in April.

We have one thing on our Side & that is, that their is no Order Issued, stating that the 3 Year's men shall stay till the date of Muster. Col. Holt is doing all he can for us.

The ones that are most positive that we will not go out in April are the Veterans. Yet they admitt that their time begins with their enlistment. I have seen men this week, Descharged from date of Enlistment.

But a few days will prove if it is April or June.

My cousins passed through Pittsburgh on their way to Annapolis Maryland a few days ago. One of the Boys informed me, that he saw my Father at Cowlins. I should think he could stay away from their.

I am glad to hear that times are so good at Pittsburg.

We have had very bad weather this Month. rain, all the time & it is raining now.

The Suttlers have been all ordered away. But I hear they are to remain another week.

We was reviewed last Thursday By Genl. Hancock & the Division looks first rate. Well I have no more news. So I will conclude,

Hoping I may be home in a few Days. to partake of some of the Ale in the celler.

Your affectionate Son,
Alfred K. Oates

Do not answer this letter till I write again For I will let you know as soon as they decide on it.

The company woke up filled with excitement. They had heard nothing as to when they would be discharged, but would find out one way or another today. The day was April 22nd, and the men hoped to be civilians by the end of it.

Their muster out cards were filled out and ready to be submitted. The lieutenant commanding the company had gathered the forms from the men and was about to go to division headquarters in the morning. The men lined up around the lieutenant and wished him well. They wished themselves well also. Their fate for the next two months lay in his hands. The men sat around waiting for an answer, only to be met by the lieutenant returning with no response, only orders. The whole corps would be reviewed today, he said, to which the groaning men stood and assembled to duty. They were on tenterhooks, having to wait while their future was being decided at the division headquarters.

The review went well, the men thought, and the corps looked ready to fight. But they did not want to fight. They might be free of further service to the government within hours, or they might still have two months left. There was no doubt in the men's minds that fighting would happen that spring, within the next two months. For the whole winter it seemed that the leaders were preparing for the great battle that would end the war. Ulysses S. Grant, the Butcher of Shiloh and Conqueror of Vicksburg had been promoted to General-in-Chief of all Union armies and he had taken office in the field with the Army of the Potomac. He was one of the few Union generals who had enjoyed consistent success, even if that success often came with large numbers of casualties. The army had been reorganized leaving three corps, the Second, Fifth and Sixth and a semi-independent Ninth attached to the army. The Third Corps, decimated at Chancellorsville and Gettysburg was summarily folded into the Second, forming the third and fourth divisions of that corps. The men of the old Third Corps despised the move, ripping them from their old unit, but they were allowed to continue wearing their diamond patches, which allayed some of their anger.

However, that was not a real concern to Oates. If he were lucky, he would neither be in the Second Corps nor need to concern himself with Grant's plans. He had fought under McClellan, Pope, Burnside, Hooker and Meade and he had done his duty. Now he wanted to go home. But as he returned to camp that night he heard disappointing news: everyone at the divisional headquarters had been at the review and there had been no action on the company's concern.

Oates went to bed that night with the tent buzzing with talk. Everyone had strong hopes that they would be released this month, and they thought it would be a "bad job for the Government if they keep the men till the date of muster."[82] He went to bed that night with dreams of being home in time to see the Sanitary Fair and following the Union army in the papers and not on the road. The next morning Oates woke up and the men poured out of their cabins ready to hear the news. All they heard was that the company had been detailed to go on picket for two days; there would be nothing done until the 25th. The men had to wait and wonder.

Two days later the men returned to their camps dirty and tired. They saw around them signs that the army was about to move. Marching orders had been issued, supplies were being loaded on wagons, and the weather had warmed enough to provide perfect campaigning weather for the army. Still, the veterans of Company A waited for word from division headquarters.

The next day the men were called out to the parade ground. This was it. They knew it. Now they would find out where they would be for the next two months. Now they would find out if Col. Holt's pressure had helped, if their prayers had helped. Now they would find out if Company A, 74th New York Volunteers, Second Brigade, Fourth Division, Second Corps, Army of the Potomac, would exist any longer.

The officer pulled out a piece of paper and began to read. Oates could barely contain himself as he urged the officer to get to the point. Then he heard it, and his heart fell and shoulders drooped. The company was stunned into silence at what they now faced. Terms of service began with the date of muster in, the officer read, and that meant that the company would not be dismissed until the 22nd of June. Also, the company should clear out all unnecessary baggage, as the army would soon be on the move to open the new campaigning season.[82]

Camp on the field May 11th
9 O'clock

Dear Mother

As the Christian Commission
is going to take some letters home
I take this oppertunity to let you
know I am still in good health
We have had 7 days of hard
fighting. We have only lost 2
wounded out of our company.
You must excuse this short
letter for I expect we will be
moving soon.
                    from your affictionate
        Son
            Alfred K Oates

Chapter Twenty

The Last Battles

Wilderness Campaign

May 4 — June 22, 1864

ates pulled a small piece of paper from his pocket. It was torn at one end from being ripped out of a friend's journal to provide him with something to let his family know he was still in the land of the living. The mail was going out this morning and there was a sense of foreboding of yet another terrible battle. Oates hurriedly dashed off a few lines home now should he be unable to later.

Camp on the Battle Field,
May 17th.

Dear Mother . . .

Oates dragged the pencil across the paper with his tired hands. His whole body was weary and worn down like everybody in the army. For the past two days the Army of the Potomac, 118,000 strong at the beginning of the campaign but now considerably less, had been busy making entrenchments while their generals planned. The men expected the fighting to resume any moment. During this campaign, only two weeks' old but seemingly having lasted forever, two days without massive casualties was a reprieve.

The army had left camp on May 4th and crossed the Rapidan River to begin its first campaign of 1864. The soldiers passed through the Wilderness, the dense woods that lay south of the river. The men recognized the land around them and they realized they were being led right through the Chancellorsville battleground. Scattered amongst the bushes and thickets were skulls and bones of former soldiers, and when they stopped for a rest, the men found the graves of those with whom they had fought. Soldiers visited their old friends, men they had grown up with, served with, and who they could only hope would be looking after them during the upcoming days.

The march continued and the men escaped from the trees only to receive orders to turn around and plunge back into them. Gen. Grant had hoped to pass through the Wilderness before meeting the Confederates, but elements from the Fifth and Sixth Corps ran into advance Confederate positions before the army had entered open farmland. The order was given to mass for battle, and for two days, May 5th and 6th the armies hammered at each other in a series of attacks and counter-attacks that got lost in the thick woods and stopped by entrenchments and massed volleys. On the first day the Excelsior Brigade had made an attack with the rest of the division but their lines had become disrupted and disarrayed from the undergrowth. Unseen Confederates unleashed volleys on them and after a tough firefight, the division was forced to fall back after sustaining heavy losses.

When fighting ended on the 6th it became apparent to Grant that he could not push the Confederates out of their positions in the Wilderness; he had already lost more than 17,000 men trying to with no success. He therefore disengaged and swung south. He made for the hamlet of Spotsylvania Court House but Lee, surmising his opponent's destination, beat him there. Fighting continued off and on as the armies maneuvered themselves into position. Then came May 12th. The Confederates had entrenched themselves in lines with a broad salient, "the Mule Shoe" as it was called. On May 10th a Union attack against the Mule Shoe had proven initially successful but was fought back when expected reinforcements did not arrive. Grant hoped that a larger attack would smash the Confederate lines and on the 12th ordered the entire Second Corps to throw themselves at the Confederate works with other corps performing ancillary attacks.

Oates wrote that the battle of May 12th, 1864 was, *"the hardest fighting I ever saw."*[83] At 4 A.M. the brigade charged the Confederate works and for seventeen hours the battle raged.[84] There was dreadful slaughter on both sides, and for hours the enemies were yards away firing point-blank. The Excelsior Brigade fought at a section in the lines later to be termed the "Bloody Angle." "Never before, since the discovery of gunpowder, had such a mass of lead been hurled into a space so narrow as that which now embraced the scene of combat," wrote one observer.[85] A large tree, two feet in diameter, was cut down by musket fire alone. The slaughter of Williamsburg, the close quarter fighting of Bull Run, the panic of Chancellorsville and the fury of Gettysburg were all at Spotsylvania and all multiplied.

Oates fought while trying to become as small as possible to avoid the tonnage of lead that was being thrown into the air. The military forces of an entire continent, the hatred and animosity that had caused this great war, the lives of thousands of America's citizens were all thrown into that Bloody Angle of a few hundred square yards. Both sides attacked each other and men died rather than cede ground. Units charged into the battle, pausing only to reload and receive fresh cartridges and, when possible, to help the wounded. The attack began before dawn and continued until after nightfall. By 9 P.M. the men were spent. The attack had killed thousands but had not broken the rebels in their entrenchments. The men slept in the field waiting for another attack to come.

The next day was rainy and no fighting came. The day after that, the 14th, the army began to slip to the left trying to outflank the rebels. Skirmishing was constant as the soldiers constructed earthworks and inched their way south. Oates had never seen so much fighting for so long. Since the 5th almost every day had been another battle, and while the fighting of the 5th and 6th would be called the Battle of the Wilderness and that of the 10th through 12th the Battle of Spotsylvania, to the soldiers on the field it had simply been one long week of marching and fighting. To Oates, taking a short break behind the entrenchments, it had been an abrupt and harsh renewal of the war. He had lost his friend Jake, one of his mess, in the first day of fighting, probably captured. The small regiment had lost 40 men since the start of May. The Army of the Potomac had suffered casualties of more than 30,000. And the fighting was nowhere near finished.

Oates finished his letter to his family and put it away in his coat to be sent home for him in the next mail or to be sent home by someone else if he were not to be so lucky. He fell asleep hoping he would survive until June when these three years of suffering and death would be over.

Oates stood on the hot field covered in dirt and tired to his bones. The campaign that started the Fourth of May had not yet finished. It did not look like this campaign could ever be considered truly finished. The army no longer filed out to battle, fought, and then returned to camp as it had done in prior years. After a battle, as long as there were still men standing, they disengaged and marched to another piece of Virginia to fight again. There was never an end, only brief pauses of a few days in which the armies gathered themselves for the next time they would smash against each other. On May 20th the Union army had moved south again, trying to slip by the Confederate flank. The two sides met on the North Anna River where battle ensued. Unable to drive out the Confederates, the Army of the Potomac had disengaged and moved south again. They found the rebels blocking their path at the crossroads of Cold Harbor and on June 1st, 2nd, and 3rd tried to break through the entrenched Confederates. When the smoke cleared there were 2,000 Confederate casualties and more than 7,000 Union dead, along with another 5,000 wounded.

Fortunately for the Excelsior Brigade they did not participate in the fighting at Cold Harbor. They were especially fortunate not to be in the attack of June 3rd in which 7,000 Union soldiers were mortally wounded in a half-hour. But even after the horrific butchery of Cold Harbor the campaign was not over, and after a few days the army again marched south. A month of constant fighting, in which the Army of the Potomac "literally marched in blood and agony from the Rapidan to the James," left the soldiers exhausted but stumbling towards yet another battle.[86]

The army crossed the James River in a flawless operation on June 14th and headed for Petersburg, a rail hub south of Richmond. The Excelsior Brigade was among the units who charged at the Virginia city's defenses. Neither side had much spirit left in them by this point. The optimism that had accompanied each army before most of its battles had disappeared. It was obvious to all that Grant's strategy was to hammer at the Army of Northern Virginia until nothing was left of it. Grant would pave the road to Richmond with the bodies of American soldiers, both Union and Confederate. The ordinary soldier now focused on doing what was asked of him and praying that he would not fall and become one more paving stone towards the termination of the war.

At Petersburg the Excelsior Brigade fought no longer as the brave legions of Sickles, their banners flying proudly in the air, but as exhausted and dirty shells of men who could barely remember a time when life did not consist of marching down dusty roads, biting bitter cartridges, or feeling the sore kick from the musket thud into one's aching body. The Union forces captured some of the fortifications around Petersburg, but the Confederacy rushed in enough reinforcements to prevent the city from falling. The sides took another pause to take stock of their accomplishments since leaving camp. Union forces were close to Richmond but with Confederates were still blocking their way and the end of the war was a long way off. The spring campaign had been difficult for both sides. During these two months the Army of the Potomac had lost 50,000 men, the Confederate Army of Northern Virginia, 30,000. Half of each army was now in prisoner camps, hospitals, or graves.

All this fighting left Oates standing on the open field under a southern sun still wearing the same uniform in which he had passed the tangle of the Wilderness and the killing fields of Spotsylvania. He had not taken a bath since leaving winter quarters — none of the men in the army had — and they were all dirty, hot, and tired. But now he would be free of the dirt and the blood. It was the moment that he had been hoping to come two months earlier. It was June 22nd and he was about to be mustered out.

The time between April and June had been without doubt the hardest months he had ever served. In the six weeks of constant fighting and marching the regiment had lost 53 men, some of those from Company A hoping they could have missed the fighting entirely. In the Wilderness, at Spotsylvania, on the North Anna, at Cold Harbor and before Petersburg the Excelsior Brigade had shown its worth. Its time of glory was past and most of its men gone. Its founder had been wounded the year before and no longer took the field of battle with them. Direct attacks had replaced skilled maneuvering as the mode of fighting and there was little for a brigade to do when all orders were to attack fortified positions and kill as many enemies as possible. Nonetheless the brigade fought on. It had stood up to the difficulties of the march and the horrors of combat and those who survived knew that they had without doubt served their country.

For three years they had fought with the Army of the Potomac, and shed blood in every one of its battles except First Bull Run and Antietam. At some battles, Williamsburg, Bristoe Station, and Whapping Heights, they fought almost alone. At others, Chancellorsville and Gettysburg, they fought among thousands of others, but fought best and on the hottest part of the field.

Three years earlier a crisis had swept the nation that threatened the very existence of the Republic. These men had done what the brave men of every generation and civilization have done since the start of time, and they answered the call to defend their homes. With the soaring words of Sickles ringing in their ears they had come together to save their nation. In the course of saving it there had fallen five hundred and ninety-five men who had once shouted their names at the twilight roll calls of the Fifth Regiment.

Ninety had died with musket in hand fighting the enemy. Thirty-six survived from wounds long enough to die in hospital tents reeking of gangrene and death. Sixty-nine fell sick and were claimed by the unseen enemies of dysentery, cholera, and malaria while they watched for Confederates. Many more had been wounded and fought for survival. If they were lucky they lived, broken and often missing limbs, but still alive. The little band standing before Petersburg carried the banners for all 900 who had set out from the Crosby St. barbershop with their young hearts full of fire.

Now their war was over, their contract with their country fulfilled. Oates had decided when he was 25 that he would put his life on hold to serve his nation. He had seen death and war and privation first-hand. He had marched across Pennsylvania, Maryland and Virginia. He had seen men, with whom the night before had shared his supper, shot dead beside him. He had not seen his family for two years, and even then only for a few weeks. He was 28 now, older, stronger, and infinitely more experienced in the world. He had given part of his youth to his country and when he read newspaper accounts of the glorious Excelsior Brigade he knew that the contribution was well received. But now his duty was complete and he was released from service. He would think no more of fighting, feel no more the fear when bullets whizzed by his head, and suffer no more the privations or the loss that accompanied the war, the daily dance with death and dullness. On that day outside of Petersburg, the lieutenant slowly read off the names of the men to be honorably discharged from service in the armed forces of the United States of America.

The lines were short and many were not there to be discharged. Charley Preston was dead, buried somewhere in the Bull Run mountains near where he fell capturing meaningless heights. Oates' messmate Jake was languishing in some Confederate jail and hoping the war would end before his life did so he could see Allegheny once more. Archy Robinson was in a hospital someplace fighting infection and gangrene. But Oates was there, still alive and still in good health.

Three years in the army had given him bouts of malaria and dysentery, but twenty-three battles had left him unharmed. He was fabulously lucky, more than any soldier could ever expect. He turned in his rifle, part of him for the last three years. He was given his papers of discharge. He was now, at last, out of the army and there would be no more war for him. There would be no more night marches, no more struggling through mud, no more Rebel yells preceding Rebel volleys. The 28 year old could now return to his house on the East Commons in Allegheny City and partake of the ale in his parents' cellar. He could return to his family and think about raising one of his own. No longer would he live day to day and hour to hour. He could lay down his tools of destruction and begin to build his life over again.

The men turned around, weights lifted off their backs, and they walked across the field. The dust had turned to golden earth and the oppressive heat to a soothing warmth. The former soldiers dispersed onto ships and railcars, all headed north. The Excelsior Brigade, the collective endeavor of five thousand men dedicated to preserving the freedoms they and their families cherished, was ended. The former warriors had handed the war over for another generation of young faces to finish. They had done their part and were done with fighting.

Oates boarded the ship and felt the rocking of the waves signal the end of his struggle. He was a free man once more, no longer subjected to the hardships and deprivations of the army. He turned his face northward, to family and to Allegheny City. After three terrible years for him and his country, the affectionate son, Alfred Kingston Oates, was finally going home.

Epilogue

Gettysburg, Pennsylvania

July 2, 1888

Oates removed his hat and bowed his head as the breeze coming off Seminary Ridge like the Rebel advance tousled his graying hair. The chaplain took the platform and spoke:

"As we to-day lay the corner stone of the monument which is to be erected in commemoration of the courageous deeds and painful sacrifices of our heroic dead, grant that the record thereof may be not merely chiselled upon marble tablets and columns, but inscribed also upon our loving and grateful hearts. May we all be preserved for years yet to come and be privileged often here to meet again and recount the story of our battle and triumph. May our children's children read, on all the monumental memorials, on this and every other field of our great strife, and upon the pages of history, the records of sacrifices, sufferings and deaths endured for their benefit, so that the spirit of a pure patriotism, of fidelity to truth, of devotion to freedom, and of love to our Union, may be cherished in their hearts down to the very latest generations."[87]

Excelsior Brigade monument at Gettysburg. Situated near Trostle Lane, it has five pillars representing the five original regiments of the brigade with a plaque for each detailing their performance at Gettysburg. Courtesy Gettysburg NMP.

Oates looked at the ranks of the former Excelsiors around him. They were no longer the young men who had charged into the abatis at Williamsburg with him. The twenty-five years since the Battle of Gettysburg had seen these men age and continue on with their lives. The boys that had once written home to their mothers and fathers saw time take away one generation and begin another. Since the war Oates had buried his parents, who had both lived into their eighties, and had started a family of his own. Soon after he returned from Petersburg he married Sarah Whittaker, two years younger than himself, and she gave birth to four children, George in 1865, twins Mary and Elizabeth in 1873, and William in 1875.

These children grew up in a time of prosperity and peace. The economy was booming, industry had led America to the forefront of the world, and there would be no more major wars until Oates' children were well into middle age. Oates had returned home, traded in his rifle for a blacksmith's hammer and spent his days creating and repairing.

"As our five regiments were always united in service and sentiment, it was fitting that their survivors should unite in consolidating their interests in this enduring monument. May it help to perpetuate the memory of the Excelsior Brigade, and of the sturdy soldiers of which it was composed."

For almost fifteen years after the war there was little interest in remembering the years when America had almost destroyed itself. In the South the countryside had been ravaged and the area was still under Reconstruction. The former Confederacy had battles yet to fight and would do so for years. In the North the soldiers became civilians and were too busy enjoying the freedom they had won and rebuilding their own lives to look back on what they had done.[81]

Then, around 1880 the men began to remember. The former soldiers found that with their lives in place once more, tied down by jobs and children, the most exciting times of their lives might be behind them. They thought less of the sufferings of war and more of the friends they had, of the fun times they had enjoyed in

Plaque from Excelsior Brigade Monument at Gettysburg detailing the regiment's role in the battle. The Excelsior monument contains five such plaques, one for each regiment.
Courtesy Gettysburg NMP.

camp, of the deeds they had done to shape this prosperous country. They realized that they had done something great in their youth that their own children would neither face nor understand. They began to remember and reacquaint themselves with former comrades. Military societies sprang up across the country, veterans' groups took hold, and the soldiers, lest their accomplishments fade from memory, began to populate the former battlefields with monuments.

It was for that reason that the Excelsior Brigade was there at Gettysburg on the 25th anniversary of that battle — to lay the cornerstone for their own monument. Made of marble, with five pillars representing the five regiments supporting a roof and an eagle, it was to mark for all time what the men of the brigade had done on that day on that field.

"If I cannot recite the history that lay behind us on the 2d of July, 1863, still less can I call up in separate mention the men by whose toils and deeds it had eliminated . . . But many, alas, many more, were absent from us in another and sadder separation. We had left them behind sleeping in soldiers' graves. Under the pines of Williamsburg, beside the flowing stream of the Chickahominy and the Rappahannock, and on Manassas Plain, we had laid them down with tears and farewells. If the dead are mindful of the living and can visit them, may we not think that their dear spirits hovered over us that day and kept its viewless company while we moved out to battle . . . A long and shining list it was already, the roll of our heroic fallen, ere it was augmented by the names which that dread afternoon was to hallow with its deathless renown."

With remembering the war came remembering their fallen companions. While they had emerged from the fires of their youth to live once more and run the full course of life, many who they once knew and served with would never leave the war. While Oates had been able to go home and see his family again, to enjoy the delights of life, to have children and raise them in peace, there were those like Charley Preston who would never leave the battlefield. They would never enjoy what they had fought for, never age, never be anything more than the young men who had given the last full measure of devotion to their country. All that the old men standing around the monument's cornerstone had done in the past twenty-five years was possible only through the sacrifices of those who were not there. The survivors had been the lucky ones, for whom the war was a chapter in life and not the end of it.

"A common sentiment and a common experience, in hardships, in peril, in successes, in reverses, in joy and in grief, have long ago fused all differences, dissolved all prejudices, and they are of one mind and one heart, brothers of the flag together, bound each to each in the indissoluble bond of that comrade sympathy that passes the love of women, and that is stronger than death."

The connection Oates had to the Excelsior Brigade, that entity that lived in the minds of a few thousand men across the country, who had joined together to defend their country, who had endured three years together, was one that could never be broken. He would live on for many more years, dying at the age of 71 in 1907 at a veterans' home in Ohio, but never forgetting his time in the brigade. Dan Sickles would continue his controversial ways, alleged affairs with a Queen of Spain, another trip to Congress, and an embezzling scandal, but through it all he appeared to have true affection for his men. The man who always was working for himself, always trying to further his career, seemed to possess true selflessness and devotion for his men and their memory, be it in Congress or on the New York Monuments Commission. His men, in return, always cared for him. They knew that years before, when Sickles was drawn and pallid from loss of blood after Gettysburg, the doctors could discern from his feverish murmurings, "God Bless the Third Corps, God Bless the Third Corps."

Sickles the general and Oates the private had both made it through the war and were both back at the former battlefield to reunite with their Excelsior family. Before the war Oates had separated himself from his family to defend them. After the war he returned to them. During the war he had found another. Now, long after he last left them, Oates was back among those with whom he had shared three trying years, the brothers he had found and lost, those who had survived to return to peace like him, and those who had found peace through pain and battle.

"No graves were ever so eloquent as these. What do they say? 'Hear us, ye living, who once pressed our hands. We died while our blood was leaping in the pulses of our prime. Let your hearts beat ever true response to the high calling of a patriot's duty. We gave our lives; give yours freely, wholly, purely to the service of God and Right and Liberty.'

In the heat and burden of our remaining day, my comrades, let our ears be always open to this voice crying to us from the ground. May we hear it from out the distant years behind us, saluting us and cheering us on, mingling in one harmony with the Divine voice from the heavens above, that ever more bids us endure hardness as good soldiers on this whole field of life's campaign."[65]

The speeches ended and the cornerstone was laid. Oates looked out across the landscape. It was lovely ground, the trees green and swaying gently in the breeze, the sky clear and the sun lending its warmth to the former soldiers. Peaches from the orchard where men had once fought and died by the thousands were ripening and nearly ready to be carted off to the market. The slope behind him was no longer a mass of young men shooting, stabbing and clubbing each other in furious violence. It was a field of green grass, a backyard once more. Home was only a short train ride away. Through the sacrifices of those absent, perpetual youths, through his own sacrifices and those of the men around him, Gettysburg was not a place of fear and danger, but one of community, where men from across all of America could come together and remember past days in peace.

Oates made his way through the crowd, greeting those he had not seen in years. The time now was for remembering and enjoying the life they were lucky enough to have. They left it up to Sickles and others who continued to serve them to establish monuments so that long after they had settled into graves of their own the three years of privation and loss they gave to their fellow man would be remembered by those who had benefited from their efforts. That would be the job for years to come, but not for that day. That day was for finding old friends and sharing a laugh. They had done their duty and their story was finished.

Appendices

Appendix A

Commanders of the Excelsior Brigade

Col. (later Brig. Gen.) Daniel Edgar Sickles. May 1861 - April 6, 1862; May 23 - July 1862.

Col. Nelson Taylor. April 6 - May 23; July - October 1862.

Col. George B. Hall. October - December 1862.

Brig. Gen. Joseph W. Revere. December 1862 - May 4, 1863.

Col. J. Egbert Farnum. May 4 - mid-May 1863.

Col. William R. Brewster. May 1863 - Muster out in July 1864.

Appendix B

Commanders of the Fifth Regiment, Excelsior Brigade

Col. Charles K. Graham. June 1861 - April 1862, May - July 1862.

Lt. Col. Charles H. Burtis. April - May 1862

Capt. Henry M. Alles. early August 1862

Maj. Edmund Price. late August 1862

Lt. Col. William H. Lounsbury. Sept 1862 - May 4, 1863; November 1863 - March 1864.

Maj. Henry M. Alles. May 4, 1863; November 1863 - March 1864 when Lt. Col. Lousbury was often ill.

Capt. Francis E. Tyler. May 4 - late May 1863

Lt. Col. (later Col.) Thomas Holt. May, 1863 - July 2 1863; April - June 1864.

Capt. William Conway. July 2, 1863 - October 1863

Major Abram L. Lockwood. June 1864 - July 1864

Appendix C

Company Profiles

Company A
Raised in New York City and Pittsburgh, PA
Mustered out June 21, 1864

Company B — Formerly Co. C, U.S. Zouaves
Raised in New York City and Pittsburgh, PA
Mustered out June 26, 1864

Company C
Raised in Long Island and Staten Island
Mustered out July 6, 1864

Company D
Raised in Cambridgeport, MA
Mustered out June 19, 1864

Company E
Raised in New York City
Mustered out August 3, 1864

Company F
Raised in Tidioute, PA
Mustered out August 3, 1864

Company G
Raised in New York City (Brooklyn Navy Yard Dockworkers)
Mustered out June 28, 1864

Company H
Raised in New York City (Brooklyn Navy Yard Dockworkers)
Mustered out August 3, 1864

Company I
Raised in New York City (Brooklyn Navy Yard Dockworkers)
Mustered out August 3, 1864

Company K
Raised in New York City (Brooklyn Navy Yard Dockworkers)
Mustered out August 3, 1864

Appendix D

Full list of engagements and expeditions of Fifth Regiment[5]

Expedition to Lower Maryland	Sept. 15 - Oct. 2, 1861
Expedition to Matthias Point, Va.	Nov. 9
Advance on Manassas, Va.	March 10-13, 1862.
Expedition from Dumfries to Fredericksburg, Va.	March 18
Reconnaissance from Liverpool Heights to Stafford Court House, Va.	April 4
Skirmish, Stafford Court House	April 4
Peninsular Campaign	April 10 - July 1
Siege, Yorktown	April 10 - May 4
Battle, Williamsburg	May 5
Battle, Fair Oaks	May 31 - June 1
Seven Days' Battles	June 25 - July 1
Engagement, Oak Grove	June 25
Engagement, Savage Station	June 29
Engagement, Glendale	June 30
Battle, Malvern Hill	July 1
Reconnaissance, Malvern Hill	Aug. 5
Campaign, Second Bull Run	Aug. 16 - Sept. 2
Engagement, Bristoe Station	Aug. 27
Battle, Second Bull Run	Aug. 29 - 30
Operations on Orange & Alexandria Railroad near Fairfax Station, Va.	Nov. 10 - 12
Battle, Fredericksburg	Dec. 2 - 15
Burnside's Mud March	Jan. 20 - 24, 1863
Operations at Rappahannock Bridge and Grove Church, Va.	Feb. 5 -7
Chancellorsville Campaign	April 27 - May 6
Battle, Chancellorsville	May 3 - 5
Gettysburg Campaign	June 11 - July 24
Battle, Gettysburg, Pa.	July 1 - 3
Pursuit to Manassas Gap, Va.	July 5 - 24
Engagement, Wapping Heights	July 23
Bristoe Campaign	Oct. 9 - 22
Advance to line of the Rappahannock	Nov. 7 - 8

---

5   Taken from Seventy Fourth New York Infantry Capsule History, compiled by John Walter.

Engagement, Kelly's Ford	Nov. 7
Mine Run Campaign	Nov. 26 - Dec. 2
Engagement, Payne's Farm	Nov. 27
Demonstration on the Rapidan	Feb. 6 - 7, 1864
Wilderness Campaign	May 4 - June 12
Battle, Wilderness	May 5 - 7
Combat, Po River	May 10
Battle, Spotsylvania (Bloody Angle)	May 12
Engagement, Harris Farm	May 19
Operations on the line of the North Anna River	May 22 - 26
Operations on the line of the Pamunkey River	May 26 - 28
Operations on the line of the Totopotomoy River	May 28 - 31
Battles about Cold Harbor	June 1 - 12
Assault, Petersburg	June 16
Engagement, Jerusalem Plank Road	June 22
Demonstration on north side of James River	July 27 - 29
Engagement, Deep Bottom	July 27 - 28

Appendix E

Casualty list of Fifth Regiment[6]

Place.	Date	Killed. Officers	Killed. Enlisted men	Wounded. Died. Officers	Wounded. Died. Enlisted men	Wounded. Recov'd. Officers	Wounded. Recov'd. Enlisted men	Missing. Officers	Missing. Enlisted men	Aggregate
	1861.									
Near Matthias Point, Va.	Nov. 9									
At Matthias Point, Va.	12									
	1862.									
Stafford Court House, Va.	April 6									
Siege of Yorktown, Va.	April 10 - May 4			1						1
Williamsburg, Va.	May 5		41		8	3	43	1	47	143
Fair Oaks, Va.	May 31 - June 1		5		3	1	16			20
Fair Oaks, Va.	June 12									
Seven Days Battle, Va.	June 25 - July 2				3					
Oak Grove	June 25	1	2		1		32		15	55
Glendale	30									
Malvern Hill	July 1				1					
Gen. Pope's Campaign, Va.	Aug. 26 - Sept. 2									
Kettle Run	Aug. 27	2	9	1	4	9	53		12	98
Groveton	28		6		2					
Bull Run	30									
Fredericksburg, Va.	Dec. 11 - 15									
	1863.									
Chancellorsville, Va.	May 1 - 3		3		2	3	17		15	40
Gettysburg, Pa.	July 1 - 3		12	1	5	5	63		3	89
Wapping Heights, Va.	23	2	2				7			11
Kelly's Ford, Va.	Nov. 7									
Mine Run Campaign, Va.	Nov. 26 - Dec. 2									
Locust Grove	Nov. 27		1		1		8			10
	1864.									
Wilderness, Va.	May 5 - 7		1		2		14			17
Spotsylvania Courthouse, Va.	6 - 21									
Landiron's Farm	10	1	2		1	1	10		1	16
Salient	May 12									
North Anna, Va.	22 - 26									
Totopotornoy, Va.	27 - 31					1	6		5	12
Cold Harbor, Va,	June 1 - 12			1						1
Before Petersburg, Va.	June 15 - Aug. 12									
Assault of Petersburg, Va.	June 15 - 19									
Weldon Railroad, Va.	21 - 23		2		1		7			10
Deep Bottom, Va.	July 27 - 29						1			
Loss at minor affairs							1		1	2
Total loss		6	82	3	33	24	277	1	99	525

---

6   From New York in the War of the Rebellion, 3rd ed. by Frederick Phisterer.

Citations

1. Keneally, T., *American Scoundrel: The Life of the Notorious Civil War General Dan Sickles*. 1st ed. 2002: Nan A. Talese. 400.
2. Mark, S., (2000). *In 1859, Capital Was a Wild, Wild, Washington*. The Washington Post. Washington. A01. 7/17/2000.
3. Launer, T., (1861). *Gen Sickles' Excelsior Brigade*. The New York Times. New York. June 4, 1861.
3a. Uncited, (1861). *A New Volunteer Company*. The New York Times. New York City. April 18, 1861.
4. Oates, A.K., *#1 Camp Scott*, July 5, 1861.
5. Oates, A.K., *#63 Camp Excelsior*, March 31, 1863.
6. Billings, J.B., *Hardtack and Coffee*. Lakeside Classics, ed. R. Hartwell. 1960, Chicago: The Lakeside Press. 483.
7. Oates, A.K., *#2 Camp Scott*, July 25, 1861.
8. Nemo, (1861). *Reconnoissance of the Excelsior Brigade in Southern Maryland*. The New York Times. New York. Oct. 3, 1861.
9. Guerney, W.S., Nov. 2, 1861.
10. Oates, A.K., *#3 Port Tobacco*, November 7, 1861.
10a. Uncited, 1861, *Jack Tars, Ahoy*, New York City. Baker & Godwin, Printers. Recruitment Poster for Co. I, 5th Reg., Excelsior Brigade.
11. Graham, C.K., *Report of the 74th New York Infantry's Expedition to Matthias Point*. 1861, Official Records of the War of the Rebellion.
12. Oates, A.K., *#66 Camp 5th Excelsior*, April 22, 1863.
13. Nemo, (1861). *The Lower Potomac*. The New York Times. New York. Nov. 7, 1861.
14. Cedma, (1861). *From the Lower Potomac*. The New York Times. New York. Dec. 11, 1861.
15. Oates, A.K., *#5 Camp Magaw*, January 20, 1862.
15a. Uncited, (1862). *Wikoff and Sickles*. The New York Times. New York. Feb. 15, 1862.
15b. Uncited, (1862). *Gen. Sickles' Farewell to his Soldiers*. The New York Times. New York. Apr. 10, 1862.
16. Oates, A.K., *#10 Some place in Virginia*, April 14, 1862.
17. Oates, A.K., *#14 Camp Winfield Scott near Yorktown*, May 3, 1862.
18. Oates, A.K., *#13 Camp Winfield Scott near Yorktown*, April 29, 1862.
19. Oates, A.K., *#12 Camp Winfield Scott near Yorktown*, April 19, 1862.
20. Oates, A.K., *#15 Mortar Battery Attack Plan for Attack on Yorktown*, May 2, 1862.
21. Oates, A.K., *#18 Place not listed*, May 12, 1862.
22. Burtis, C., *Report of the 74th New York Infantry at Williamsburg*. 1862, Official Records of the War of the Rebellion.
23. Oates, A.K., *#19 Camp near West Point*, May 12, 1862.
24. Sigourney, L.H., *Lieut. Frank Howard Nelson, of the 1st Regt. Excelsior Brigade, N.Y.: died at the Battle of Williamsburg, Virginia, aged nineteen*. 1862, Hartford, Conn.: Privately published.
25. Oates, A.K., *#21 Williamsburg*, No date given. Early May 1862.
26. Cedma, (1862). *Return of Gen. Sickles to his Brigade - His Enthusiastic Reception - How his Command Feel Toward him*. The New York Times. New York. May 31, 1862.

27. Ellis, T.T., *Leaves from the Diary of an Army Surgeon: or, Incidents of Field, Camp, and Hospital Life*. 1863, New York: John Bradburn.
28. Oates, A.K., *#28 Fair Oaks*, June 5, 1862.
29. Oates, A.K., *#29 Camp near Fair Oaks*, June 19, 1862.
29a. Uncited, (1862). *News from the Peninsula*. The New York *Herald*. New York. June 20, 1862.
30. Oates, A.K., *#25 Chickahominy Swamp*, May 29, 1862.
31. Sickles, D.E., *Report of the Excelsior Brigade at Oak Grove*, July 7, 1862.
32. Oates, A.K., *#36 Camp near Harrison Landing*, July 13, 1862.
33. Sickles, D.E., *Report of the Excelsior Brigade on the 1st of July (Battle of Malvern Hill)*, July 9, 1862.
34. Burton, B.K., *Extraordinary Circumstances: The Seven Days Battles*. 2001, Bloomington: Indiana University Press. 524.
35. Sickles, D.E., *Report of the Excelsior Brigade on the 29th and 30th of June (Battle of Glendale)*, July 9, 1862.
36. Oates, A.K., *#41 Harrison Landing*, August 7, 1862.
37. Oates, A.K., *#35 Malvern Hill*, July 6, 1862.
38. Oates, A.K., *#39 Camp near Harrison Landing*, July 31, 1862.
39. Oates, A.K., *#37 Camp near Harrison Landing*, July 19, 1862.
40. Oates, A.K., *#43 Near Alexandria*, September 8, 1862.
40a. Uncited, (1862). *Military Movements in the City*. The New York *Times*. New York City. Aug. 7, 1862.
41. Cedma, (1862). *The Excelsior Brigade*. The New York *Times*. New York. Sept. 28, 1862.
42. Oates, A.K., *#42 Near Alexandria*, September 5, 1862.
43. Oates, A.K., *#45 Camp near Fort Lyon*, September 11, 1862.
43a. Uncited, (1862). *The Excelsior Brigade*. The New York *Times*. New York City. Aug. 9, 1862.
43b. Uncited, (1862). *The Excelsior Division*. The New York *Times*. Sept. 8, 1862.
44. Oates, A.K., *#46 Camp near Alexandria*, September 19, 1862.
45. Oates, A.K., *#47 Camp near Alexandria*, September 30, 1862.
46. Oates, A.K., *#53 Camp near Falmouth*, December 22, 1862.
47. Oates, A.K., *#55 Camp near Falmouth*, January 10, 1863.
48. Oates, A.K., *#56 Camp near Falmouth*, January 18, 1863.
49. Mitchell, R., *Civil War Soldiers*. 1988, New York: Viking Publishing, Inc.
50. Oates, A.K., *#64 Camp near Falmouth*, April 9, 1863.
51. O'Hagen, J.B., S.J, *The Diary of Joseph B. O'Hagen, S.J., Chaplain of the Excelsior Brigade edited by the Rev. William L. Lucey*. Civil war history, 1960. VI: p. 402-409.
52. Chapman, F.G., (1864). *How the Army of the Potomac Enjoys Itself*. The New York *Herald*. New York. March 23, 1864.
53. Oates, A.K., *#68 Camp 5th Excelsior*, May 10, 1863.
53a. Uncited, (1863). *Our Special Army Correspondence*. The New York *Times*. New York. May 10, 1863.
54. Coyne, J.N., *Oration at the Dedication of the Excelsior Brigade monument at Gettysburg, July 2, 1888*, in *New York at Gettysburg*. 1900, J. B. Lyon Co.: Albany. p. 586-596.
55. Oates, A.K., *#71 Camp 5th Excelsior*, May 19, 1863.
56. Revere, J.W., *Report of the Excelsior Brigade during the Chancellorsville Campaign*. 1863, Official Records of the War of the Rebellion.
57. Cook, T.M., (1863). *Very Important Return of Hooker's Army to their Camps at Falmouth*. The New York *Herald*. New York. May 8, 1863.

58. Oates, A.K., *#72 Camp 5th Excelsior,* May 25, 1863.

59. Oates, A.K., *#54 Camp near Falmouth,* January 1, 1863.

60. Oates, A.K., *#73 Camp near Falmouth,* June 6, 1863.

61. Brown, H.L., *History of the Third Regiment Excelsior Brigade 72nd New York Volunteer Infantry 1861-1865.* 1902, Jamestown, NY: Journal Print Co.

62. Oates, A.K., *#76 Gum Springs, 5th Excelsior,* June 23, 1863.

63. Oates, A.K., *#75 Camp near Centerville,* June 18, 1863.

64. Rice, G., *Devil Dan Sickles' Deadly Salients,* in *America's Civil War.* 1998. p. 10.

65. Twichell, J.H., Chaplain of the Second Excelsior, *Oration at dedication of Excelsior Brigade Monument at Gettysburg, July 2, 1888,* in *New York at Gettysburg.* 1900, J. B. Lyon Co.: Albany. p. 575-582.

66. Pfanz, H.W., *Gettysburg - The Second Day.* 1987, Chapel Hill: University of North Carolina Press. 601.

67. Brewster, W.R., *Report of the Excelsior Brigade at Gettysburg.* 1863, Official Records of the War of the Rebellion.

68. Oates, A.K., *#77 Camp 5th Excelsior,* July 13, 1863.

69. Farnum, J.E., *Report of Excelsior Brigade at Wapping Heights.* 1863, Official Records of the War of the Rebellion.

70. Cook, T.M., (1863). *The Battle of Wapping Heights.* The New York *Herald.* New York. Aug. 1, 1863.

71. Oates, A.K., *#80 Camp near Beverly Foard,* August 4, 1863.

72. Oates, A.K., *#82 Camp at Freeman Foard,* August 22, 1863.

73. Oates, A.K., *#44 Camp at Freeman's Foard,* September 10, 1863.

74. Oates, A.K., *#78 Camp 5th Excelsior, near Middleborough,*

75. Oates, A.K., *#89 Camp near Brandy Station,* December 11, 1863.

75a. Uncited, (1863). *Patriotic Offer to the Government.* The New York *Times.* New York. Nov. 9, 1863.

75b. Uncited, (1863). *Re-enlistment of Troops - An Important Movement in the Army.* The New York *Times.* New York. Nov. 9, 1863.

76. Oates, A.K., *#87 Camp near Culpepper,* October 5, 1863.

77. Oates, A.K., *#91 Camp near Brandy Station,* January 24, 1864.

78. Oates, A.K., *#92 Camp near Brandy Station,* February 2, 1864.

79. Oates, A.K., *#93 Camp near Brandy Station,* February 13, 1864.

80. Oates, A.K., *#94 Camp near Brandy Station,* February 20, 1864.

81. Linderman, G.F., *Embattled Courage: The Experience of Combat in the American Civil War.* 1987, New York: The Free Press.

82. Oates, A.K., *#99 Camp near Brandy Station,* April 23, 1864.

83. Oates, A.K., *#70 Camp on the battlefield,* May 17, 1864.

84. Heslin, J.J., *From the Wilderness to Petersburg: The Diary of Surgeon Frank Ridgeway.* The New-York Historical Society Quarterly, 1961. **45**(2).

85. Walker, F.A., *History of the Second Army Corps.* 1886, New York: Charles Scribner's Sons. 737.

86. Bowman, J.S., ed. *The Civil War Day by Day.* 1989, Brompton Brooks Corporation: Printed in China. 224.

87. Bulkey, C.H.A., Chaplain of the First Excelsior, *Invocation at dedication of Excelsior Brigade Monument at Gettysburg, July 2, 1888,* in *New York at Gettysburg.* 1900, J. B. Lyon Co.: Albany. p. 574-575.

Bibliography

The largest sources of information for this book have been the 99 of Alfred Oates' letters that survived to be found in my aunt's attic, newspapers reports from the era and campaign reports written by Oates' commanders and collected in *The War of the Rebellion: A Compilation of the Official Records of the Union and Confederate Armies*, a 128 volume set published between 1880 and 1901. Oates' letters and the newspaper articles give most of the details for the camp sections. The letters, articles, and reports all contribute greatly to the information for the battles, especially for action below the brigade level. What these sources did not provide was supplied by the following list.

The Battle Atlas of the Civil War. Time-Life Books. 1991, Barnes & Noble: New York. 320.

Arnold, J. and R. Wiener, *Gettysburg July 2 1863 Union: Army of the Potomac*. Order of Battle, ed. J. Moore. 2000, Oxford, UK: Osprey Publishing. 96.

Benedict, G.G., *Letter to Free Press Nov. 3, 1862*, in *Army Life in Virginia: Letters from the Twelfth Vermont Regiment and Personal Experiences of Volunteer Service in the War for the Union, 1862-63*. 1895, Free Press Association: Burlington, VT.

Billings, J.B., *Hardtack and Coffee*. Lakeside Classics, ed. R. Hartwell. 1960, Chicago: The Lakeside Press. 483.

Bowman, J.S., ed. *The Civil War Day by Day*. 1989, Brompton Brooks Corporation: Printed in China. 224.

Brandt, N., *The Congressman Who Got Away With Murder*. 1991, Syracuse: Syracuse University Press.

Brewster, W.R., *Letter to Adjutant-General of the United States Army*. 1863, Printed in The New York *Times* of Nov. 9, 1863 in article "Patriotic Offer to the Government."

Brewster, W.R., *Report of the Excelsior Brigade at Gettysburg*. 1863, Official Records of the War of the Rebellion.

Brewster, W.R., *Report of the Excelsior Brigade from July 9 to July 26, 1863*. 1863, Official Records of the War of the Rebellion.

Brown, H.L., *History of the Third Regiment Excelsior Brigade 72nd New York Volunteer Infantry 1861-1865*. 1902, Jamestown, NY: Journal Print Co.

Bulkey, C.H.A., Chaplain of the First Excelsior, *Invocation at dedication of Excelsior Brigade Monument at Gettysburg, July 2, 1888*, in *New York at Gettysburg*. 1900, J. B. Lyon Co.: Albany. p. 574-575.

Burns, J.R., *Battle of Williamsburgh, with reminiscences of the campaign, hospital experiences, debates, etc.* 1865, New York: Privately published.

Burtis, C., *Report of the 74th New York Infantry at Williamsburg.* 1862, Official Records of the War of the Rebellion.

Burton, B.K., *Extraordinary Circumstances: The Seven Days Battles.* 2001, Bloomington: Indiana University Press. 524.

Catton, B., *The American Heritage New History of the Civil War.* 1996, New York: Viking.

Cedma, (1861). *From the Lower Potomac.* The New York Times. New York. Dec. 11, 1861.

Cedma, (1862). *The Excelsior Brigade.* The New York Times. New York. Sept. 28, 1862.

Cedma, (1862). *Sickles' Division.* The New York Times. New York City. Nov. 16, 1862.

Cedma, (1862). *Return of Gen. Sickles to his Brigade - His Enthusiastic Reception - How his Command Feel Toward him.* The New York Times. New York. May 31, 1862.

Chapman, F.G., (1864). *How the Army of the Potomac Enjoys Itself.* The New York Herald. New York. March 23, 1864.

Cook, T.M., (1863). *Very Important Return of Hooker's Army to their Camps at Falmouth.* The New York Herald. New York. May 8, 1863.

Cook, T.M., (1863). *The Battle of Wapping Heights.* The New York Herald. New York. Aug. 1, 1863.

Coyne, J.N., *Oration at the Dedication of the Excelsior Brigade monument at Gettysburg, July 2, 1888,* in *New York at Gettysburg.* 1900, J. B. Lyon Co.: Albany. p. 586-596.

de Fontaine, F.G., *Trial of Dan Sickles etc.* 1859, New York: R. M. De Witt.

Eicher, D.J., *The Longest Day: A Military History of the Civil War.* 2001, New York: Touchstone Books.

Ellis, T.T., *Leaves from the Diary of an Army Surgeon: or, Incidents of Field, Camp, and Hospital Life.* 1863, New York: John Bradburn.

Farnum, J.E., *Report of Excelsior Brigade at Wapping Heights.* 1863, Official Records of the War of the Rebellion.

Fowler, W. and E. Kerrigan, *American Military: Insignia, Medals and Decorations.* 1st ed. 1995, Edison, New Jersey: Chartwell Books. 160.

Fox, W.F., *Regimental Losses in the American Civil War, 1861-1865: A Treatise on the Extent and Nature of the Mortuary Losses in the Union Regiments, with Full and Extensive Statistics Compiled from the Official Records on File in the State Military Bureaus and at Washington.* 1889, Albany: Albany Publishing Co.

Graham, C.C.K., *Report of the 74th New York Infantry during the Seven Days Battles,*

Graham, C.K., *Report of the 74th New York Infantry's Expedition to Matthias Point.* 1861, Official Records of the War of the Rebellion.

Graham, C.K., *Report of the 74th New York Infantry at Seven Pines.* 1862, Official Records of the War of the Rebellion.

Guerney, W.S., Nov. 2, 1861.

Hart, O.H., (1862). *Military Announcements*. The New York Times. New York. Sept. 25, 1862.

Hennessy, J.J., *Return to Bull Run: The Campaign and Battle of Second Manassas*. 1993, New York: Simon & Schuster. 607.

Heslin, J.J., *From the Wilderness to Petersburg: The Diary of Surgeon Frank Ridgeway*. The New-York Historical Society Quarterly, 1961. **45**(2).

Howland, E.N.W., *Letter to Joseph Howland, Aug. 10, 1861*, in *Letters of a Family during the War for the Union 1861-1865*. 1899, Privately published. p. 360.

Hudson, C.O., Jr., *Civil War Williamsburg*. 1997, Mechanichsburg, PA: Stackpole Books.

Keneally, T., *American Scoundrel: The Life of the Notorious Civil War General Dan Sickles*. 1st ed. 2002: Nan A. Talese. 400.

Launer, T., (1861). *Gen Sickles' Excelsior Brigade*. The New York Times. New York. June 4, 1861.

Linderman, G.F., *Embattled Courage: The Experience of Combat in the American Civil War*. 1987, New York: The Free Press.

Livingston, B., *Civil War New York*. 1998, Robert E. Lee Civil War Round Table.

Lounsbury, W.H., *Report of the 74th New York Infantry at Fredericksburg*. 1862, Official Records of the War of the Rebellion.

Lounsbury, W.H., *Report of the 74th New York Infantry during the Mine Run Campaign*. 1863, Official Record of the War of the Rebellion.

Mark, S., (2000). *In 1859, Capital Was a Wild, Wild, Washington*. The Washington Post. Washington. A01. 7/17/2000.

McAfee, M., *Zouaves: The First and Bravest*. 1991, Gettysburg, PA: Thomas Publications.

McAllister, R., *The Civil War Letters of General Robert McAllister*, ed. J.I. Robertson, Jr. 1998, Baton Rouge: Louisiana State Univeristy Press.

Mitchell, R., *Civil War Soldiers*. 1988, New York: Viking Publishing, Inc.

Mitchell, R., *The Vacant Chair*. 1993, New York: Oxford University Press.

Nemo, (1861). *Reconnoissance of the Excelsior Brigade in Southern Maryland*. The New York Times. New York. Oct. 3, 1861.

Nemo, (1861). *The Lower Potomac*. The New York Times. New York. Nov. 7, 1861.

O'Hagen, J.B., S.J, *The Diary of Joseph B. O'Hagen, S.J., Chaplain of the Excelsior Brigade edited by the Rev. William L. Lucey*. Civil war history, 1960. **VI**: p. 402-409.

Pfanz, H.W., *Gettysburg - The Second Day*. 1987, Chapel Hill: University of North Carolina Press. 601.

Phisterer, F., *New York in the War of the Rebellion*. 3rd ed. 1912, Albany: J. B. Lyon Co.

Prince, H., *Report of the Second Division, Third Corps during the Mine Run Campiagn*, Dec. 6, 1863.

Program), C.B.S.A.B.P., *Bristoe Station*, Heritage Preservation Services.

Revere, J.W., *Report of the Excelsior Brigade during the Chancellorsville Campaign.* 1863, Official Records of the War of the Rebellion.

Rhea, G.C., *The Battle of the Wilderness: May 5-6, 1864.* 1994, Baton Rouge: Louisiana State University Press. 512.

Rice, G., *Devil Dan Sickles' Deadly Salients*, in *America's Civil War.* 1998. p. 10.

Sears, S.W., *To the Gates of Richmond: The Peninsula Campaign.* 1992, New York: Ticknor and Fields. 468.

Sears, S.W., *Chancellorsville.* 1996, Boston: Houghton Mifflin. 593.

Sickles, D.E., *The Republic is Imperishable: Speech Delivered in House of Representatives, Jan. 16, 1861*, Located in New York Public Library.

Sickles, D.E., *Report of the Excelsior Brigade at Fair Oaks*, June 7, 1862.

Sickles, D.E., *Report of the Excelsior Brigade on the 29th and 30th of June (Battle of Glendale)*, July 9, 1862.

Sickles, D.E., *Report of the Excelsior Brigade on the 1st of July (Battle of Malvern Hill)*, July 9, 1862.

Sickles, D.E., *Report of the Excelsior Brigade at Oak Grove*, July 7, 1862.

Sickles, D.E., *General Sickles's Memorable Interview with Mr. Lincoln*, in *The Religion of Abraham Lincoln.* 1900, G. W. Dillingham Company: New York.

Sickles, D.E., *Leaves from My Diary.* Journal of The Military Service Institution of the United States, 1902. **vi**(22).

Sigourney, L.H., *Lieut. Frank Howard Nelson, of the 1st Regt. Excelsior Brigade, N.Y.: died at the Battle of Williamsburg, Virginia, aged nineteen.* 1862, Hartford, Conn.: Privately published.

Smith, C., *Chancellorsvile 1863.* Osprey Military Campaigns, ed. L. Johnson. 1998, London: Osprey Military. 96.

Stackpole, G.E.J., *Chancellorsville.* 2nd Edition ed. 1958, Harrisburg, PA: Stackpole Books. 398.

Steere, E., *The Wilderness Campaign.* 1960, Mechanichsburg, PA: Stackpole Books. 522.

Sutherland, B., *Pittsburg volunteers with Sickles' Excelsior Brigade.* Western Pennsylvania historical magazine, 1962. **XLV**: p. 47-68, 342-362.

Taylor, N., *Report of the Excelsior Brigade at Williamsburg*, May 8, 1862.

Taylor, N., *Report of the Excelsior Brigade during the 2nd Bull Run Campaign*, Sept. 8, 1862.

Twichell, J.H., Chaplain of the Second Excelsior, *Oration at dedication of Excelsior Brigade Monument at Gettysburg, July 2, 1888*, in *New York at Gettysburg.* 1900, J. B. Lyon Co.: Albany. p. 575-582.

Tyler, C.F.E., *Report of the 74th New York Infantry during the Chancellorsville Campaign.* 1863, Official Records of the War of the Rebellion.

Uncited, (1861). *Local Military Movements.* The New York Times. New York. July 17, 1861.

Uncited, (1861). *The Sickles Brigade - Another Disaffected Company.* The New York

Times. New York. July 1, 1861.

Uncited, (1861). *A New Volunteer Company*. The New York *Times*. New York City. April 18, 1861.

Uncited, 1861, *Jack Tars, Ahoy*, New York City. Baker & Godwin, Printers. Recruitment Poster for Co. I, 5th Reg., Excelsior Brigade.

Uncited, (1862). *The Excelsior Brigade*. The New York *Times*. New York. Aug. 22, 1862.

Uncited, (1862). *The Excelsior Division*. The New York *Times*. Sept. 8, 1862.

Uncited, (1862). *From Albany: Gen. Sickles' Excelsior Brigade -- Gen. Busteed Making Arrangements for the Draft*. The New York *Times*. New York. Sept. 18, 1862.

Uncited, (1862). *Wikoff and Sickles*. The New York *Times*. New York. Feb. 15, 1862.

Uncited, (1862). *Gen. Sickles' Farewell to his Soldiers*. The New York *Times*. New York. Apr. 10, 1862.

Uncited, (1862). *Military Movements in the City*. The New York *Times*. New York City. Aug. 7, 1862.

Uncited, (1862). *News from the Peninsula*. The New York *Herald*. New York. June 20, 1862.

Uncited, (1863). *Engagement at Manassas Gap*. New York *Daily Tribune*. New York. August 1, 1863.

Uncited, (1863). *The Excelsior Brigade and the Conscripts*. The New York *Times*. New York. Aug. 22 1863.

Uncited, (1863). *Our Special Army Correspondence*. The New York *Times*. New York. May 10, 1863.

Uncited, (1863). *Re-enlistment of Troops - An Important Movement in the Army*. The New York *Times*. New York. Nov. 9, 1863.

Uncited, (1863). *Patriotic Offer to the Government*. The New York *Times*. New York. Nov. 9, 1863.

Uncited, *Daniel Edgar Sickles Biography*. 2002, Arlington National Cemetary Website.

Uncited, *Fort Ward History on City of Alexandria, Virginia Website*. 2003.

Walker, F.A., *History of the Second Army Corps*. 1886, New York: Charles Scribner's Sons. 737.

Walter, J.F., *Capsule History of the Seventy-Fourth New York Infantry*. 1983.

Walter, J.F., *Seventy-Fourth New York Infantry Official History*. 2002. p. 30.

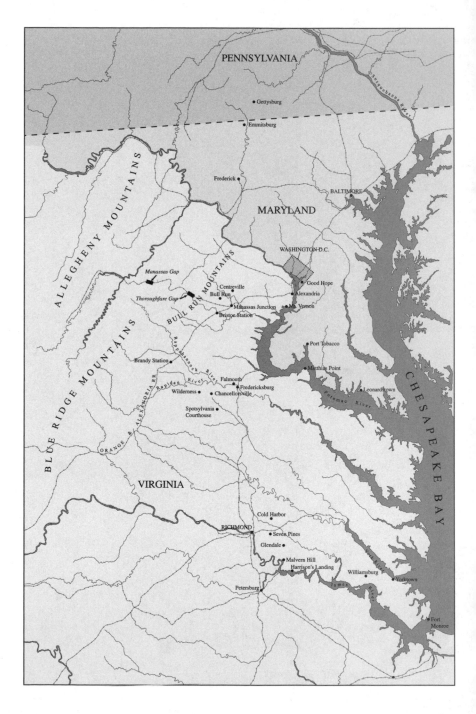